PROGRAMS FOR LADIES
VOLUME 3

BY
TERESA BOHANNON
and
BARBARA WESTBERG

Themes and Complete Banquet Programs
Skits and Dramas
for Ladies' Retreats and Conferences

Adaptable for Large or Small Groups, Special Services,

Showers, Socials, and Ladies' Ministry Meetings

PROGRAMS FOR LADIES
VOLUME 3

BY
TERESA BOHANNON
and
BARBARA WESTBERG

Themes and Complete Banquet Programs
Skits and Dramas
for Ladies' Retreats and Conferences

Adaptable for Large or Small Groups, Special Services,

Showers, Socials, and Ladies' Ministry Meetings

Programs for Ladies

Volume 3

by Teresa Bohannon and Barbara Westberg

©2001, Word Aflame Press
Hazelwood, MO 63042-2299

Cover Design by Paul Povolni

All Scripture quotations in this book are from the King James Version of the Bible unless otherwise identified.

All rights reserved. No portion of this publication may be reproduced, stored in an electronic system, or transmitted in any form or by any means, electronic, mechanical, photocopy, recording, or otherwise, without the prior permission of Word Aflame Press. Brief quotations may be used in literary reviews.

Printed in United States of America

Library of Congress Cataloging-in-Publication Data

Westberg, Barbara.
    Programs for ladies vol. 3 / by Barbara Westberg.
        p. cm.
    Includes bibliographical references.
    ISBN 1-56722-565-9
    1. Women, Pentecostal—Societies and clubs. 2. Holidays—Exercises, recitations, etc. 3. Pentecostal churches—United States—Membership.   I. Title.
BX8762.Z5W47   1990
246'.7—dc20   89-49113
                                                                                                                              CIP

Contents

Banquet Programs
    Building on a Firm Foundation 9
    By Their Shoes Ye Shall Know Them 15
    Chosen Vessels 21
    Christmas Tea. 27
    Fifties Sweetheart Social 35
    Gift Baskets 47
    Hand 'n Hand 55
    Home Tweet Home 61
    Psalm 23 Picnic 69
    Say It with Flowers 75
    Sunbeams and Rainbows 85

Mini-Dramas
Synopses of Mini-Dramas 93
    The Bridge Builders. 95
        Scene I: The Past Bridge Builder's Values
        Scene II: The Present Bridge Builder's Sacrifice
        Scene III: The Future Bridge Builder's Vision
    The Parable of the Teacup 111
        Scene I: Chipped
        Scene II: Empty
        Scene III: Restored
    Treasures of the Heart. 127

Dramas
Synopses of Dramas 143
    A Wake-up Call 145
        Act I: Martha's Garage Sale
        Act II: Jael's Moving Sale
        Act III: Not for Sale
        Act IV: Moving Day
    The God of Hagar 187
        Act I: Coffee Break
        Act II: Just Practicing
        Act III: The Valley of Baca
        Act IV: Water in the Wilderness

Women of the Kingdom 225
    Act I: Waiting for the Kingdom
    Act II: Working for the Kingdom
    Act III: Weeping for the Kingdom
    Act IV: Welcome to the Kingdom

Miscellaneous
    Monologue: A Daughter's Day 273
    Skit: The Party Line. 277
    Just for Fun Games. 283
    Potpourri of Ideas 293
    Recipes
        Desserts. 299
        Drinks 301
        Finger and Snack Foods 302
        Soup and Salads 304
    Resources 307
    Answers to Games and Puzzles 309
    Patterns 315
    Index 321

Banquet Programs

Building on a Firm Foundation

"He is like a man which built an house, and digged deep, and laid the foundation on a rock: and when the flood arose, the stream beat vehemently upon that house, and could not shake it: for it was founded upon a rock" (Luke 6:48).

Since women often do the planning of the banquets for the men, here is an idea for a father-son banquet.

The family is like a building, fitly framed together, solid and secure, when built on the right foundation.

Decorations
Sawhorses and tools.

Centerpieces
Small toolboxes and scraps of wood.

Favors
2 x 4 candy bars and chocolate tools (made from candy melts).

Door Prizes
Have slips of paper and pencils sitting beside a paint bucket on a table near the entry. As the men and boys enter, give each one two slips of paper. On one he writes his Social Security number. On the other he writes his birth date (i.e., 10/4/58). Slips are folded and placed in the basket.

Purchase five or six inexpensive tools.

To give these away during the program, play a game. Draw a slip from the paint bucket. The player whose Social Security number or birth date is called chooses a tool. When all the tools have been chosen, continue drawing. When a player's number or date is drawn, he can claim a tool from someone who has it. "I want the screwdriver *(Max)* has." The catch is that he must remember who has what tool. Players can hide the tools they have so the other players cannot see them. For a small group, all slips can be drawn. In a large group, set a time limit. When time is called or the slips are all drawn, the players with the tools get to keep them.

Programs for Ladies

Games

Drive It In. Bring several scrap pieces of 2 x 4's, 16-penny nails, and hammers. Divide into teams of not more than ten. On one end of the room, place the wood and nails on the floor. Place a stack of newspapers or magazines under the wood to help deaden the sound.

The teams line up, and the first person in each line is given a hammer. He runs to the other side of the room, picks up a nail, and whacks it one time into the stacked 2 x 4's. He runs back to his team, passes the hammer to the next person in line, and the race is on. Each person can hit the nail one time only. The winning team is the one who drives the nail the deepest into the wood. If one nail is driven in before each team member has a turn, the next team member starts with a new nail.

Identify It. Place a bag of assorted nails on each table; each bag contains the same number and size of nails. Allow three minutes for the teams to identify the types of nails (6p, 16p, finishing, etc). The first team to correctly identify all the nails wins.

Construction Crews. Divide into teams. Give each team a pile of Legos, Lincoln Logs, or blocks. Allow two minutes for the teams to build a building. Judges will award ribbons or certificates for (1) most creative, (2) best use of materials, and (3) most likely to withstand a storm.

Identify the Tool. Gather a variety of antique tools. Give each player a paper and pencil. Fathers write on their papers the use of each tool. Sons write on their papers a creative use for the tool.

After all the tools have been shown, hold each one up again, asking for answers. The sons will learn about tools-of-old, and the fathers will enjoy hearing their sons' creative suggestions.

Songs

"He's Still Working on Me" (by Bill Gaither)

"Kids under Construction" (by Bill Gaither)

"The Wise Man and the Foolish Man" (Let the grandfathers sing this one, complete with motions.)

Precious Moments

Beforehand ask a grandfather, father, and son to be prepared to tell about something that they built with their father/grandfather that created a special memory. It might even be humorous because not all building projects are successful.

BANQUET PROGRAMS

Chalk Talk

The Wise Man and Foolish Man

Bring a dry erase board, dry erase markers, Vis-a-Vis markers, and a spray-bottle filled with water.

Tell the story of the foolish man building his house on the sand and draw a picture of a house built on the sand with the Vis-a-Vis marker. Next draw a picture of the house built on the rock with the dry erase marker. Spray water from the bottle onto the dry erase board while you talk about the rain coming down.

The house on the sand will disappear, while the house on the rock will remain.

Monologue

Sunny Skies

PROPS:

    Nail apron
    Carpenter's cap
    Newspaper
    Chair

INSTRUCTIONS:

Make a tape of the sounds and the man's voice at the end of the skit. Arrange for someone behind the scene to play the tape. Make a copy of the script for him to follow.

MAN ENTERS, *removing his nail apron and cap.*

Ah-ha! Finally, it is finished. And what a fine house I have built. Look at that foundation. You'll not find a more solid rock this side of Gibraltar.

Too bad about that guy down on the beach. Everyone knows it is stupid to build a house on the sand. *(chuckles)* He's headed for a big fall.

I'll just sit here and wait for the storm.

(Sits down and picks up a newspaper) Might as well check the weather map. *(flips through the paper and reads silently for a few*

Programs for Ladies

seconds) What? Sunny skies all week? *(throws down the paper and gets up)* Well, sooner or later it's got to storm. Then all my labor will pay off, and that guy down there sure will be sorry.

(Walks over and pretends to peer out a window) Look at that house. Looks just as nice as mine, but I know it's not! I know about his foundation! Ha! He thought he was being smart, saving time and money, but inferior construction always shows up sooner or later. Yep, sooner or later, it will storm, and that house will fall!

***EXITS**, then **ENTERS**.*

Been a month and still no storm!
SOUND: Hammering (background)

Ahhh, what's that I hear? Sounds like thunder. *(runs to the pretend window, looks up)* Sun's still shining. What's that noise? *(looks down)* Oh, no! Don't tell me! That guy on the beach is adding a sun porch to his house. Guess he'll be putting in a hot tub next. And on that shaky foundation, too! He'll be sorry, but I won't! I'm the wise guy. He's the fool.

(Sits down and waits) I'll just wait . . . and wait . . . and wait.
(Several seconds of silence, signifying passing of time)
SOUND: Laughter (background)

(Jumps to his feet) What's that? *(peers out the window)* Who's laughing? Why, it is that guy down on the beach with all his friends. They're having a party! They shouldn't be having a party! Their world ought to be falling apart! It's not fair! Those cheapskates shouldn't be happy. *(stomps from the room)*
SOUND: Wind and Rain (background)

***ENTERS**, running and clapping his hands.*

It's raining! It's raining! Listen to that wind! Man, what a storm. I've been waiting for this. Wonder how my neighbor's doing now? *(peers out the window, mouth falls open)* Why, it's not even raining down on the beach! They're sitting on their porch watching it storm up here on the rock.

It's not fair! It's not fair! Sure my house is standing firm, but now I'll have to clean the gutters and patch the roof, while my neighbor in that house on the shaky foundation has a party and swims in the sun. It's not fair!

Their house was supposed to fall!

***EXITS** and **ENTERS**, carrying a suitcase.*

I've had it. I'm moving. Everyone can tell that the storm is not coming. I've waited and watched. I've worked and repaired. The storm always hits me, while that fool down on the beach never gets hit. I'm moving down on the beach with the party crowd.

EXITS.
SOUND: Storm and Loud Crashing
MAN'S VOICE on tape: Yep, you guessed it! That night the storm hit—the beach and the rock. The house on the sand fell, the empty house on the rock stood firm.

By Their Shoes Ye Shall Know Them

"How beautiful are the feet of those who preach the gospel of peace, who bring glad tidings of good things" (Romans 10:15, NKJV).
"Then had the churches rest . . . walking in the fear of the Lord, and in the comfort of the Holy Ghost" (Acts 9:31).

"Our lives are like shoes, to be worn out in the service of God" (Spencer W. Kimball).

Decorations
Shoes. Collectors of miniature shoes often have an oversize shoe that is used as a display. Borrow one of these and set it on a table near the door. Drape the table with a table skirt and cloth. If a large shoe is not available, make a shoe display using ceramic shoes or interesting shoes the ladies may have in their closets.

Centerpieces: small collectible shoes, available at dollar stores and collectible shops. Stack small boxes and drape with fabric. Set the shoes on the fabric.

Favors
Plastic shoes (available at party supply stores by the dozen) filled with mints or bath salts. Tie circles of tulle around the shoes. Attach a card printed with Romans 10:15.

Programs for Ladies

Puzzles/Quizzes for the Printed Program

Find the Shoes

P	U	M	P	S	F	I	O	S	X	K	R	P	H	W	W	G
U	N	B	E	X	L	Z	Z	W	T	L	L	H	E	O	H	A
G	E	N	D	T	L	G	E	S	H	A	O	U	E	H	K	L
H	Q	W	V	U	M	D	G	G	T	U	X	O	L	Q	E	O
O	H	B	V	S	G	N	N	F	S	D	Y	D	S	A	F	S
P	U	G	G	E	I	I	O	E	T	C	H	Y	Z	Q	B	H
Y	T	O	S	L	N	R	S	Z	G	B	Z	I	U	C	D	E
Z	L	F	S	N	M	H	N	A	I	O	W	X	K	S	W	S
C	Y	S	U	S	O	J	B	K	N	E	Y	N	Q	R	S	A
Z	E	R	P	E	E	T	P	U	R	U	F	P	M	E	R	F
M	Y	F	S	O	L	S	E	W	Q	G	M	N	H	K	E	V
V	C	I	T	W	L	O	L	N	Y	Y	A	T	T	A	P	S
M	U	J	K	G	B	F	A	A	N	S	S	M	L	E	P	Q
X	B	I	F	S	W	A	P	F	D	I	T	T	A	N	I	U
Y	N	H	Z	O	L	C	X	I	E	N	S	O	A	S	L	W
S	P	C	N	H	F	W	H	O	L	R	A	P	O	L	S	W
S	X	Q	F	D	Y	V	M	G	A	F	S	S	C	B	F	S

BOOTS	HEELS	RUNNING	TENNIS
CLOGS	HOUSESHOES	SANDALS	WEDGES
FLATS	LOAFERS	SLINGS	
FLIPFLOPS	PLATFORMS	SLIPPERS	
GALOSHES	PUMPS	SNEAKERS	

Bible Trivia—Feet

1. What animal in Genesis found no rest for the sole of its foot?
2. Before the Israelites could enter the Promised Land, where did the priests have to place the soles of their feet?
3. In the New Testament, who prophesied of the Messiah that He would guide their feet into the way of peace?
4. Who did not want Jesus to wash his feet?
5. Where was the lame man Peter and John healed when he leaped to his feet?
6. Who did not receive enough inheritance to set his foot on?
7. Who gathered up his feet in his bed before he died?
8. Balaam's donkey crushed Balaam's foot against what?
9. What did Moses put on the "great toe" of the right feet of Aaron and his sons?
10. According to Ephesians 6, we should have our feet shod with what?
11. What did not happen to the feet of the Israelites during the forty years in the wilderness?
12. Who put himself in danger when he "went in to cover his feet"?
13. Which son of Jacob did Moses prophesy would "dip his feet in oil"?
14. "Loose thy shoe from off thy foot; for the place whereon thou standest is holy." These words were spoken to two people in the Bible. One was Moses. Name the other.

Games

Let's Race. Divide into two teams. Each team has a pair of large high-heeled shoes. The first player puts them on, runs to the other end of the room and back. She takes the shoes off and hands them to the next person in line, who repeats the above. The first team finished wins.

Variation: use several types of shoes such as high heels, swimming flippers, house shoes, and flip-flops. Choose one person for each team to hand out the shoes. Keep the shoes in a box and hand out a different pair each time.

Another possibility is to put left shoes in one bag and the right ones in another. The "distributor" reaches into each bag and hands the runner a shoe. A runner may be running with a flipper on one foot and a high heel shoe on the other.

Feet in the Bible. Pass out paper and pens. Set the timer for three or five minutes. Each lady (or group of ladies) lists every Scripture she can think of that mentions feet.

Programs for Ladies

Precious Moments

Before the banquet ask two or three ladies to tell something they remember about a grandparent's, parent's, or even a special friend's shoes. This could be a funny incident. How many women have gone to town wearing mismatched shoes? Or it could be a heart-touching story. During the Depression many people patched their shoes with cardboard. Parents often wore shoes that were falling apart so they could buy school shoes for their children.

Activity

Whose Shoes? Ask several women to bring a pair of extra shoes. Any kind of shoe is acceptable; older or unusual shoes work best. Try to collect a variety, including sneakers, running shoes, hiking boots, high-heels, loafers, house shoes, galoshes, sandals, flip-flops, and slippers.

Place the shoes on a table and number them. Give each guest a piece of paper. Players number their papers and write the name of the person they think the shoes belong to next to the appropriate number. The person with the most correct answers wins.

If most of your guests are fairly well acquainted with the Bible, have them also write the name of woman in the Bible who would have worn this kind of shoe. This can be a fun challenge. Answers will vary. Examples: Mrs. Noah might have worn galoshes. Jezebel would have worn high-heels, Sarah hiking boots, Delilah sneakers. Who would have worn flip-flops? You decide.

Puppet Song

See reproducible art on page 315.

"Beautiful Feet" by Sandy Patti and the Friendship Company (available on cassette).

For unique entertainment, present this song with puppets. Make feet puppets by tracing a foot shape on poster board. Adhere the poster board to foam core with spray adhesive. Cut out the feet with a craft knife.

Paste facial features on the feet.

For the mouth use a yarn-covered elastic hair band (Scunci brand). Make two small holes, as indicated in the drawing. Push a piece of wire through one hole, around the elastic band, and back through the second hole. Twist the ends of the wire together on the back of the foot. Repeat, as indicated.

Attach a 16" piece of fishing line to the lower part of the hair band. Tie a metal washer to the end of the fishing line. Move the mouth by pulling on the washer.

Use a puppet stage if one is available. If not, use a curtain or blanket held on each side by volunteers.

This presentation may be done using neon poster board and black light, with or without a stage or curtain. If you do not use a stage or curtain, the puppeteers should dress in black or wear black robes. They sit in chairs and hold the foot with one hand, working the mouth with the other hand.

By Their Shoes Ye Shall Know Them

I. Our Shoes Tell on Us
   A. Shoes Identify Owner
   B. Shoes Reflect Character
   C. Shoes Reveal Position
II. Shoes in God's Service
   A. Choosing Your Shoes
   B. Breaking in Your Shoes
   C. Filling Your Shoes

Chosen Vessels

"If a [woman] therefore purge [herself] from these, [she] shall be a vessel unto honour, sanctified, and meet for the master's use, and prepared unto every good work" (II Timothy 2:21).
"But the Lord said unto him, Go thy way: for he is a chosen vessel unto me, to bear my name before the Gentiles, and kings, and the children of Israel" (Acts 9:15).

Decorations
Before the banquet ask ladies to bring a unique jar or bottle. Use these for decorations and centerpieces.

Favors
• Purchase small bottles from craft or discount stores. Fill these with bath salt, bath oil, or seasoned cooking oil. Attach a ribbon and a card printed with II Timothy 2:21.
• Contact a potter for small clay jars.

Precious Moment—A Chosen Vessel
Before the banquet the planning committee should choose one lady to be honored as "a chosen vessel." Or the ladies who will be attending could be asked to cast a "secret ballot" to choose this lady. She could be in leadership or perhaps a lady of silent strength whose contributions to the kingdom of God are often overlooked. She might be a prayer warrior or a wise woman whom others seek out for private counsel.

Make this a beautiful surprise presentation, with only the committee knowing the name of the lady to be honored. Have a poem (perhaps especially written for the occasion), a special song, a brief listing of this lady's good works, a letter of commendation from the pastor, and/or a word from her daughter or someone close to her.

A corsage is always appropriate when honoring a lady. For a gift give her a special "vessel" with an engraving on it:

Presented to *(name)*
A Chosen Vessel
on *(date)*
from *(Ladies' group)*

Programs for Ladies

Quiz for the Printed Program

Chosen Vessels from God's Word

The Bible tells of many women who were "chosen vessels." How many of these ladies do you know?

1. This woman hung a scarlet rope from her window and saved her family.
   (a) Eve (b) Rahab (c) Esther (d) Sarah

2. This woman bore a child in her old age and became the mother of a mighty nation.
   (a) Miriam (b) Sarah (c) Athaliah (d) Sapphira

3. This woman was in business with her husband, making tents.
   (a) Jezebel (b) Salome (c) Delilah (d) Priscilla

4. This woman was the great-grandmother of King David.
   (a) Michal (b) Abigail (c) Ruth (d) Leah

5. This woman won a beauty contest and later saved her people from destruction.
   (a) Delilah (b) Rachel (c) The queen of Sheba (d) Esther

6. This woman loved to play the tambourine.
   (a) Miriam (b) Dinah (c) Melissa (d) Eve

7. With a tent peg and a hammer, this woman put the finishing touches to a great victory.
   (a) Delilah (b) Athaliah (c) Jezebel (d) Jael

8. This woman prevented much bloodshed by her quick thinking and wise words.
   (a) Jezebel (b) Eve (c) Abigail (d) Sapphira

9. This woman was a *succourer* (help in time of distress) of many, including the apostle Paul.
   (a) Ruth (b) Phebe (c) Hagar (d) Jezebel

10. This woman was a judge in Israel and went into battle with them.
    (a) Rachel (b) Elisabeth (c) Deborah (d) Martha

BANQUET PROGRAMS

Games
How Many? Teams (tables) have an allotted time to list various kinds of vessels. Remind them that not all vessels are used in the kitchen (e.g., a blood vessel, a rowboat, a vessel of mercy). The group of women with the longest list wins.

Make a Vessel. Give each player a sheet of copy paper. Instructions: holding the paper behind your back, tear a vessel (any kind of vessel) from the paper. Let the ladies at the head table (or a specific table) serve as judges. Give a small prize to the lady who made the most outstanding vessel.

Sharing Time
Allow time for the ladies to share the history of the jars they brought.

Songs
"The Potter"
"He Didn't Throw the Clay Away"

Skit

Choose Me, Lord

The person playing the voice of God should have a reverb microphone and be out of sight. The Saint kneels in prayer, facing the audience.

SAINT: Lord Jesus, I do so want to be used by You.

VOICE: You do?

SAINT: Oh, yes, I do. I am volunteering to do anything You say. I want to be a chosen vessel.

VOICE: That's great. I could use you.

SAINT: Oh, wonderful! I want to be a vessel that pours out blessings on multitudes. I want the whole world to hear the gospel.

VOICE: That is My plan, too.

SAINT: I know, and I do so want to be part of Your plan. I dream of the day when I go to the Bahamas to teach the gospel to—

Programs for Ladies

VOICE: Wait just a minute. Let's talk about your neighborhood.

SAINT: My neighborhood? But, Lord, everybody in my neighborhood knows the gospel. It's the poor, starving children in the Bahamas who need—

VOICE: What about the clerk at the convenience store where you buy gas?

SAINT: Oh, You mean . . . uhhhh . . . old-uhhh what's her name?

VOICE: Yes, her. She's lonely and needs a friend.

SAINT: She needs something. She never smiles, never, and do You know—oh, I guess You do know—anyway, the other day she shorted me a quarter! I intend to tell her boss.

VOICE: As I said, "She needs a friend." And remember Casey?

SAINT: Casey? Casey who?

VOICE: Think a minute.

SAINT: *(wrinkles brow; hand under chin)* Casey? Casey Jones? Casey? Who is Ca . . . oh, now I remember. How could I have forgotten? Casey is my paperboy. He never gets it on the porch. If there is a mud puddle anywhere in the yard, he hits it. One time I found my paper on the roof! His supervisor heard about that!

VOICE: I know. You hit the roof, too, didn't you?

SAINT: Well, what would You have done? Never mind. Don't answer that one.

VOICE: Did you know that Casey has never heard the gospel?

SAINT: Probably wouldn't sit still long enough to listen. You know how hyper kids are these days. That's why I gave up my Sunday school class. Those kids wouldn't do a thing I told them to do.

VOICE: Hmmm . . . I can relate to that. I have a few disobedient children, too.

SAINT: I'm sure You do.

VOICE: Now about Casey—

SAINT: But we were talking about me being a chosen vessel for You.

VOICE: That is what I am talking about.

SAINT: What's Casey got to do with it? Just think of all the people I can reach with the gospel, Lord, if You will send me to the Bahamas. I could start a beach ministry. Just think—

VOICE: Just think about Casey.

SAINT: Yeah, Casey. But, Lord, what about the world?

VOICE: Think about it. Think about it.

Illustrated Sermon
Give It to God

Give each lady an index card with a hole punched in one corner. Bring a helium balloon for each lady. Tie a balloon to the back of each chair.

Read and discuss II Kings 4:1-7.

This widow used what she had and was given more.

How much oil is in your vessel? Are you down to your lowest level? God wants us to willingly give Him everything: possessions, relationships, time, talent, and problems. When we give everything, we, too, will be blessed beyond measure.

II Timothy 2:21 tells us we will be prepared unto every good work. Sometimes it is hard to see how a situation can work for our good, but God can and will work on our behalf.

Ask each lady to write on the index card something that is troubling her. Perhaps she has a problem that she cannot totally surrender to the Lord. Tie the card to the balloon.

Go outside and form a large circle. Pray together, asking the Lord to move in every situation. On the count of three, release the balloons. Sing a chorus of surrender such as "I'm Yours, Lord" or "I Give All My

Programs for Ladies

Problems to You, Lord," as the balloons float upward, carrying the problems with them. They cannot be retrieved, just as we should not retrieve a problem once we have given it to God. Have a time of praise.

Poem

Reproof

As children bring their broken toys,
    With tears, for us to mend;
I brought my broken dreams to God
    Because He was my Friend.

But then instead of leaving Him
    In peace to work alone,
I hung around and tried to help
    With ways that were my own.

At last, I snatched them back and cried,
    "How could You be so slow?"
"My child," He said, "what could I do?
    You never did let go!"

—Author Unknown

Christmas Tea

"For unto you is born this day in the city of David a Saviour, which is Christ the Lord" (Luke 2:11).

The best Christmas tea I have been privileged to attend was at Apostolic Temple in Pasadena, Texas. Pastor's wife Joyce McClain and the ladies of Apostolic Temple worked for weeks to insure the success of this annual event. Many of the ideas here are from their tea. Thanks, ladies, for a lovely time.

Teresa Bohannon

Decorations

Ask for volunteers to decorate tables—one or two ladies per table. The tables will not match, and there are only two prerequisites for each table: (1) it must have a theme and (2) it must be set with fine china. Set clear plastic plates inside the china.

The favors for each table are the responsibility of the hostess for that table. The favors correspond with the table's theme.

Ideas for Table Décor, Centerpieces, and Favors

Angels
Nativity Sets
Poinsettias
Candles
Coke Memorabilia

White and Gold: For favors purchase gold metal boxes from the dollar store. Fill with potpourri or candy.

Greenery and Ribbon: For favors use a paint pen to write the name of each person on a Christmas ornament. Write the occasion and date on the back of the ornament. Set these in napkin rings or wreaths made from strips of greenery.

Stockings: Place stocking containing gifts or small items in the center of table. For favors cut small stockings from felt and sew together. Insert napkins and flatware in the stockings.

Gingerbread Men: For favors give Little Debbie's® Gingerbread Men snacks. Tie a red ribbon around their necks. Wrap assorted gift boxes in coordinating paper. Trim with ribbon and stack in center of table.

Programs for Ladies

Angels

Favors

Teapot Favors can be made from round Christmas bulbs and polymer clay. Cut a piece of clay 1/4" thick. Roll the clay and pinch it to form a handle and a spout to fit on the ornament. Roll a narrow strip to fit around the hanger. Bake the clay according to instructions on the clay package. When cool, hot glue the handle, spout, and lid to the ornament. Decorate with paint pens or rub-on transfers.

Puzzle/Quiz for Printed Program

These quizzes can be copied onto the printed program or separate sheets. The ladies can work on them as they wait for the program to begin. The answers are on page 310-11.

Programs for Ladies

Christmas Wordies

Each answer is a Christmas hymn, saying, or a portion of Scripture from the Christmas story.

bethlehem

BANQUET PROGRAMS

Where's My Line?

The following lines or phrases are taken from familiar Christmas songs. Can you name the songs?

1. As the shoppers rush home with their treasures. _____

2. Jump in bed and cover up your head. _____

3. Say hello to friends you know and everyone you meet. _____

4. Then one foggy Christmas Eve. . . . _____

5. Gonna find out who's naughty and nice. _____

6. From now on, our troubles will be miles away. _____

7. What a laugh it would have been, if Daddy. . . . _____

8. Yea, Lord, we greet Thee. _____

9. But the fire is so delightful. _____

10. And wild and sweet the words repeat. _____

11. O tidings of comfort and joy. _____

12. Joyful all ye nations rise. _____

13. While fields and floods, rocks, hills, and plains. _____

Programs for Ladies

14. You can plan on me. _____

15. Holy Infant so tender and mild. _____

16. Above thy deep and dreamless sleep. . . . _____

17. On Mary's lap is sleeping. _____

18. A thrill of hope the weary world rejoices. _____

19. Following yonder star. _____

20. Laughing all the way. _____

Activity

Teacup or Gift Exchange. Each lady brings a teacup, wrapped and tied with a bow.

Everyone sits in a circle, holding the gift that they brought for the exchange. Someone reads the story (see below) slowly so the gifts can be passed out. Every time RIGHT is read, the gift goes to the right. Every time LEFT is read, the gift goes to the left. Whatever gift a lady has at the end of the story is hers, providing it is not the gift she brought.

Right or Left?

On a hillside just outside of Bethlehem shepherds LEFT their sheep sleeping around them as they gathered by the campfire.

A young shepherd gazed RIGHT into the fire and quietly asked the chief shepherd who sat RIGHT beside him: "Master Jeremiah, do you think the prophecies are RIGHT? Will the Messiah ever come? Or has God LEFT us?"

The older man shook his head. "God has never LEFT His people. Why should He do so now? The Messiah will come. The prophecies are RIGHT." He pushed a glowing ember RIGHT back into the fire.

Suddenly, the sky was ablaze. As the shepherds looked RIGHT up into the heavens, they were almost blinded.

"Fear not," the angel said. "I bring you tidings of great joy. RIGHT this night in the city of Bethlehem the Savior has been born. You will find Him wrapped in swaddling clothes, lying in a manger RIGHT where His mother has laid Him."

Then RIGHT beside the angel was a heavenly host, praising God and saying, "Glory to God in the highest, and on earth peace, good will toward men."

As soon as the angelic host LEFT, the shepherds said to each another, "Let us go RIGHT now to see the Savior."

So they LEFT their flocks and went RIGHT into Bethlehem.

As they returned from worshiping the Savior, the young shepherd turned to the chief shepherd and said, "You were RIGHT. God has never LEFT His people, and He never will."

As the shepherds returned to the field where they had LEFT their flocks, the chief shepherd smiled and answered, "RIGHT."

Precious Moments

Beforehand choose five ladies to speak briefly on one of the following subjects.

(1) My favorite Christmas memory.
(2) The best Christmas gift I have ever given anyone.
(3) The best Christmas gift I have ever received.
(4) The happiest Christmas my family has ever had.
(5) My dream of a "perfect" Christmas.

Fifties Sweetheart Social

"Beloved, if God so loved us, we ought also to love one another" (I John 4:11).

Encourage the attendees to dress in 50s styles: rolled-up jeans and leather jackets for the men and poodle skirts and sweaters for the ladies. Of course, bobby socks and saddle oxfords complete the outfits.

Decorations

Fifties ice cream parlor or drive-in. Party stores have many items for this theme, as do prom supply catalogs.

Use small round tables covered with red and white or black and white checked cloths. Checked tablecloths are available in plastic from party supply stores or in vinyl from discount stores. Vinyl tablecloths are usually cheaper than plastic.

Hang records on the walls, and use them for centerpieces. If model cars from the 50s are available, display them.

Coca-Cola™ or Pepsi™ memorabilia would also add to the décor.

Programs for Ladies

Centerpieces

Paint several bamboo skewers black. Glue or tape one to the back of each 45-RPM record, leaving two to three inches sticking below the record. Place Styrofoam blocks inside cardboard soda cartons. Insert the records and silk greenery into the Styrofoam.

Fill glass soda bottles with lamp oil. Mix red and green oil to attain the color of cola, and pour it into the bottles. Insert floating wicks in the bottles. These are glass tubes and wicks, available at Hobby Lobby or a candle shop. Place one bottle on each side of the centerpiece and light the wicks.

Music

Play fifties religious music. If a record player is available, bring it for playing records and appoint a DJ. If not, find someone with a stereo who will tape the records for you.

Games and Entertainment

Prizes: Candy bars from the fifties, such as Big Hunk, Payday, Hershey, Abba Zabba.

Know What I Did? This game is guaranteed to get laughs and get people up and moving. It can be played by five or six people or each table can play, following the group in the front of the room. Two people are required to demonstrate this game. Choose four or five people to come to the front.

Demonstrate the following:

First Person: Do you know what I did when I got up this morning?

Second Person: No, what did you do?

First Person: I brushed my teeth. *(acts as if brushing teeth)*

Second Person: You brushed your teeth? *(does same motion as person 1)*

First Person: I brushed my teeth. *(keeps acting as if he is brushing teeth throughout the game).*

Second person turns to the third person, and they repeat the above. Last person in line tells it to person 1.

First person adds another motion.

First Person:	Do you know what I did when I got up this morning?
Second Person:	No, what did you do?
First Person:	I brushed my teeth and combed my hair. *(continues to brush teeth, runs hand above head from front to back)*
Second Person:	You brushed your teeth and combed your hair? *(does same motions)*
First Person:	I brushed my teeth and combed my hair.

Third line: I brushed my teeth, combed my hair, and did my exercises. *(adds knee bends to the other motions)*

Fourth line: I brushed my teeth, combed my hair, did my exercises, and ran around the block. *(adds circular hip motion to the other motions)*

Precious Moments

Ask two married couples to participate in a quiz. The women sit at a table on one side and the men at a table on the other side. Give each participant a paper and pencil for writing his/her answers.

If this is a banquet for unmarried sweethearts, revise the questions to fit the occasion.

Ask the following questions:
1. What first attracted you to your spouse?
2. What did your spouse want to be when he/she was growing up?
3. What is your spouse's pet peeve?
4. What was your spouse's mother's maiden name?
5. Who was your spouse's first boy/girlfriend?
6. What is your spouse's favorite magazine?
7. What is your spouse's favorite thing to do for relaxing?
8. What is your spouse's dream vacation?
9. How long has it been since you told your spouse, "I love you"?
10. If your spouse could change one thing about you, what would it be?

Go back over the questions and compare the answers.

Programs for Ladies

Skit
Let Me Call You "Uhhh, Sweetheart"

CAST:

    Henry, dressed in old-fashioned, Sunday best attire, carrying a cane
    Sadie, dressed in old-fashioned, Sunday best attire
    Waiter, dressed in formal attire

PROPS:

    Card table
    2 Chairs
    Tablecloth
    Table set-up (2 menus, silk flower in a vase, 2 bowls, 2 spoons, 2 napkins, 2 glasses of water)
    7 real or play $10.00 bills
    Wallet
    Dish of lemon slices

INSTRUCTIONS:

Set up a card table and two chairs on one side of the room. Cover the table with a cloth. Place two menus and a silk flower in a vase in the middle of the table. Copies of the script can be on the table.

HENRY ENTERS, *putting on bow tie, fastening suspenders.*

HENRY: *(singing)* "Henry went a courtin'; he did go . . . over to Miss" . . . now what is that woman's name? Oh, well, I'll think of it sooner or later.

    I declare, ever' time I go on a date, I get so nervous I almost ferget to put my teeth in. One of these days I'm gonna get my nerve up and ask that old gal to marry me—if I can ever think of her name.

    Now where does she live? Somewhere on Maple, I think . . . or is it Walnut? Or Pine or Oak or Cherry? I declare, I know she's up a tree somewhere. Or is it her cat that's up a tree? Where does that woman live?

(Pulls out wallet) I think I got her address somewhere in my wallet. Hmmm . . . gettin' more expensive all the time to court a woman. Wonder if I got enough money fer takin' her out to one of them fancy cafes? *(takes seven bills out of his wallet, holds them up close to his eyes, while also holding them so the audience can see that they are $10.00 bills)* Three . . . four . . . five . . . six . . . seven dollars. Why, that oughta be plenty. Never spent $7.00 on no girl back when I was datin' in high school. *(puts money back in wallet and wallet in pocket)*

Now, let's see, where was I goin'? *(wanders around a bit)* Oh, yeah, I was goin' to pick up . . . up . . . up my sweetheart. Sure wish I could remember her name.

Now where does she live? Oh, yeah, that's why I was diggin' out my wallet. Got her address here somewhere. *(pulls out his wallet again)* Seems like she lives on some street with a tree name, or was it a dog's name . . . Cocker? No, that ain't it . . . Chow? No, that don't sound right either. *(takes a slip of paper out of his wallet)* Aww, here it is. 711 East Sic-a-more. *(chuckles)* That's right good memory association. A tree and a dog—a dog up a tree, Sycamore. Got it, Henry, old boy?

(Looks around) Henry, old boy? Who am I talkin' to anyway? *(scratches head)* Henry? Who's he? Ain't nobody here but me. Me? Oh, yeah, Henry, that's me.

(Looks at watch) Gotta hurry or I'm gonna be late. Not that I can remember what time I told what's her name I'd be there.

(Pretends to be peering at house numbers) 701, 705, 709, 711 . . . ahhhh, here it is. *(knocks on door)* Sure wish I could remember her name. Oh, well I'll just call her . . . uhhh Sweetheart. Ever' woman likes to be called . . . uhhhh Sweetheart.

ENTER SADIE, *answering the door.*

HENRY: *(sings in a cracking voice)* "Let me call you Sweetheart."

SADIE: Oh, Henry, that's so rheumatic. You're makin' me have heart pap-er-tations. *(gets right in his face)* I'm almost breathless.

HENRY: *(backs away from her and turns up his nose)* Yeah, but not quite. *(aside)* Garlic tablets!

SADIE: What did you say, Henry?

HENRY: I said, "Darlin', you're a habit with me."

SADIE: Oh, Henry, that's so rheumatic. I declare I think your croonin's gonna make me swoon.

***SADIE** swoons. **HENRY** drops his cane and tries to catch her. They almost fall. She holds him up.*

HENRY: Come along. Come along. I got us conservations at this fancy café.

SADIE: Special conversations just for us? My, it must be a fancy restaurant you're takin' me to. Oh, Henry, that's so rheumatic.

*As **THEY EXIT, SADIE** says, "I think I'll have hamburger steak with lots of onions."*

***ENTER WAITER.** He adds silver to the table set-up.*

WAITER: Next customer's mine. I sure hope I get a big tipper this time. I wanta get my girl a box of fancy chocolates.

ENTER HENRY and SADIE.

WAITER: *(looks at Henry and Sadie; slaps his forehead)* Oh, no! Here's my big tipper. Maybe if I ignore 'em, they'll go away.

HENRY: Well, I guess this is one of them fancy places where ya get to sit wherever ya want to, Mab . . . I mean, Joy . . . I mean, uhhh Sweetheart. Let's just sit at that table over there.

***HENRY and SADIE** go to the table. **WAITER** turns his back to them. **HENRY** sits down while **SADIE** stands beside her chair and waits.*

HENRY: Somethin' wrong with this table?

SADIE: There's nothin' wrong with the table.

HENRY: *(looks around for the waiter)* Wonder how ya get waited on in this place? *(looks at Sadie)* Somethin' wrong with your chair?

SADIE: Nothin's wrong with my chair. *(remains standing)*

HENRY: *(picks up the menu and reads)* Coffee or tea, $1.25. Bowl of onion soup, $2.95. Hamburger steak, $7.95. *(gulps loudly; says to self)* Let's see, how much money do I have? $7.00. Hmmm, that ain't enough! *(looks at Sadie)* Something wrong with your seat?

SADIE: There's nothin' wrong with my . . . why, I've never been so insulted in my whole life! I oughta walk outta here right now.

HENRY: *(grabs his cane and starts to get up)* Now, that's a right good idea!

SADIE: *(sits down quickly)* Oh, Henry, you're such a tease. *(grabs a menu)* Awww, here it is . . . hamburger steak.

HENRY: Uhhhh, yeah, hamburger steak. I was wonderin', Clara . . . I mean, Minnie . . . I mean, uhhhh Sweetheart, if you wouldn't like to have a bowl of onion soup? Got lots more onions in it than hamburger steak. Last time I was here their hamburger steak was half-cooked.

SADIE: Oh, that's just the way I like it—half-raw.

HENRY: Did you think I said, "Half-cooked"? I said, "Over-cooked."

SADIE: Oh, well, that's okay. I can just tell them how I want it cooked. You probably didn't order it right when you were here before.

HENRY: *(aside)* How'm I gonna get outta this one? How do you talk a woman into orderin' somethin' she don't want?

SADIE: *(looks around for the restroom sign; puts hand to mouth and whispers loudly)* Henry, I uhhh . . . I uhhhh . . . I gotta . . . gotta go to the powder room. You just go ahead and order fer me. Okay? I'll take a hamburger steak, medium-rare—don't ferget, medium-rare—and double the onions, and iced tea, and *(checks the menu again)* a double fudge cake.

HENRY: *(gulps)* That's all?

SADIE: *(gets up)* Yeah. That's enough. Don't wanta ruin my figure.

SADIE EXITS.

HENRY: Yeah, or my wallet. *(sings to the tune of "Oh, What a Beautiful Morning")*

> Oh, what a bad situation.
> I've got myself in a fix.
> Dating a starvin' woman
> And a flat wallet don't mix!

WAITER *turns around.*

WAITER: Well, there's nothin' to do, but wait on 'em. *(takes water to the table)* Are you ready to order, sir?

HENRY: Yeah, I guess so. *(searches the menu again)*

WAITER: *(clears his throat, waits a few seconds, then clears it again)* Are you ready to order, sir?

HENRY: Uhhhh, yeah.

WAITER: Let's start with the drinks. What would you like to drink?

HENRY: Oh, we'll just drink water—water with lemon slices.

WAITER: I knew it! Anything else, sir?

HENRY: Yeah, the lady will take a cup of onion soup and . . . let's see . . . $2.95 by 2 that's about $6.00 plus tax. Yep, I'll take a cup of onion soup, too. *(winks at the Waiter)* Self-defense, you know.

WAITER: *(sarcastically)* Excellent choice, sir. It's the house specialty. Just what I order for my girlfriend.

WAITER EXITS, *stiffly.*

SADIE RETURNS *and stands by her chair.*

HENRY: You got a problem with that chair?

SADIE: No! I got a problem with you!

HENRY: Huh?

SADIE: In my day the boy pulled out the chair fer the girl.

HENRY: *(stumbles to his feet)* Oh, yeah! Well, I'm comin'. Don't know why I can't date one of them women libbers. They know how to pull out a chair.

HENRY *gets up, pulls her chair out, and* **SADIE** *starts to sit down. He pulls it out from under her. Pandemonium for a while. Finally, they are seated.*

WAITER *brings two cups of soup and lemon slices.*

SADIE: *(sniffs)* Onion soup. My, that smells good. I didn't know we got an appetizer with our dinner.

HENRY: *(chuckles)* Marybell . . . I mean, Judith . . . I mean, uhhh Sweetheart, that ain't an appetizer. It's your dinner.

SADIE: My dinner? But I ordered hamburger steak.

HENRY: Uhhh . . . uhhh . . . they were fresh out of hamburger. Yeah, sold the last one just 'fore we got here.

SADIE: Well, that's disappointing. I wanted hamburger steak.

Programs for Ladies

HENRY: I'm sorry, uhhh Sweetheart, but I know you love onions so I got you onion soup. It's the house specialty the waiter said. And good for your figure, too . . . *(aside)* and my wallet.
   (Sings) How'd you like to be an onion in a petunia patch?
   A petunia patch? A petunia patch?
   How'd you like to be an onion in a petunia patch?
   A cryin' . . . .
   (Stops singing) Hmm . . . maybe it's a petunia in an onion patch? Oh, it's the thought that counts.

SADIE: Oh, Henry, you're so rheumatic . . . just like Bing Crosby.

HENRY: *(wipes brow with napkin)* Whew! Got outta that one. *(slurps)* How's your soup, Petunia . . . I mean, uhhh Sweetheart?

SADIE: *(slurps)* Oh, it's wonderful. Chucked full of onions.

BOTH slurp soup loudly. **WAITER** watches in disgust.

SADIE: *(starts to take a drink)* Henry?

HENRY: Yeah . . . uhhhh Sweetheart?

SADIE: Would you call the waiter, please? He seems to have forgotten my iced tea.

HENRY: Uhhh . . . uhhh . . . he said that they were fresh outta tea, too.

SADIE: Really? What kind of a place is this?

HENRY: Expensive! Uh, I mean, mighty popular to run outta everything. So I just ordered lemon slices. You can squeeze the lemon in the water and add some sugar and make lemonade. Yeah . . . you know what they say, "When life hands you lemons, make lemonade."

SADIE: Oh, Henry, you're such a tease. That's what I love about you, your sense of humor.

BANQUET PROGRAMS

HENRY *grins and nods; pushes his chair back and motions for the waiter.* **WAITER** *comes to the table.*

WAITER: Yes, sir. May I get you some dessert?

HENRY: No! No no no! We're finished!

SADIE: But, Henry, I wanted a double fudge cake.

HENRY: Uhhh . . . uhhh . . . *(shakes head at the waiter)* they're fresh outta that, too.

WAITER: *(aside)* I knew it! This old geezer's 'bout broke.

SADIE: *(hotly)* Well, what kind of restaurant is this anyway? They are out of everything! You can be sure I'll not come back here. *(folds napkin; picks up her purse, not paying attention to Henry and the waiter)*

HENRY and WAITER: That's fine with me!

WAITER: *(hands Henry the ticket)* I'll take care of your check, sir. You can pay me.

HENRY: *(looks closely at the ticket; wipes brow; mutters)* $6.78! Whew! *(pulls out seven bills and hands them to the waiter)* Keep the change, young man. Keep the change!

WAITER: *(sarcastically)* Yes, sir. Thank you, sir. *(stands to one side, money in hand)*

HENRY: *(to Sadie)* I suppose you want me to help you outta your chair?

SADIE *stands. She takes Henry's arm.*

SADIE: That was a rheumatic meal, Henry. I shall never forget it.

HENRY: Why you are most welcome, Sadie! Sadie? Sadie, that's your name! *(puts his arm around her and sings)* Let me call you Sadie, I'm in love with you.

Programs for Ladies

SADIE* and *HENRY *lean toward each other as if about to kiss.* ***BOTH*** *pull back and turn up noses.*

SADIE and HENRY: Yuk! Onions!

THEY EXIT*, far apart.*

WAITER: *(looks at the bills in his hand; eyes get wide; waves bills as he counts)* Well, what do you know? Ten, twenty, thirty, forty, fifty, sixty, seventy! $70.00! That old gentleman just bought my sweetheart and me a fancy dinner at a first-class restaurant.

WAITER EXITS.

Menu
- Home-cooked hamburgers and french fries or chips served in napkin-lined plastic baskets.
- Sodas (complete with paper straws) served in "Coke" glasses. These can be purchased from a discount store.
- Malts or shakes.
- Make ice cream sundaes or banana splits. Check with fast food restaurants or restaurant suppliers for plastic banana split containers.

One church had their singles serve as waitresses, complete with poodle skirts, scarves, and bobby socks. They carried order pads and wrote down each person's name, what they wanted on their hamburgers, their drink and/or the flavor of malt they wanted. For large groups have a condiment table, so each person can fix his/her hamburger.

Gift Baskets

*"For as we have many members
in one body, and all members have not the same office:
so we, being many, are one body in Christ,
and every one members one of another.
Having then gifts differing according to the grace
that is given to us"* (Romans 12:4-6).

Decorations

The decorations for this banquet can also be a fundraiser for Mother's Memorial. A fun way to do this is to assign a lady or team to gather items for each basket. Teams may donate money to buy the items or contact local merchants for donations. Dollar stores are a good source for basket fillers. Give prizes to the teams (or individuals) whose baskets raise the most money at the auction. If you do not have an auctioneer, a silent auction is an alternative, although not as much fun.

Centerpieces are baskets or other containers filled with items that reflect different ladies.

• **The Creative Lady.** Include craft items such as a small glue gun, glue sticks, wreath, silk flowers, gift certificate to local craft store, craft kits, and/or craft magazines.

• **The Sewing Lady.** Include scissors (thread scissors or other unusual scissors), jar of buttons, scraps of lace, package of needles, spools of thread, any sewing notions, gift certificate to fabric or quilt store.

• **The Shopaholic.** Include shopping bags from department stores: the paper ones with handles. If you cannot find these in small sizes, make your own. Purchase small bags (8" tall) from a craft or party store. Glue labels from department stores to the bags. Arrange several in the center of the table with tissue paper sticking out of the tops. Inside the bags put slippers (to wear when her feet hurt), snacks, a bottle of water, a certificate for lunch or a snack from a mall kiosk, a gift certificate, a magnifying glass to read the fine print on the sale labels, and advertisements from local stores (Sunday paper).

• **The Junk Food Lady**. Fill basket with junk food.

Programs for Ladies

- **The Cooking Lady.** Choose a theme for this basket. If Italian, include items like a package of spaghetti sauce, French bread, parmesan cheese. For pizza, include pizza dough mix, sauce, cheese, pepperoni, pizza pan, and cutter. Other themes could be dessert, salad, or any ethnic food. Add dish towels, kitchen gadgets, and a cookbook.
- **The Baking Lady.** Include hot pads, baking mixes, icing, sprinkles, and a kitchen timer.
- **The Praying Lady.** Include a book about prayer, devotional books, prayer gift certificates from the World Network of Prayer, and/or a framed Scripture.
- **The Relaxed Lady.** Include bubble bath, lotion, a bath sponge, a candle, body spray, a book or music tape, and a box of chocolates.
- **The Musical Lady.** Include CDs and/or tapes (new or slightly used), a gift certificate to a Bible bookstore, tickets to the symphony.
- **The Gardening Lady.** She will bid high for seeds, garden tools, gloves, and plants. Put the items in a clay pot.
- **The Collector.** Include several of any type of collectible such as ceramic shoes, salt and pepper shakers, etc. Add a book or magazine about collectibles.
- **The Victorian Lady.** Arrange a porcelain doll and Victorian items on a lace doily.
- **The Coffee Break Lady.** In this container (perhaps a coffee tin) put flavored coffees, mugs, stirring sticks, creamer, coffeecake, or muffin mix.
- **The Tea Party Lady.** In a tea tin put flavored teas, a teapot and/or teacups, cloth napkins, tea cookies.

Items in the baskets/containers can be "like new" things that the ladies have at home. For example, a lady may have a teapot that she never uses, but another lady would enjoy it.

Favors

Favors at each table should match the gift basket theme. For example:

The Baking Lady: cookie cutters.

The Relaxed Lady: bath scrubbers or small bars of soap wrapped with tulle or gift wrap.

Quiz for Printed Program

Give each lady a copy of this page. Or if you prefer, read the name aloud and let each table write down their answers.

What's My Line?

Every lady is different. Each has unique characteristics, talents, callings, likes, and dislikes. Can you identify these Bible women by telling what each one did?

1. Dorcas
2. Martha
3. Mary of Bethany
4. Hannah
5. Ruth
6. Abigail
7. Miriam
8. Lydia
9. Phebe
10. Rizpah
11. Joanna
12. Deborah

Programs for Ladies

Games

Penny Game. Give each guest five pennies. They will return them at the end of the game. Each player names as many unusual things that she has done as she has pennies (e.g., had twins, gone skydiving, met the President). As a player names something, each one who has done that same thing puts a penny in a bowl. If the lady who names the thing is the only one who has done it, she keeps her penny. The person with the most remaining pennies is the winner. This helps guests get to know something about each other.

The Mystery Gift. Wrap a mystery gift in a pretty package. It should be unbreakable with some weight and possibly a little sound when shaken. Pass the gift around and allow each lady to hold it briefly and shake it gently. Give each lady a slip of paper on which to write her name and her guess. Have a drawing. The first name drawn with the correct answer receives the gift.

Precious Moments

Ask two mothers and two daughters to be prepared to talk briefly about their mother or daughter's gifts (talent, ability) and how it has been a blessing to their family.

Activity

Charades

Write each of the seven motivational gifts from Romans 12:4-8 on an index card: (1) prophesying/perceiving; (2) ministering/serving; (3) teaching; (4) exhorting/encouraging; (5) giving; (6) ruling/administrating; (7) showing mercy.

Divide into seven teams and play charades. Each team pantomimes their gift and the other teams guess what it is.

Skit

An Open Door

CAST:

> Doorkeeper (someone with a lot of facial expressions)
> Lady in search of gifts

PROPS:

> Full-size hollow core interior door (a mobile home door works best)
> Sunday school teacher's manual
> Home Bible study
> Note cards and envelopes
> Money
> Prayer cloth, tracts from World Network of Prayer (or other tracts on prayer) "How to Pray for . . ."
> Canned goods in a paper bag marked "Food Pantry"
> Church bulletin

*The **DOORKEEPER** is silent throughout the skit. She carries the door in front of her, following the lady, getting in front of or to the side of her. At the appropriate time, she drops an item in the lady's path. While the **LADY** discusses the item, the doorkeeper nods her head, makes faces, points, etc. Lots of dramatics here.*

LADY: I know there must be something I can do for the Lord. Brother Pastor said everyone has talent, but I sure don't know where mine is. *(looks up)* Lord, please show me what I can do for You.

DOORKEEPER *slides the Sunday school teacher's manual across floor in front of the lady. She moves the door so it is directly in front of the lady, sticks her head around it, and nods with satisfaction when **LADY** picks up the book.*

LADY: Ohhh, Lord, You know I can't teach Sunday school. Children make me nervous. No, I don't think that is my talent. *(carries the manual to one side of the stage and drops it; turns*

Programs for Ladies

around) Lord, I am sure there is something I can do for You besides work with children.

DOORKEEPER *drops the home Bible study in her path. Places the door three to four feet in front of lady and leans around door to point at Bible study.*

LADY: *(picks up the Bible study)* Now, Lord, You know I can't teach Bible studies. I just don't feel I am called to that ministry. It takes sooo much study and preparation. *(discards the Bible study on top of the Sunday school manual)* But, Lord, if You would open a door, I'd be glad to work for You.

DOORKEEPER *rolls her eyes and shakes her head in exasperation. She walks around the lady and drops the note cards and envelopes.*

LADY *picks up the note cards.*

DOORKEEPER *nods vigorously and smiles.*

LADY: Encourage people? Oh, Lord, You know I don't like to write notes or talk on the phone. Well, unless Sister Susie calls. She is my connection to the church grapevine, You know. No, Lord, encouragement is not my gift. Surely there is something else I can do. *(discards the note cards on the pile)* I wish You would open a door for me.

DOORKEEPER *shrugs her shoulders disgustedly. Picks up the door and walks around, dropping dollars.*

LADY *picks up the money.*

DOORKEEPER *stops, sets the door down, smiles and shakes head.*

LADY: Give in the offering? Lord, You know I gave $1.27 in the offering last week. Why, that was sacrificial giving. I mean, I was only going to give $1.00, and I gave an extra twenty-seven cents. I just don't have any extra to spare. You know I am saving so I can go to Hawaii this summer. *(tucks the money in her pocket)* I really would like to work for You, Lord, if You will just let me know what to do.

DOORKEEPER *shakes her head in amazement, picks up door, and walks around. She drops a prayer cloth and tracts.*

LADY: *(picks them up)* Lead ladies' prayer meeting? Intercede? You have got to be kidding! I just don't think it is necessary to get together and pray like that. I pray in my prayer closet. Besides, I don't have time. I have garden club on Monday morning, and I am the president, You know. Tuesday morning I do my yard work and laundry, Wednesday morning is my golf day. Thursday morning I wash my hair, and Friday morning I go to garage sales. No, there is just not time for prayer meetings. Lord, please help me find something I can do for You.

DOORKEEPER *makes faces. Picks up the door, circles around the lady, and sets bag marked "Food pantry" containing canned goods in front of her. Peeks around the door and points toward the bag.*

LADY: Help in the food pantry, deliver food to the poor? Oh, I can't do that. I just can't relate to those people. *(puts the bag with other discarded items)* Lord, there must be something I can do.

DOORKEEPER *grabs the door and stomps around, dropping the church bulletin.*

LADY: *(picks it up)* Oh, surely there will be something in here that will help me find direction. Hmm . . . "workers needed in the nursery." No thank you! *(holds nose)* No dirty diapers for me! *(reads)* "Ladies needed to help make peanut brittle." Nope, can't do that either. I might burn myself. The choir is looking for singers. No, they always give the solos to Sister Jones, and I won't sing if I can't do solos. Lord, I just don't understand why I can't find an open door to work for You. Brother Pastor said we all have a job to do, but I guess I'll just have to draw unemployment. Seems You can't find a job for me.

Programs for Ladies

DOORKEEPER *picks up the door and* ***EXITS****, shaking her head.*

LADY EXITS*, mumbling about a sale at the mall.*

Topic for Speaker

Identifying Your Gift

Ask someone to research and speak on the motivational gifts listed in Romans 12:4-8.

The Sunday School Division of the United Pentecostal Church International, 8855 Dunn Road, Hazelwood, MO 63042 offers a "Discover Your Talents and Abilities Questionnaire" for about $1.00 each. Consider ordering one for each lady. (Phone: 314-837-7300, ext. 358)

Or find a talent quiz online. Go to www.about.com and do a search on "spiritual gift test."

Most women want to know what their giftedness is. Often it helps a woman to better understand and accept herself when she recognizes her gifts. She then is able to focus her efforts in the area where she is most effective and fulfilled.

Hand 'n Hand

"Whatsoever thy hand findeth to do, do it with thy might"
(Ecclesiastes 9:10).
"She stretcheth out her hand to the poor; yea, she reacheth forth her hands to the needy"
(Proverbs 31:20).

Decorations

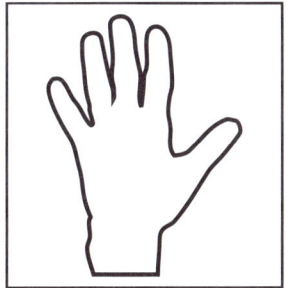
See reproducible art on page 316.

Use a copy machine to make a transparency of the hand pattern. With an overhead projector enlarge two hands to five to six feet tall. Trace on heavy cardboard, foam core, or thin plywood. Paint or cover with fabric, using spray adhesive. Embellish as desired. Tape broomsticks or a six-foot piece of 1" PVC pipe to the back of the hands with duct tape, leaving two feet sticking below the hands. Insert the sticks or pipes into a bucket of sand at a slight angle. Pull tissue paper up around the bucket. Use these behind the podium.

Centerpieces

In the center of each table, place a lady's purse with a pair of gloves draped over the top of the purse.

Ask a man who enjoys woodworking to help with this project. Use the pattern to make wooden hands. Paint or decorate as desired. Write the theme of the banquet on the hand with a paint pen. Wrap wire around a dowel rod. Drill a small hole in each side of the top of the hand. Insert the ends of the wire in the holes and hot glue in place. Put silk greenery around the base of the hand.

Purchase hatboxes and place them in the center of the table. To the back of the box attach a small dowel rod, painted to match the box. Adhere a small piece of Styrofoam inside the hatbox. Insert the dowel rod into the Styrofoam. Stuff the box with colored tissue paper, leaving the ends sticking up. Drape gloves over the edge of the box. Add scraps of lace if desired.

Programs for Ladies

Favors

• **Ladies' Gloves.** Embellish with lace, ribbon, and beads. If desired, insert a small amount of potpourri in the glove and glue the edges together. Look for gloves at garage sales, antique stores, and resale shops. Check the department store clearance tables after Easter. Child-sized gloves are fine. Place one glove at each place setting.

• **Punkydoodles**. Purchase hand-shaped Punkydoodles from a teacher supply store. Embellish as desired. Buy smaller hand shapes for name tags. Punch two holes in each hand and insert a safety pin.

• **Hand Lotion.** Purchase sample-sized bottles of hand lotion. Tie a ribbon around the neck of each bottle and place one beside each place. Check for donations with stores and individuals selling creams and lotions. They may have small containers or packets of

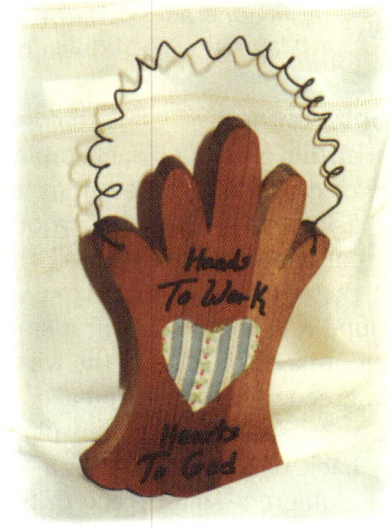

lotions. Put these in baskets, wrap in tulle or cellophane, and tie a ribbon around the top.

Activities

All Hands on Board. A couple of weeks before the banquet take pictures of the hands of a dozen or so ladies who will be at the banquet. Arrange the developed photos on a board and number them.

When the guests enter, give each a slip of paper and challenge her to identify the hands on the board. Give the one who correctly identifies the most hands a pair of gloves. In case of a tie, have a drawing.

Handy Tips. Place an index card and pencil beside each place setting. As the ladies wait for the program to begin, ask them to write a handy tip on the card. It can be humorous or serious, for saving time, removing stains, cooking, disciplining children, being a good hostess, or anything that interests ladies.

At some point during the program, appoint a team of three judges. Read the tips aloud to the ladies. The judges decide on the winners: (1) most creative, (2) most helpful, and (3) funniest. Award prizes like hand lotion, fingernail files, manicure sets, etc.

Prayer Handkerchiefs. Ask each lady to bring a handkerchief. On a table place several fabric pens of various colors. As each lady arrives, she prints her name on one corner of her handkerchief. When the handkerchiefs are dry, fold them so the names do not show and place them in a basket. At some point in the program, pass the basket and ask each lady to take a handkerchief, promising to pray for the lady whose handkerchief she has drawn. Set a time limit to this prayer activity, such as three months or even until the next banquet. (Thanks to Racquel Guerrero, Salt Lake City, Utah, for this idea.)

Programs for Ladies

Quiz for the Printed Program

Handy Answers

Each answer contains the word "hand."

1. Does not have to be dry-cleaned. _____

2. Made at home, not in a factory. _____

3. A square of cloth. _____

4. Has been used. _____

5. A famous sculpture of folded hands. _____

6. The steering device on a bicycle. _____

7. A small utensil. _____

8. A purse. _____

9. A small round object used in a game. _____

10. A female servant. _____

11. A pamphlet or brochure. _____

12. A restraining device used on criminals. _____

13. A disability. _____

14. To select personally. _____

15. A firearm. _____

16. To grasp hands in greeting. _____

17. Penmanship. _____

18. One who does odd jobs. _____

19. Freebie. _____

20. A musical instrument. _____

BANQUET PROGRAMS

Gloves

Each answer is a kind of glove.

ACROSS

4 Worn when working in the soil.
6 Worn on a diamond.
11 Throw-away.
13 An expensive fabric.
15 Both the first and last season of the year.

DOWN

1 Made from a plant that produces balls.
2 Worn when hands are on a wheel.
3 _____ and satin.
5 Synthetic rubber.
7 Worn in a ring.
8 Made from trees.
9 Worn to balls and banquets.
10 "An iron hand in a _____ glove."
12 Made from cowhide.
14 "Handle with _____ gloves."

Programs for Ladies

Game
Place eight to ten different kinds of gloves on a tray. Suggestions: work gloves, dress gloves, rubber gloves, winter gloves, driving gloves, leather gloves, baseball glove, and latex gloves.

Walk around and let the women look at the tray. Then put the tray out of sight. Give each lady a paper and a pencil. She lists the gloves she remembers seeing.

Special Moments
- Arrange for a skin care expert to present a ten-minute talk on skin care.
- Ask the ladies to share things they remember about their mothers' hands.

Songs
"Lord, Use My Hands"
"Hand in Hand with Jesus"
"Precious Lord, Take My Hand"

Home Tweet Home

"To be discreet, chaste, keepers at home, good, obedient to their own husbands, that the word of God be not blasphemed" (Titus 2:5).

From Other Translations

"To live wisely, and be pure, to take care of their homes, to do good, and to be submissive to their husbands. Then they will not bring shame on the word of God" (Titus 2:5, *NLT*).

"To be self-controlled and pure, to be busy at home, to be kind, and to be subject to their husbands, so that no one will malign the word of God" (Titus 2:5, *NIV*).

"To be sensible and clean minded, spending their time in their own homes, being kind and obedient to their husbands so that the Christian faith can't be spoken against by those who know them" (Titus 2:5, *TLB*).

Creating a Home Tweet Home is a challenge and joy to a woman. Home, like a bird's nest in a storm, should be a haven for a family. The mother is the key to making that happen.

Decorations

Plates and napkins printed with birdhouses are available at party stores or use clear or solid color plates and solid color paper place mats. Purchase a notepad in the shape of a birdhouse (from a teacher supply store) and attach it to the place mat with double-sided tape, or buy bulletin board border decorated with bird houses and attach a strip to the side or bottom of the place mat with double-stick tape.

Place birdhouses, bird feeders, and/or a birdbath on stands or sitting on columns around the room.

Centerpieces

Birdhouses. Buy them already decorated or purchase unfinished birdhouses from craft stores. Paint and add greenery as desired. Place in the center of table; intertwine silk greenery around the birdhouse.

Birdbaths. Turn a clay pot upside down. Glue a larger clay base

Programs for Ladies

(water catcher) to the clay pot. Hot glue a bird to the side of the birdbath. Place a napkin or doily in the base and use for muffins, rolls, or crackers.

Favors
- Small birdhouses purchased from dollar or craft stores.
- Make miniature birdbaths using 1-2" clay pots and saucers.

See reproducible art on page 317.

- Use the pattern to make a birdhouse. On card stock copy two birdhouses per lady. Glue the edges together, leaving the top open. Glue on a circle of a different color for the "hole." Enclose a zipper locked bag of birdseed (or mints, nuts, potpourri, or bath salts) in the house.
- Purchase birdhouse stickers. Print a Scripture on card stock. Cut into business card size pieces. Attach a birdhouse sticker to card and laminate. Glue a magnet to the back of card.

BANQUET PROGRAMS

Door Prizes

Centerpieces can double as door prizes. Birdhouse teapots or cookie jars also make good gifts. Cracker Barrel restaurants are good sources for birdhouse items.

Printed Programs

• Cut card stock into birdhouse shape. Print the program on colored paper and insert into card stock cover.

• Fold colorful papers in half and stamp the front with birdhouse stamp or stencil. Trim around the edges with decorative scissors.

Quiz for the Printed Program

Copy this quiz onto the printed program. Answers are on page 312 and may vary.

Who Lives Here?

Homes have different names, depending on who lives there. Who lives in these homes?

1. Palace
2. Nest
3. Den
4. White House
5. Roost
6. Hive
7. Colony
8. Aquarium
9. Barn
10. Stable
11. Sty
12. Cage
13. Burrow
14. Web
15. Fold
16. Shack
17. Cave
18. Prison
19. Mansion

Programs for Ladies

Music
Play a tape of bird sounds during the meal.
"His Eye Is on the Sparrow"

Demonstrations
Have demonstrations of one or more of the following:
• Setting a beautiful table. Show several tables, both formal and informal. Include napkin folding; give each lady a napkin (cloth or paper) to fold along with the demonstrator. Check at the public library for decorating books.
• Decorating tips using collections, heirlooms, candles, and books.
• Decorating your home. Contact a dealer who sells home accessories, such as Home Interiors and Gifts (www.homeinteriors.com), The Homemaker's Idea Company (www.thehomemakersideaco.com, 800 800-5452) or Country Peddler, (www.cpca-usa.com, 800 873-3537). Some furniture stores have decorators on staff that will speak to groups.
• Simple recipes/cooking for a month.
   Once-a-Month Cooking by Mimi Wilson and Mary Beth Lagerborg; Focus on the Family Publishing ISBN 1-56179-041-9
• Time-saving tips: cleaning and storage.
• Family devotion ideas.
• Hospitality: making your guests feel comfortable; how to make your guest room say "welcome." *The Role of the Shepherdess* by Roffie Ensey has a chapter on hospitality. Also *Christian Social Graces* by Gayla Baughman is full of ideas. These books are available through the Pentecostal Publishing House.

Games
A Sensitivity Test. Creating a Home Tweet Home for family and guests is a sensitive work.

For prizes bring items that relate to our five senses, such as a small hand mirror (sight), a fragrant candle or bag of potpourri (smell), a small box of chocolates (taste), a music tape or CD (hearing), and a small pillow (touch). Prizes can vary. To cut down on cost, they can even be secondhand if they are like new.

Give each lady a piece of paper and a pencil. Allow time after each statement for the ladies to reflect before answering.

The thing in my home I enjoy most looking at is

My favorite smell at my house is

My favorite home-based taste is

What I love hearing most at my house is

The thing at my house that I like most to touch is

Then call for volunteers to share their answers, one sense at a time. After each sense, let the women vote on the best answer and award the appropriate prize.

Precious Moments
Ask two or three ladies to be prepared to tell about what made their homes special when they were growing up.

Skit

No Place Like Home

CAST:

    Lady of the house
    Maid
    Narrator

PROPS:

    List
    Large safety pin
    Ink pen
    Hand mirror
    Potatoes (five or seven)
    Belt
    Can of powder
    Powder puff
    Miscellaneous items (as needed)
    Marker
    Whole baking chicken

Programs for Ladies

NARRATOR: Words have many meanings. Let's look in on Sister _____ (pastor's wife) and Gladys, her housekeeper.

LADY: Gladys, I have to go out of town. I'll be back tomorrow. Here is a list of jobs for you to do while I am gone.

GLADYS: Yes, ma'am, I'll get right on it.

LADY *picks up purse and leaves.*

GLADYS: *(looks at list and reads first item)* Pin up your hair. *(picks up safety pins and tries to pin up hair)* Wait, I know. *(sticks ink pen in hair, looks in mirror and shrugs shoulders)* What's next? Pair the potatoes. Okay. *(puts potatoes together in pairs)* Here's a pair and here's a pair. Got an extra one. What am I supposed to do with it, I wonder.
(Reads next item) Dress the chicken. *(picks up whole chicken and puts doll clothes on it)* Chicken a la King.
(Reads) Whip the potatoes. *(Picks up a belt and hits potatoes)* I guess I had better start cleaning the house. *(picks up list and reads)* Dust the furniture. *(looks puzzled)* Okay. *(picks up box of powder and starts dusting the furniture with the powder puff)*

Here are some other ideas to use in this skit:
- Snap the beans *(glue snaps on beans)*.
- Draw the drapes *(draw picture of drapes on paper)*.
- Trim the steak *(put lace on steak)*.
- Measure one cup of rice *(measure cup of rice with a ruler)*
- Baste the chicken *(use a needle and thread)*.
- Toss the salad *(toss bag of salad like a Frisbee)*.

LADY ENTERS*, after Gladys has done all the damage she can do. After she asks a few key questions about the mess, she faints.*

GLADYS: *(wrings hands)* Oh dear, what do I do when someone faints? *(thinks a minute)* I know—call 911. *(yells)* Nine one one! Nine one one! *(checks Lady)* Funny! It's not helping. What else can I do? Oh, I know. Check her pulse. *(pulls out a marker and makes a large checkmark on the lady's wrist)*

LADY *sits upright.*

LADY: *(jumps to her feet and **EXITS** on the run, calling)* Let me out of here before she gets any more ideas.

GLADYS: That was a good idea. It worked. I don't know why she is so upset.

GLADYS EXITS.

(The idea for this skit came from an Amelia Bedelia book by Peggy Parish. This series of children's books contains a multitude of ideas that can be easily adapted into skits. Check them out at your public library or any bookstore.)

Psalm 23 Picnic

"The LORD is my shepherd; I shall not want" (Psalm 23:1).
"Go to the ant, thou sluggard; consider her ways, and be wise" (Proverbs 6:6).

This picnic idea works even in the winter since it is held indoors.

Decorations

Decorate the room for a picnic. Bring in park benches, lawn chairs, quilts spread on the floor, picnic baskets, and plants. A child's wading pool makes a nice pond. Borrow small fountains and set them among the greenery.

On the serving table spread quilts. Serve everything in baskets.

Hide rubber or plastic insects in the baskets, under the tables, and throughout the room. This will add to the hilarity of the occasion.

(Alternate) Have a box supper. Each lady brings dinner in a decorated box or basket, which is auctioned to the highest bidder.

Programs for Ladies

Centerpieces
- Set baskets on baby quilts or quilt blocks.
- Or make "tranquility vases."

Tranquility Vase

Clear glass vase, eleven inches tall, with opening for a four-inch plastic tray (available at discount or craft stores. Instructions are available with the vases.)
1 yard decorative ribbon
1 package aquarium rocks
Male beta fish, also called Siamese fighting fish
4-inch plastic saucer
Ruler
Scissors
6-inch water-loving plant, such as Anthurium, Spathaphyllium, or Philodendron

INSTRUCTIONS:

Rinse the vase and rocks.

Remove the plant from the pot and thoroughly rinse all soil from the roots under lukewarm running water. Trim the roots if needed. If the plant is too large, cut it in half down the middle to make sections about two inches across at the base.

Use scissors to cut an X about 2 1/2" across the center of the plastic saucer. Gently work the roots of plant through the cuts.

Place a two-inch layer of decorative rocks or gemstones in the bottom of the vase.

Fill the vase with treated water (distilled/purified) to about one inch below neck. This leaves air space so the fish can breathe.

Gently add the fish to the vase of water, following recommended care instructions provided by the pet store.

Holding the plastic saucer over the vase, work the roots into the vase. Once the roots are in the water, rest the plastic saucer securely in the opening of the vase. Fill the plastic saucer with the remaining rocks.

Tie a decorative ribbon around the vase.

To feed the fish, gently grasp the plant by its stems and lift it along with the plastic tray to drop in the food. If the water becomes cloudy, temporarily transfer the fish to another bowl and replace the treated water. Trim the roots if they become too large.

Favors

Sheep. Make a pompom with white yarn. Cut a pipe cleaner in two three-inch pieces. Twist around the pompom to form legs. Cut a face from black fun foam and glue to the pompom.

Baskets. Line small baskets with red and white checked pieces of fabric. In the basket, place anything related to a picnic (e.g., plastic dinnerware, small cans of bug spray, wet-wipes).

Games

- **Find the Insects.** Announce at the beginning of the picnic that the one who finds the most insects will receive a prize. Rule: they cannot search for the insects. They must simply come upon them as they play games, eat, and visit.
- **Herd the Sheep.** Blow up two balloons. Draw a face on each balloon. Glue cotton balls to the balloon if desired. These are the sheep. Fold two pieces of 10" x 25" poster board into thirds. Tape the side of each piece together to form a triangle (tunnel). Set these tunnels on the floor near the center of the room.

Divide into two teams. Half of each team is at one end of the room, half at the other. Give each team a broom and a balloon. Assign each team a tunnel. The first person puts the balloon on the floor and hits it with the broom. She must "herd" the sheep to the other end of the room, going through her team's poster board tunnel. When she has herded the sheep over the line, she hands the broom to another player, who then herds the sheep back to the other side of the room. This continues until all the players have had a turn. First team finished wins.

Ants. A picnic is not complete without ants. In three minutes list words that include the word ant (plant, can't, slant, cantaloupe). Give a small prize to the one with the longest list.

Memory Ball. No picnic is complete without a ball game. This game can be played in a variety of ways with a variety of balls. A beach ball works well indoors.

Players stand in a circle. They are to quote Psalm 23. The first player quotes the first phrase, "The Lord is my shepherd." She then tosses the ball to another player (anyone in the circle). The player catches the ball and quotes the next phrase, "I shall not want." Then she tosses the ball to another player. Anyone who cannot quote the next phrase correctly, or misses the ball, is out. The goal is to correctly quote the chapter before everyone drops out.

(Alternate) Players quote any verse from their memory, not necessarily verses from a specific passage.

Programs for Ladies

Basketball Relay. Divide into two teams. You need a basketball for each team. Within the teams, players divide into pairs (players of approximately the same size). The teams line up on one side of the room. Designate a finish line on the other side of the room.

The first pair on each team stands back to back. Place a basketball between them in the small of their backs. The goal is to cross the room and return, keeping the basketball between them. If the players drop it, they return to the starting line. If after three tries, they have not reached the goal, they pass the ball to the next pair and return to the end of the line for another turn. Players keep their arms folded in front of them and cannot use their elbows to hold the balls in place.

If the players are taking too long, set a time limit. When time is called, the winning team is the one with the most pairs who have reached the goal.

Precious Moments

Have a story-telling contest. Offer a prize to the one who tells the craziest true picnic story.

Activities

Have an old-fashioned sing-along. Each table chooses one chorus or song and starts singing. Everyone sings along. When that song is finished, the next table starts their song.

A fun variation to this is to play musical charades. Each table decides on a song and motions. One person at each table is designated as the "song leader." Instead of singing, the teams pantomime the song, keeping time in their minds. Ladies at the other tables guess the song.

Consider the Ant

Instead of having a special speaker for such an informal occasion as a "picnic," divide into teams. Give each team a large index card with a characteristic of the ant on it. Set a time for each team to brainstorm to draw spiritual parallels. Ask, "What does the ant teach us?"

When time is called, a spokeswoman for each team shares their conclusions with the group. Limit responses to two or three points and minutes.

Characteristics of the ant for the index cards. Write one characteristic per card/team.
- The worker ants are all female. (Enjoy this one!)
- Every ant in the colony has a specific job. Some tend the nurs-

ery. Some carry out trash. Some guard the door, etc.
- Harvester ants actually plant and harvest a crop. Each ant has a job in the harvest.
- To safely ride out a flood, fire ants form a ball around the queen and are carried by the flood.
- Ants recognize one another by their smell and are loyal to their colony.
- Ants gather their food in the harvest and store it for the winter.
- Every ant has two stomachs, one private stomach for their food and a public stomach, much like a backpack. When they eat, they do not eat just for themselves. They eat to carry nourishment back to the babies and the ants at work in the colony.

If you have more than seven teams, check the children's department at the public library for more facts about ants.

Menu
- Chips, dips, sandwiches
    Hurt Yourself Dip (See page 302 for the recipe.)
    Queso (See page 303 for the recipe.)
- Fried chicken or ham, potato salad, baked beans, and slaw.

Say It with Flowers

"The flowers appear on the earth; the time of the singing of birds is come, and the voice of the turtle is heard in our land" (Song of Solomon 2:12).
"And the LORD shall guide thee continually, and satisfy thy soul in drought, and make fat thy bones: and thou shalt be like a watered garden, and like a spring of water, whose waters fail not" (Isaiah 58:11).

As every flower lover knows, flowers have a language of their own. Create an English flower garden where flowers speak to the heart.

Decorations

Programs for Ladies

Bring in plants and flowers of all types. Garden or park benches, lattice, teacarts, etc., help set the atmosphere of an English flower garden.

Each table features a different flower.

The flowers on this list express sentiment. The ladies can choose for their table the flower that expresses the characteristic or emotion on which they want to focus. One lady from each table could tell what the flower represents and why they chose it.

Use plates, napkins, painted/printed with that flower if possible.

Alyssum	Worth beyond beauty
Bluebell	Constancy, humility
Camellia (white)	Perfection, excellence
Carnation	Joy
Chrysanthemum (white)	Truth
Crocus	Gladness
Daffodil	Respect
Daisy	Innocence, purity
Freesia	Trust
Heather	Admiration
Iris	Promise
Lilac	Beauty
Lily	Devotion
Lily (white)	Purity, sweetness
Lily (yellow)	Gratitude

Lily of the Valley	Happiness
Mimosa	Sensitivity
Mum	Hope
Oleander	Caution
Orchid	Thoughtfulness
Pansy	Merriment
Peony	Compassion
Rose (red)	Passion
Rose	Love
Snapdragons	Strength
Sweet Pea	Blissful pleasure
Tiger Lily	Prosperity
Tulip	Luck
Violet	Virtue, modesty
Violet (blue)	Faithfulness, watchfulness
Water Lily	Purity of heart
Wisteria	Welcome
Zinnia (scarlet)	Constancy
Zinnia (white)	Goodness

Programs for Ladies

Centerpieces

Real or silk arrangements, featuring the chosen flower for each table.

Inexpensive watering cans in plastic or metal are available at discount stores. Set these in the center of the table. Place a flowerpot with the chosen flower on the table two to three inches from the spout of the watering can.

Mylar balloons and latex flower-shaped balloons are available at florists or specialty shops. Add balloon flowers to the centerpieces.

Favors

Silk Flowers. Purchase silk blooms of each flower. Pull the blooms off the stems. Push a stiff wire (eight inches long) through the bottom of the flower and wrap with green floral tape. Add a leaf halfway down the stem.

Bend the wire into a circular shape and set on the table. May be placed around a napkin.

Dirt Cake. This is both a dessert and a favor. (See the recipe on page 299.)

Serve the cake in small clay pots or plastic cups. Purchase silk flower bunches of each type of flower. Cut the flowers apart so each flower has its own stem. Insert the stem into the dirt cake.

Bedding Plants. Purchase flats of bedding plants at a nursery. Cut floral foil into squares. Set one bedding plant in the center of the foil. Pull the edges of the foil up around the plant. Make bows from narrow floral ribbon. Tie off the bow with the wire. Insert the wire into the soil.

Flower Bulbs. Wrap flower bulbs in tulle and tie with 1/4" ribbon.

Packets of Seed. Glue a small silk flower to a matching packet of seeds. Glue 1/4" ribbon to the top of the packet to form a hanger.

Precious Moments

Set up a lattice arbor with greenery climbing it. In front of it, place a park bench. Arrange for a professional photographer, or someone with a good camera and artistic eye, to take pictures of mother-daughter(s), family groups, individuals, etc., to record this precious moment.

More Precious Moments

Call for volunteers to tell about a time someone said something special to her with flowers or about a time she said something special to someone with flowers.

Programs for Ladies

Quizzes for the Printed Program

This quiz can be copied for the ladies to work as they wait for the program to begin. Patterns on pages 318 and 319.

Identify the Flowers

On this page there are ten different flowers. How many can you identify?

BANQUET PROGRAMS

Phonetically Speaking

Put the pictures in each frame together to find the name of a flower.

  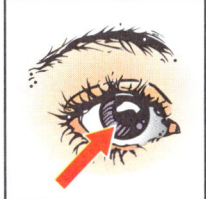

Programs for Ladies

Games

Can You Remember? Give each player a piece of paper and a pencil. Tell the players to list as many flowers as they can in three minutes. When time is called, ask the lady with the longest list to read the flowers on her list. When this lady names a flower that someone else has listed, that person who has listed it also calls out, "Got it," and it must be marked off of all the lists. Go around the room with ladies naming the flowers left on their lists. The winner is the lady who wrote the most flowers on her list that no one else remembered. Give a small prize.

A Flowery Answer. Copy this quiz and pass it out to the players. Allow five to seven minutes for them to write their responses. Appoint two or three judges before calling for answers. Since there are no correct/incorrect answers, give prizes for the most creative answer and the funniest answer. This will work best with a group of less than twenty. If you have more, consider dividing into pairs. Otherwise, judging the responses could be too time-consuming.

Say It with Flowers

Beside each statement, write the name of a flower that you would send to say it.

"I'm sorry I was so snappy." _____

"I love you." _____

"My heart is broken." _____

"I promise not to tell." _____

"It's your fault!" _____

"Congratulations on the new baby." _____

"Sorry your cat died." _____

"Thanks for the delicious meal." _____

"Hurry up and ask me!" _____

"Merry Christmas." _____

"Sending you kisses." _____

"I miss you." _____

"You're daffy, but I love you." _____

Bird Watching. Place a strip of masking tape on the floor, or draw a straight line with chalk. If marking on the floor is not feasible, bring a six-foot 2 x 4. The object is to walk a straight line while looking through a pair of binoculars backwards.

Song
"In the Garden"
If someone in your group does signing for the deaf, ask her to sign this song as it is sung. This should make an impressive presentation. Or it could be presented as a musical (brass, harp, or even guitar and harmonica)—anything "special."

Skits
"A Petunia in an Onion Patch," from *Programs for Ladies*, page 11.
"Fretful Flowers," *Programs for Ladies, Volume 2*, page 13.

Menu
Set up a salad bar. Serve each item in clay or plastic pots—a large pot for the lettuce, smaller pots for other vegetables and condiments. Put ice in oblong planters or wallpaper trays and insert the pots into the planters.

Serve drinks from watering cans.

Serve crackers in clay saucers.

For dessert, serve Dirt Cake. (See the recipe on page 299.)

Sunbeams and Rainbows

"Ye are the light of the world" (Matthew 5:14).
"I do set my bow in the cloud, and it shall be for a token of a covenant between me and the earth" (Genesis 9:13).

When a sunbeam passes through drops of water, it bends (refracts) and what do we see? A rainbow—a beautiful arch of color. Often in the rainy seasons God sends a "sunbeam" to brighten our days and to bring color to our lives. In this program those "sunbeams" are honored.

Rainbow Facts

The colors in the rainbow always appear in the same order: red on the top, then orange, yellow, green, blue, and purple.

The rainbow is known by many different names. Italians call it "the flashing arch." In Sanskrit, it is "the bow of India." The people of Annam call it "a little window in the sky." North African people greet the rainbow as "the bride of the rain." In the various languages of central Europe the rainbow is called "the bridge of the Holy Spirit" and "the girdle of God." (World Book Encyclopedia @1983)

Decorations

Rainbows. Use the six colors of the rainbow throughout the room.

Balloon Arch. Purchase ten-inch balloons in the six rainbow colors. Inflate the balloons, using an air compressor; helium is not needed. Tie the end of each inflated balloon. Insert one end of a large paper clip through the ends of four balloons of the same color. Twist the balloons around 1/2" CPVC pipe. (This pipe is flexible and will bend to form an arch.) Repeat with the next color and continue until all colors are used. Continue until the arch is the desired size.

Insert the ends of the CPVC in two buckets of sand. Cover the buckets with tissue paper.

CPVC is available at home improvement stores. Balloon arch frames are available at wedding rental stores.

Helium-balloon Arch. Inflate the balloons with helium two to

Programs for Ladies

three hours before the banquet. Balloon tape is available at balloon stores for this project. If cost is an issue, tie matching ribbon to each balloon: six-foot length of ribbon to the red, five-foot to the orange, four-foot to the yellow, three-foot to the green, two-foot to the blue, and one-foot to the purple.

Tie the balloons to an eight- to ten-foot ribbon. Secure the ends of the ribbon to stationary objects. (Microphone stands work well.) The balloons will form an arch or rainbow.

Table Settings

Use tablecloths, paper plates, and napkins in rainbow colors or place mats in rainbow colors with clear plates. Start with red, the next place setting is orange, then yellow, and continue in rainbow order. If you prefer, each table can be a different color (one all red, one all purple) with rainbow napkins.

Favors

• **Promises.** Print promise Scriptures on card stock. Cut into 1" x 3" pieces. Glue a rainbow eraser (available from Oriental Traders) or sticker to the corner of each card. Glue a magnet to the back.

• **Rainbows.** Notepads, erasers, key rings, and a variety of items with rainbows on them are available at discount stores. Purchase an assortment of these for favors.

Puzzle for Printed Program

Copy this onto the printed program (or separate sheets of paper) for the ladies to work as they wait for the program to begin. On each table place a mug filled with crayons or markers. Pattern on page 87.

A Color-full Puzzle

Add color to each picture to complete a saying. For example, color the cross red to get the "Red Cross."

Add color to each picture/word to complete a saying.

BANQUET PROGRAMS

Programs for Ladies

Games

Arrange the tiles to reveal a message. The letters are in the proper order on each tile.

ND I	ME	SET	EART
NANT	WEEN	LOUD	MY
SIS	BE F	I DO	TOK
AND	S, A	IN T	THE
EN O	T SH	F A	9:13
GENE	COVE	HE C	H.
OR A	BET	ALL	BOW

Precious Moments

• Before the banquet arrange for two or three ladies to tell about someone (also present) who brought a ray of sunshine into their lives at a dark time. Have happy face stickers for them to present to their "sunbeams."

• Before the banquet let the ladies who will be attending the banquet vote to choose the "Sunbeam" of your church. Of course, this is someone with a happy smile, a positive attitude, and a cheerful disposition. At the banquet announce the winner and present her with a yellow corsage and a gift matching her personality and tastes.

Songs

"Jesus Wants Me for a Sunbeam"
"Light Your World"
"Smile Awhile"

An Allegory

The Cave and the Light

Once upon a time a cave lived under the ground, as caves have a habit of doing. It had spent its lifetime in darkness.

The cave heard a voice calling, "Come up into the light. Come and see the sunshine."

He replied, "Light? What is light? I don't see anything but darkness."

The voice persisted, "Come and see. Come and see the light."

Finally, the cave became so curious that he ventured forth from his dark hole to see the light.

Looking up at the sun, he said, "Come with me and see what darkness is."

The sun replied, "Darkness? I do not know what darkness is."

The cave repeated, "Come with me and see."

So one day the sun accepted the cave's invitation. As the sun entered the cave, he said, "Now show me your darkness."

But there was none.

Outline

Sunbeams

I. The Power of a Sunbeam
   A. Drives out Darkness
   B. Produces Energy
   C. Brings Beauty
II. Be a SONbeam
   A. Drive out Darkness
   B. Tear Down Strongholds
   C. Reflect the Light

Menu

Use as many rainbow colors as possible.
- Finger sandwiches. Check with bakeries for colored bread.
- Vegetable trays.
- Fruit trays.
- Rainbow Jell-O or cookies.

Mini-Dramas

Synopses of Mini-Dramas

The Bridge Builders

Three monologues relate how each generation builds a bridge for the succeeding one. Because of the commitment, integrity, convictions, and faith of the grandmother and mother, the daughter overcomes her fear of the future.

Humor and truth are mixed to make this an enjoyable production. Approximate time: forty-five minutes.

The Parable of the Teacup

Mildred, having tea with her friend, Victoria, learns a lot about herself as she hears the story of a teacup that was chipped, emptied, and then restored. Although the story is fiction, the restoration of the teacup is typical of what happens to damaged china at Replacements Limited in Winston-Salem, North Carolina. The restoration of lives that Mildred experienced happens daily around the world at altars of repentance.

A serious message in a light three-scene setting. Approximate time: forty-five minutes.

Treasures of the Heart

Since Eve, women have collected valuables in the treasure chests of their hearts. "For where your treasure is, there will your heart be also." The members of the Collectors' Club, while showing their findings at a meeting, learn that the treasures we keep are the ones we give away. Amid the laughter the audience is challenged to look into their hearts and check their treasure chests.

One act. Approximate time: twenty-five minutes.

The Bridge Builders

CAST:

Grandmother, Past Bridge Builder
Mother, Present Bridge Builder
Daughter, Future Bridge Builder

PROPS:

Telephone
Telephone ringer
Walking cane (optional)

INSTRUCTIONS:

This drama is presented as three monologues.

SCENE I

The Past Bridge Builder's Values

<u>SOUND: Telephone</u>

ENTER GRANDMOTHER, *tottery, looking for the telephone.*

I'm a comin'. I'm a comin'! Where is that phone? That's the trouble with those newfangled pot-able phones. They're never in the same place twice. Now where is it?

<u>SOUND: TELEPHONE keeps ringing (at regular intervals) until she answers it.</u>

Ahhh, there it is. *(picks up phone; holds it upside down to ear)* Hello? Hello? I can't hear ya. Probably didn't push the right button. *(moves the phone away from ear and examines it, pushing buttons; turns it right side up)* Let's try it this way.

Hello? It's about time you answered. Where have you been? . . . Waiting for me to answer the phone? Well, I answered. Now where are you? Home?

Who is this anyway? . . . Sarah Lee? *(scratches head)* Sarah Lee? Oh, yeah, the lady that bakes those frozen cakes. Are you calling to get the recipe for my famous chocolate cake? Well, I can't give it to you. It's a family secret—

You know that? How'd you know it was a family secret? Oh, you're not Sara Lee, the baker. You're Sarah Lee, my daughter?

Daughter? *(Scratches head again and looks perplexed)* My daughter Sarah Lee? Oh, that's right. Well, I had you a looong time ago. You don't expect me to remember everything, do you? Why that was over fifty years ago. . . . What? Well, fifty or forty . . . At eighty ten years ain't much.

Why are you callin'? . . . You're gonna do what? Build a bridge? And you want me to what? Help you? Help you build a bridge?

Honey, the only bridge I've got is in my mouth! And I don't think I could build one of those, and neither could you. You went to Bible school, not dental college.

We're living in what? . . . Oh, yeah, the end times. Seems like I did hear somethin' about that. . . . What's that? We need to build a bridge for Emilie and all the little Emilies that follow? We've gotta help 'em get from here to there without drowning in worldliness and what? New Age fill-fill? New Age fill? Oh, New Age fill-os-ofee. Honey, in my day we just called it what it was—false doctrine!

Well, buildin' a bridge sounds well and good, Sarah Lee, but the truth is—you're no engineer, and I'm not either. Remember when we tried to put up that shelf in the bedroom?

Oh, you're talking about a spiritual bridge? Well, I hate to tell you this, honey, but we're not spiritual engineers either. We are just ordinary moms and grandmoms who love God and try to live right, but make lots of mistakes.

You've got a plan? Sarah Lee, I remember the last time you had a plan, it cost me $652.38, and I still haven't figured out where it went.

What? How can I remember amounts of money to the penny when I can't even remember my own daughter? . . . Well, I guess "economics" comes before "kids," you know, "e" before "k," in my mental file. *(taps head)* My mind's just like a stuffed file cabinet. Things are crammed in there. You see a lot, hear a lot, learn a lot . . . forget a lot in eighty years. Sometimes it's kinda hard to find the right file at the right time.

All right! All right, I'm listening.

(Nods) Uh-huh. The end times . . . Uh-huh. Families . . . Uh-huh. A bridge . . .

Share what with you? . . . My values? *(scratches head)* Hmmm . . . The biggest value I can think of off the top of my head was when I bought that bedroom suite at that garage sale back in 1958 for—

Oh, you're not talking about bargain values? You're talking about values? Values like what?

Values like commitment? Commitment? Sarah Lee, that was your Aunt Sadie who was committed, and they didn't keep her long. Said she was stupid, but she wasn't crazy.

Oh, you mean commitment—like to your dad? Sixty-three years married to the same man? Well, when I took him to raise, I figured it would be a lifetime project, and it has been. I'm still workin' on him.

Bein' married is kinda like bein' on a roller coaster that never stops. You could jump off, but the fall would be worse than the ride. So you just hang on and pray for the best!

And my commitment to God? Honey, it's more like God's commitment to me. Been pretty easy fer me to stick to Him. I reckon He's the one that's had to be committed to put up with me.

Programs for Ladies

Thirty-five years of cleaning the church every week? Why, Sarah Lee, that was a privilege. Some of the best blessings I ever got in my life, I got cleanin' the church and prayin' for the saints as I swept 'round their pews and talkin' to God about those little Sunday school kids as I picked up their gum wrappers and paper wads.

You say commitment's a pretty rare commodity these days. . . . Well, that's too bad 'cause commitment's really just love with Super Glue on it.

Sure, use it. Pour good old-fashioned commitment into one of them bridge piers.

What else have I got that you need for that bridge? Integ— what'd you say? In-teg-rity. Oh, that's just one of them fancy words . . . Oh!— *(holds phone away from ear)*

What's that bumpin' on my line? . . . You think I've got another call? But I don't have another phone.

What? Call waiting? Oh, yeah, I think your dad did say something about gettin' Call Waiting. So now what do I do?

Hang up on you? Why, honey, that wouldn't be nice. You know I never hang up on anybody, not even them tell-a-bunch people.

Oh, just pretend like I'm hangin' up on you? Well, that might be okay.

Push the hang-up button . . . let it up . . . and the other person will be on the line? But what'll happen to you? You'll just wait for me to hang up on them, and you'll still be here? Well, that's nice of you. Hang on. I'll try it.

(Pushes button) Hello? Hello? *(changes phone to other ear)* Hellooooo? Hello, whoever you are! *(takes phone away from ear and talks to it)* So you hung up on me! That sure wasn't nice. You interrupt my conversation with Sarah Lee and then you hang up before I can get to you. You know what I think about you, Call Waiting? I think you're rude!

MINI-DRAMAS

Now how do I get back to Sarah Lee? *(starts pushing buttons and checking the phone with each push)* Hello? Hello? Sarah Lee, where'd ya go? Hello? *(finally gets connected)*

Ahhh, there you are. Now what were we talkin' about before we were so rudely interrupted?

Oh, yeah, puttin' integrity in that bridge pier. Integrity's just one of them fancy words for being honest—telling the truth, even when it means admitting that I'm forty pounds heavier than it says on my driver's license; paying my bills, even when it means passing up that sale at Dillard's; keeping my word, even when it means helping at the bake sale when I'd rather turn over and go back to sleep.

Integrity's just doing what's right.

Sure I think integrity would make a good pier in that bridge. Integrity's pretty strong stuff, got lots of steel in it.

Now you've got commitment and integrity. How many piers you gonna put under that bridge? . . . Four? . . . What else have I got that you need?

Convictions? Hmmm. The other day I heard this professional gal in her suit carryin' one of them briefcases say that convictions are a thing of the past . . . old-fashioned, out-of-style, okay for grandma, but not for her. Said things have changed.

Said somethin' 'bout sit-u, sit-u, situ-ations . . . Oh, what did she call it? . . . Situational ethics? Yeah, that's the term. What's that mean, Sarah Lee? . . . Means right or wrong is determined by the situation? Baloney! Right and wrong is determined by the Word of God!

This little gal said, *(mimics)* "After all, this is the twenty-first century!"

Well, I got news for her, people is people, no matter what the century.

Honey, pour a double weight of convictions in that bridge pier. I've got a feeling our kids comin' after us are gonna need lots of good, strong, old-fashioned convictions if they're gonna survive the flood of worldliness that's sweepin' this generation!

Oh, no, don't tell me somebody's bumpin' in on my line again? Not my line? It's yours? Will I hold? Hold what? Hold the phone? Honey, I'm holdin' the phone right now. You mean wait while you answer that other call? Well, I reckon I will, but in my day we were taught not to be interrupting other folk's conversations. . . . All right! All right, I'll hold.

(To audience) Seems to me, the more machines we get, the ruder we get. Can you believe that the other day a computer called me to ask me to vote for some guy? I'd never vote for a guy that had to have a computer do his talkin'. Then I tried to call this business, and it took ten minutes to get to a real live body. Then—

(Looks at the phone) Well, what am I doin' standin' here holdin' the telephone? Was I callin' somebody or answerin' it? Hum!

Hello? Hello? Nobody's there. I musta been callin' somebody, but who? Oh, hi, Sarah Lee? Why did I call you? Funny thing I never heard your phone ring. . . . Oh, now I remember I was talkin' to you, and you put me on hold so you could talk to somebody else. That was not nice. When I was a kid we were taught . . . Yeah. How'd you know? Oh.

Well, what were we talkin' 'bout? Oh, yeah, building this bridge. You're gonna build those piers outta commitment, and uhhh, integrity, and uhhh, what else? Oh, yeah, convictions. That's three piers. What you gonna put in the last one?

Faith? Well, honey, I don't have a lot of faith. I'm not a candidate for the hall of faith. Seems to me that this business of faith is blowed all outta proportion. Faith's just believin' God's not a liar, that He's gonna do what He says.

Sure, I remember that time we prayed and God healed you of

spinal meningitis. But He said we'd lay hands on the sick and they'd recover. So we did, He did, and you did. That's faith.

Yeah. Yeah, I remember the time in the Depression your dad couldn't get a job. We didn't have anything to eat, and we prayed. The next day the neighbors moved to California—and gave us their cow and chickens. Said they were payin' us back for all the times we'd helped them. We never went hungry again.

Faith's not some high-powered evangelist in alligator shoes hyping up a crowd. Faith's just believing that what God says He'll do, He'll do.

Don't know how somethin' so simple got made so complicated.

Sure, put faith in your bridge. Faith is simple, but it's powerful! Can't no flood shake it. Build that bridge on faith, and it'll hold any weight that crosses it.

Commitment . . . integrity . . . convictions . . . faith—pretty strong stuff! Kept me steady through poverty and prosperity, joy and sorrow, and all the highs and lows of life these eighty years. Those values will keep that bridge standing no matter how bad the flood gets. Yeah, that's right. Just remember, Sarah Lee—

Oh, no! Somebody bumpin' in on us again, and I'm gettin' tired of it so I'm just gonna go bake that famous chocolate cake. Good-bye, Sarah Lee, and whoever else you are that's callin'.

GRANDMOTHER *hangs up the phone and* **EXITS.**

SCENE II

The Present Bridge Builder's Sacrifice

PROPS:

Table covered with tablecloth
Chair
Handkerchief

MOTHER dressed in robe with scarf on her head, yawning and peering at her watch through half-open eyes.

What time is it anyway? Two-thirty-five? *(yawns)* I sure wish I could sleep. I'm so worried! *(big yawn)* So much to worry about.

(Draggy) I guess God wants me to pray. Must be why I can't sleep. I'm sure it's not that pepperoni pizza.

Did I take my hormone pill yesterday?

I better not kneel, or I'll go to sleep for sure.

(Starts to sit down at the table, almost misses the chair, and finally sits down. Puts chin in hands and yawns) Now let's see; what was I was worrying about? Oh, yeah, this bridge project. It's up to me to do it. Mother's too old, and Emilie's too young.

(Wails) But, Lord, I've never built a bridge before! I don't know where to start. And what if I don't do a good job, and the bridge collapses, and my kids drown in materialism and humanism and all the other "isms" of the end time?

Oh, Lord, why me? Like Mom said, I'm not a spiritual engineer.

I can't even turn on a computer. I've never gotten an e-mail in my life. FAX? What's a FAX? I'm so out-of-touch with today's world, how can I ever build a bridge to get my kids through adolescence with their values intact? *(slaps face lightly)* I feel so not-with-it.

(Yawns) God, would . . . You . . . tell me. . . . *(eyes close)* zzzzzzz.

(Snorts. Shakes head) Let's see. Where was I? Oh, yes, praying about building that bridge. God . . . *(looks up, blinks)* God? What? Did You say something?

"I'm not praying? I'm worrying?" Well, yeah, but . . . *(still looking up, blinks, shakes head)*.

But, God? . . . "Worrying aloud is not praying? I'm . . . on the wrong track?" *(nods, takes deep breath)* Well, okay, I'll try again.

(Folds hands in prayer position. Closes eyes. Prays in a measured way with each word carefully thought out and pronounced) Dear God . . . uhhhh . . . uhhhh *(to self)* start with praise. Oh, yeah! *(back to prayer)* Uhhh . . . dear God, thank - You - for - giving - me this project. I don't know how I'll ever . . . *(shakes head)* No! No! Not that way! *(takes big breath)* I know it's a big responsibility and *(sighs heavily and nods)* a wonderful privilege; I am honored. *(looks up)* Is that better?

(Hands back in prayer position. Eyes closed) I . . . uhhhh . . . uhhhh . . . I know it will require tremendous dedication and sacrifice. But I am willing, Lord. Use me. *(looks up and smiles)* Okay?

(Eyes closed) "[I] present [my] bod[y] a living sacrifice, holy" . . . *(whines)* well, I try to be holy . . . *(prayer tone of voice)* "and acceptable". . . *(whines)* I hope . . . *(prayer voice)* "unto [You], which is [my] reasonable service."[1]

(Yawns. Straightens shoulders. Nods firmly) Lord, I'll build that bridge for You, or I'll die trying. *(eyes pop open)* Die? Well, I don't mean that literally, Lord. You know what I mean.

I mean, I'll die out to . . . I'll die out to . . . to my own . . . to . . . my . . . own . . . will? I guess. Maybe. That is, if You don't expect me to fast too often. You know, not over twice a year, or pray too much . . . like every day.

But wait a minute, You didn't say "a dying sacrifice," You said "a living one." Hmmm . . . *(wails)* but, Lord, I don't know anything about sacrifice—dead or alive! I've never done anything great for You. I can't build a bridge!

(Stands and starts walking) I've never given up my home to go to the mission field. I've never been persecuted or thrown in jail for my faith.

How am I ever going to teach my kids about sacrifice? How am I ever going to build a bridge? *(on the verge of tears)* I know my mom has given me her values, but Lord, I don't know how to use them.

(Stops and looks up) What, Lord? What about the Sundays Don and I have stayed home to teach our Sunday school class when his folks begged us to go to the cabin with them? But, Lord, that wasn't a sacrifice. When Don and I took that class, we committed to be there on Sunday morning for those kids. I mean, we love to teach Sunday school. Being faithful to church and our Sunday school class is not a sacrifice.

Paying our tithes? Lord, You know we always pay our tithes and give in the offerings. You don't have to remind me to do that. Oh, You weren't reminding me? You're commending me— You're commending me for paying tithes? Lord, You don't have to commend me for that; that's my duty. It's only reasonable. Reasonable? Ohhhhh . . . *"I beseech you therefore, brethren, by the mercies of God, that ye present your bodies a living sacrifice, holy, acceptable unto God, which is your reasonable service."*[2] "Reasonable service." Now that's interesting . . . reasonable. Wonder why I never noticed that word before?

Anyway, Lord, You've always blessed us and blessed us and blessed us. For every penny we've given, You've given us back at least a dime. So I don't think that qualifies us for martyrs.

See what I mean, Lord? I don't know anything about sacrificing.

What did You say, Lord? "Staley Corporation?" That's where Don used to work. Is there somebody there I'm supposed to pray for?

No? You're just thinking about the time Don and I decided he shouldn't take that big promotion because he would have to miss church too much? And besides, his supervisor was always wanting him to pad his expense account and tell little lies on the phone and . . . yeah, I remember when they fired him because he wouldn't do those things. But we figured his integrity was worth more than that job.

We were worried for a little while, but everything turned out okay. You gave him a much better job. That's just like You, Lord. Thanks again.

But I don't know how we got on this subject. We were talking about *(panic in voice)* that bridge I've got to build! God, You've gotta help me. . . . You're trying? Keep listening?

(Sighs and sits down) Okay.

You want me to look at my convictions!? Well, if I can. I . . . don't really know how. What convictions are you talking about? Godly dress? Avoiding the appearance of evil? Separation from the world?

Yes. I remember that time we refused to let the kids have that new game, and when we wouldn't let them go to that gospel rock concert, and lots of other times when we said "No," even though some of our friends, even our church friends, were saying "Yes." Emilie pouted for a week when I made her take back that low-necked dress she had bought.

But we just stood for our convictions, Lord. Not to be goody-goody, but just because we had to!

But I don't know what this has got to do with building a bridge!

(Yawns and rubs eyes) Lord, I'm not here to play "Do You Remember?" I need help.

Okay, I'm listening. But, Lord, please talk loud. *(yawns again)* I'm getting sleepy.

Faith? Did You say "faith"? Have I got faith? A little bit.

(Nods) Yes, I remember. I remember when You healed Emilie's ears, and she didn't have to have surgery. And I remember when You gave Don that good job. And I remember when You filled his dad with the Holy Ghost just before he died. That was wonderful. Thank You for Your amazing grace.

And I remember—but, Lord, those are things You did. Not what I did.

(Wails) I'm the one that's got to build the bridge. How am I going to do it?

(Listens intently and blinks) Just . . . keep . . . doing . . . what I'm doing? Is that what You said? Just keep doing what I'm doing? *(yawns, stands up)*

Just keep doing what I'm doing. . . . *(starts to exit)* "Reasonable service." There's something in that. *(yawns again)* If I weren't so sleepy, I think I might get it. Maybe in the morning it'll all make sense.

Good night, Lord. Thanks for sitting up with me.

EXITS.

SCENE III

The Future Bridge Builder's Vision

PROPS:

Blindfold

DAUGHTER ENTERS, *wearing a blindfold. Minor mood music plays to set the scene, then fades out as she starts to talk. As she talks she stumbles around, tripping over things, almost falling. Stands frozen for a while, then tries a step or two forward, then freezes again. (Will have to play this by ear according to the setting.)*

(Trembles and shakes, voice quivers) Ooooohhhh, it's so scary! I'm so afraid! I'm afraid to look! I'm afraid to take one step forward, but I'm afraid to stand still, too. It's so frightening! This has got to be the beginning of the great tribulation!

The end of the age is coming and nobody knows what's going to happen. Computers are going to shut down. Airplanes are going to crash. Respirators are going to stop. People are going to die.

The banks are going to crash! I won't be able to get my $17.21 out of the bank. I'll lose everything!

The Antichrist is coming and the mark of the Beast! *(holds hand up in front of blindfolded face; panic-stricken)* My hand! I can't see my hands. I haven't taken the mark, have I? Tell me I haven't. Tell me I haven't!

(Grabs chest) Oh, I think I'm having a heart attack!

Has anybody got a paper sack? I'm about to hyperventilate. *(gasps for breath)*

I've got to get a hold of myself. I've got to get control! Oh, I can't think about it. I just can't think about the future. It's too dark and frightening.

But I can't go on like this either. I've got to see . . . I've got to look or I'm going to break my neck!

I guess I can choose: take off the blindfold, look at the future, and die of a heart attack or leave on the blindfold and die of a broken neck! Oh, what does it matter? I'm going to die anyway! Heart attack, broken neck, or starvation when I refuse to take the mark of the Beast.

I can't stand this darkness! *(reaches to remove the blindfold)* I've got to take off this blindfold. *(takes hand down)* But I can't stand to look either.

Oh, Lord, what am I going to do?

(Cries out) Mamma! Mamma! Where are you?

(Sternly to self) Emilie, stop that! You're acting like a baby. You are a grown woman, a young lady, in control of yourself.

Oooohhhh, I've got to take off this blindfold. *(reaches for the blindfold again)* I've always been afraid of the dark. *(counts slowly)* One . . . two . . . I can't!

(Sternly to self) Yes, you can, Emilie. Yes, you can. Just look behind you. Don't look ahead.

Yes, yes! That's what I'll do. I'll look behind me. *(takes off the blindfold, turns slightly and looks behind her)*

Ahhhh! That's so much better.

And look! There's my grandmother.

GRANDMOTHER ENTERS, *dressed in white robe, appears behind Daughter. Walks slowly across the platform. As* **GRANDMOTHER** *walks across the platform,* **DAUGHTER** *turns to watch her. This may mean turning her back to the audience, but that's* *okay, because at this point, the focal point is the Grandmother.*

> What a lovely Christian lady grandma was, so dedicated to God and committed to my grandfather. Why, they were married sixty-three years before she died. That's almost unheard of today. And she was still cleaning the church when she was seventy-five years old. Lots of congregations have to pay someone to clean the church.
>
> And I remember if grandma promised me something, I got it—whether it was baking cookies or a spanking. Grandma kept her word.
>
> Grandma believed every word of the Bible, too. Her whole lifestyle was based on "thus saith the Word"—no wishy-washy relativism, situational ethics stuff for grandma. Right was right. Wrong was wrong, no matter who it involved or what the situation. Grandma always stood for her convictions.
>
> And faith, oh what faith my grandma had! She prayed for food on the table, healing for the kids. Whatever she needed, she believed that God would supply it. And He did!
>
> Was life really easier for Grandma, or does it just seem like it to me?
>
> And look!

MOTHER *appears on edge of stage, dressed as she was in the second scene. She simply stands frozen in place.*

> There's my mother. What an example she has been. She and Dad are so committed to that Sunday school class and our church. I remember one time when there was not enough money to buy groceries, but they paid their tithes. I wonder how we got through till the next payday. Hmmm. I can't remember, but somehow we did.
>
> And talk about integrity and convictions. *(smiles)* I remember when my mother made me take back a dress I had bought because the neckline was too low. Boy, did that make me mad!

Now I know why she did it.

Just like Grandma, Mother has a lot of faith, too. She prays about everything: my earaches when I was a kid, Dad's job, Grandpa's salvation, even when everyone else thought he was too old to change.

Looking back almost gives me enough courage to look ahead. I wonder if Grandmother and Mother were ever afraid of the future? Was their faith in God always so strong that they faced tomorrow without fear? I doubt it. They probably had their fears, too.

But I'm facing the end of the world—the Antichrist, the mark of the Beast, the great tribulation! It's overwhelming!

But I can't go through life backwards—I've got to look forward! I've got to!

(Turns slowly to face the audience) Why, look! Look! There's a beautiful golden bridge. It has four majestic pillars under it. *(with eyes ahead, walks slowly toward edge of the platform, points)* And look! Look on the other side!

I see a glorious sunrise, a new day filled with opportunities and victories for the church. A new age. And I don't see the Antichrist. I see Jesus Christ and I hear—

SOUND: TRUMPET

SONG: "What's That I Hear?"

GRANDMOTHER *comes from one side;* ***MOTHER*** *from the other. They join the* ***DAUGHTER*** *in rejoicing, then march off victoriously.*

---

[1] Romans 12:1
[2] Ibid.

The Parable of the Teacup

CAST:

    Mildred, the Guest
    Victoria, the Hostess
    Teacup (voice only, always on reverb mike)
    Woman (dressed in black, pantomimes with a cup as the Teacup tells its story)

PROPS:

    2 tables (card tables will work)
    2 chairs
    2 tablecloths and napkins
    Centerpiece
    3 elegant china teacups and saucers, spoons
    Sugar, cream, lemon
    Teapot and tea
    Serving tray
    Large carry-on bag
    Miscellaneous trinkets (coins, buttons, etc.)
    Dark-colored box
    Basket of junk
    Table (for garage sale)
    Garage Sale sign and tape
    Newspaper
    Small box (sized to hold the Teacup)
    Sticker and marker
    Tissue paper

STAGE SET-UP:

    On one side set up a table and two chairs for tea.
    On the other side set up a table covered with a dark, solid-colored tablecloth. On it set the Teacup. The action is pantomimed on this side. A woman dressed in black stands behind the table holding the

Programs for Ladies

Teacup. She acts out the parable as the Teacup tells it. Other trinkets needed in the first scene are in a dark-colored box sitting beside the cup on the table. Hidden under the table are a basket of junk, a small packing box, a newspaper, sticker, marker, tape, tissue paper, and a garage sale sign. A bare table for a garage sale is placed to one side of this table.

The setup is the same for all the scenes.

SCENE I

Chipped

ENTER VICTORIA, *carrying a tray with items for tea.*

VICTORIA: *(looks at watch as she sets the table)* Mildred should be here by now. She said two o'clock, and it is five after. She's usually very punctual.

ENTER MILDRED, *like a whirlwind, lugging a huge, heavy carry-on case (unknown to the audience, the case is not fastened and she is holding it shut).*

VICTORIA: Oh, here she is now.

VICTORIA *goes to the door.*

VICTORIA: Come in! Come in! My, you are loaded down. Why are you carrying your luggage? Are you taking a trip?

MILDRED: *(highly offended)* Certainly not. I'm too busy to go anywhere. Why, if I left town, there's no telling what would happen! That's not my luggage. It's my attaché case.

VICTORIA: Attaché case? *(looks puzzled)* Oh, you mean, your briefcase?

MILDRED: Attaché case . . . briefcase . . . call it what you will. It has all my . . . *(drops the carry-on case; papers fly everywhere; wails)* important papers in it!

WOMEN *pick up the papers while* ***MILDRED*** *wails that all her important files are getting mixed up. They ad-lib.* ***MILDRED*** *jumps around trying to catch her "pet cricket" that fell out of the case.*

VICTORIA: Finally! That's the last one! My, Mildred, where are you going with all these important papers? Have you gotten a job?

Programs for Ladies

MILDRED: Oh, no, not a paying job anyway. I have lots of important jobs. I'm president of the PTA, treasurer of the Committee to Restore Brick Streets to America. I belong to the Society for the Salvation of Crickets, and I'm thinking about starting a Shoppers Anonymous support group. I know all about the "mall mania" and addiction to shopping.

VICTORIA: My, you are busy! Sit down here. Let's have a cup of tea. Nothing soothes frayed nerves better than a cup of tea—nothing, that is, except a prayer meeting.

MILDRED: Prayer meeting? Oh, yeah, I knew you'd get around to that. I just didn't know it would be in the first scene.

WOMEN *are seated.*

VICTORIA: I have been missing you at prayer meeting. *(pours tea, asking for preferences, sugar, cream, lemon, etc.)*

MILDRED: *(states her preferences)* Well, I decided if I can't sing, I won't pray.

VICTORIA: *(shocked)* Did I hear you right? If you can't sing, you won't pray?

MILDRED: That's what I said.

VICTORIA: I don't get it. In the first place, you can sing. You have a lovely voice.

MILDRED: Tell that to Brother Carlton. Do you realize he hasn't asked me to sing in *(counts on fingers)* one, two, three, four, five, six, six and one-half weeks—that's twenty services!

VICTORIA: But, Mildred, there are a lot of people in our church who can sing. I'm sure he prays about whom he uses and—

MILDRED: *(sarcastically)* Oh, I'm sure he does. And the Lord tells him, "Don't use Sister Mildred. She has an attitude."

VICTORIA: *(shocked)* Mildred!

MILDRED: Well, if the Lord doesn't tell him that . . . his wife does!

VICTORIA: Mildred!

MILDRED: She does! *(voice takes on whine and ends in sob)* Sister Madge told me that Sister Janice told her that Sister Betty told her that Sister Mary said that Sister Carlton said . . . that she said that . . . that I . . . that I—

VICTORIA: That you what?

MILDRED: *(sobs and chokes)* That I . . . That I . . . oh, I can't remember what she said. It was too long ago. *(angrily)* But I know she shouldn't have said it. *(whines)* It hurt my feelings—really bad.

VICTORIA: But if you can't remember what she said, how can you—

MILDRED: Let's talk about something else. It hurts too much to talk about that! *(blows her nose on a napkin, holds up her teacup, examines it)* This is a lovely little teacup . . . so exquisitely perfect.

VICTORIA: Yes, but it hasn't always been that way. This little teacup has quite a story behind it. Would you like to hear it?

MILDRED: Yes, I would. *(looks at watch)* That is, if it is not too long. I am on my way to a meeting.

VICTORIA: It won't take long. Just sit back and relax while the little teacup tells its story. I call it "The Parable of the Teacup."

SPOTLIGHT *shifts to focus on the other table.* **WOMAN** *standing at the table, holds up the cup, runs her finger over the lip of the cup, etc., as the Teacup speaks from the background.*

TEACUP: *(reverb mike)* I am a vessel, a lovely, delicate, fragile china teacup. I am hand-crafted, hand-painted, unique—yet one of a set, a family, matching and belonging.

I was given to the bride on her wedding day. I was loved, treasured, displayed in a hutch in a prominent place, reserved for

Programs for Ladies

special occasions, filled with only the finest, fragrant, refreshing teas.

Then one day I was bumped . . . knocked from my saucer . . . and chipped. It was just a little hurt, a chip on my lip.

MILDRED: A chip on the lip, huh? I've heard of chips on the shoulder, but this is the first time I've ever heard of a chip on the lip!

TEACUP: It wasn't a big chip, but it marred my perfection. No longer was I a showpiece. I was moved to the back of the hutch, used only as a last resort.

MILDRED: Boy, I know how that feels. When everyone else has laryngitis, Mildred gets to sing.

TEACUP: Even in emergencies, I was only used by my mistress, never by the guests!

One day I was taken from the hutch in the dining room and placed on the dresser in the back bedroom. I was filled with trinkets, odd buttons, safety pins, paper clips, pennies.

As worthless trinkets were dropped into me, I was chipped, cracked, stained—hurt, oh so hurt. No one saw my beauty or remembered my value. *(slowly and firmly)* I was reduced to the worth of my contents. Once a valuable, handcrafted, lovely, fragile teacup, I had now become a pot of trinkets. I was full, but oh so empty!

MILDRED: A pot of trinkets? I wonder what that means. *(stands up)* A cute little story, but I've just got to go.

Where's my attaché case? I do hope my valuable files aren't too scrambled. I sure would hate to give my thesis on saving the crickets when I'm suppose to be giving the annual financial report to the Committee to Restore Brick Streets to America.

Thanks for the tea, Victoria. I've got to run.

VICTORIA: *(stands up)* But, Mildred, that's not the end of "The

Parable of the Teacup."

MILDRED: But I must not be late for my important meeting. We can finish the story over tea tomorrow. I am invited back for tea tomorrow, aren't I? *(whines)* You don't believe what Sister Madge said that Sister Janice told her that Sister Betty . . . or was it Sister Lucy . . . told her that Sister Mary said that Sister Carlton said about me, do you?

VICTORIA: Mildred, I don't even know what they said.

MILDRED: Well, if anyone tells you, don't believe a word of it. I'll see you tomorrow and the Teacup can finish its story. It's a cute story, although I really don't get the point. *(starts to leave)* Oh, one more thing, if anyone tells you what they're saying about me, will you tell me?

VICTORIA: Mildred, I—

MILDRED: See you tomorrow.

EXIT MILDRED.

VICTORIA: *(walks over to the other table and picks up Teacup)* Little Teacup, may God anoint your story because I have a feeling that someone needs to hear it.

SONG: "Fill My Cup, Lord"

SCENE II

Empty

ENTER VICTORIA, *singing, "Fill My Cup, Lord," carrying a tea tray with tea items on it. Begins setting the table.*

ENTER MILDRED, *empty-handed, walking slowly, head down. Knocks.*

VICTORIA *goes to the door, greets Mildred cheerfully. Mildred responds dully.*

VICTORIA: Come in, Mildred. Where's your attaché case?

MILDRED: My what? Oh, you mean my carry-on bag? At home.

VICTORIA: Have a seat. I'll pour you a cup of tea. Let's see, you like it with *(preferences from Scene 1)*.

WOMEN *sit down.*

MILDRED: Thank you. *(wipes tears, sniffs loudly)*

VICTORIA: Mildred, what's wrong?

MILDRED: *(dissolves into tears)* What's wrong? I thought you'd never ask! It would be easier to tell you what's right. We . . . *(chokes)* . . . we . . . Joe and I . . . we . . . we are . . . are going to file for . . . going to file for—

VICTORIA: Not a divorce!

MILDRED: No. Not a divorce, at least, not now. That may come later. Things are not good between Joe and me. We are going to file for bankruptcy. *(wails loudly)* We're going to lose everything! And Joe says it's all my fault! And the bad part of the whole thing is . . . he's right! I can't stand it when he's right!

VICTORIA: I'm so sorry.

MILDRED: Me, too! I wish just once he'd be wrong! This whole thing would be a lot easier to take if he wasn't always so right! And I'm always so wrong!

VICTORIA: *(gets up and pats Mildred on the shoulder)* Mildred . . . Mildred, I wish I could help. *(returns to seat)*

MILDRED: That's not all. Last night we found a bag of white stuff in little Joey's room. I think he's taking drugs, and I've been too busy saving the crickets to see what was happening to my own son!

VICTORIA: What can I say?

MILDRED: I'll tell you one thing not to say.

VICTORIA: What's that?

MILDRED: Don't quote Romans 8:28 at me.

VICTORIA: Romans 8:28? Oh, yes. *"All things work together for good."*

MILDRED: I said, don't quote it! It also says, *"To them that love God, to them who are the called according to his purpose."* *(sobs)* I'm not sure I'm either one!

VICTORIA: Yes, you are, Mildred. You love God . . . just not enough. And He has a purpose for your life. You've just gotten off track somewhere.

MILDRED: *(holds up teacup)* What did little Teacup say yesterday, "Full, but oh so empty"? Makes more sense today than it did yesterday.

VICTORIA: Maybe it's time for you to hear some more of "The Parable of the Teacup."

MILDRED nods.

Programs for Ladies

SPOTLIGHT *shifts to the second table.*

TEACUP: *(reverb mike)* My world was falling apart.

MILDRED: Boy, do I know about that!

*As the **TEACUP** talks, the **WOMAN** pulls the basket of junk from under the table. She does as Teacup "instructs." Places a garage sale sign on or above the sale table.*

TEACUP: Everything around me was picked up, sorted, and packed or discarded. It was moving day.

> I was lifted, turned upside down, and everything in me—all my trinkets—were dumped . . . into the trash.
>
> I was chipped, cracked, stained, and empty.
>
> I trembled with weakness and fear . . . and something else . . . a sense of loss. I felt so worthless and empty, alone and afraid.
>
> I was tossed into a basket of junk and carried out to a table on the driveway. There were no napkins or linen cloth, no crystal or silver. It was bare wood, piled high with junk—junk like me that used to be someone's treasure but now was only used, ugly, dirty junk.
>
> Someone stuck a sticker on my side, "fifty cents." This was my first experience with a garage sale.

MILDRED: A garage sale? That's where my valuables are going!

TEACUP: The next day I was picked up, examined, set aside . . . again and again.

> To pass the time and control my fears, I daydreamed—of the days of my glory, when I was treasured and protected, when I was used and admired, when I belonged to a set and had a mistress who loved me.
>
> I tried to remember the feel of warm, fragrant tea filling me.

I looked back because I dared not look forward.

MILDRED: Oh! I know about that, too.

TEACUP: The sun was hot. The day was long. Near evening the table was less cluttered. I sat beside a scratched picture frame and a tattered ribbon.

Then someone picked me up. This time the touch was different; it was gentle. I was turned slowly from side to side, upside down, right side up. Turned so the light shone into my soul, exposing every jagged crack and ugly stain. The tiny chip on my lip seemed gigantic—to me.

MILDRED: *(runs her finger over her lips; then thoughtfully to her self)* The chip on my lip.

TEACUP: I heard a soft sigh, felt the sunlight of a smile. I was paid for, wrapped in old newspaper, and packed carefully in a box.

The trip was long and dark. I was tossed, turned, and tormented. Why was I in this dark place? Where was I going? What awaited me?

MILDRED: I'd like to know that, too, little Teacup. What's going to happen to my son, to my marriage, to my home?

TEACUP: Was this the end? Was I no longer of value to anyone—not even as a pot for trinkets?

The movement stopped, and there was nothing! Nothing but silence and stillness. Nothing. Was I to die here in this dark, silent, lonely place?

Then the box was ripped open, I was lifted out . . . out into the blinding light of . . . of . . . where was I? It was not a home, not a garage. What was this place?

It was a warehouse . . . a huge, cluttered, bright warehouse. All around me were vessels like me—chipped, scarred, stained, empty; cups, saucers, plates, glasses; crystal, silver, china—

Programs for Ladies

things that were once valuable but now were stained by usage, chipped by accidents, scarred by pain.

I did not know what the future held, but for the first time in a long time, I was filled with a sense of belonging. These were my kind. They understood. They had known the pride of the china hutch, the joy of service, the pain of rejection.

Then I saw a sign on the wall. It said, "Replacements Limited." I had heard about this place. It was a saving station for lost, homeless, scarred vessels like me. I can't tell you how glad I was to be here.

MILDRED: Replacements Limited? Is there such a place, Victoria? What is the cup talking about?

VICTORIA: In Greensboro, North Carolina, there is a place called Replacements Limited. As a hobby, the owner, an accountant, would go to garage sales, flea markets, and estate sales on weekends. He would pick up odds and ends of china, crystal, silver. His friends started asking him to look for certain pieces to replace ones that they had broken or lost.

Eventually, he realized that there was a definite need for such a business. In 1981 he quit his job and with one part-time employee started Replacements Limited.

Today, he has a huge warehouse with over two million pieces of dinnerware in it. He has over 500 employees and 1,500 suppliers around the world who are constantly looking for the odd and ends of china and other dinnerware.

MILDRED: That was the gentle hand at the garage sale? The hand of a supplier?

VICTORIA: Right. She was looking for pieces to send to the warehouse in Greensboro.

MILDRED: But who would put a scarred, chipped, cracked piece of china in with her good set? They might be the same pattern, but they wouldn't match if one was scarred and the others well cared for.

VICTORIA: In this warehouse there are master craftsmen who restore worn and dull vessels.

MILDRED: That's how I feel . . . worn and dull. Guess I've "a chip on my lip," too.

VICTORIA: Mildred, I know a place where you can be restored. The hurts can be healed. You can get rid of that chip. The ugly stains of bitterness can be washed away.

MILDRED: Yes, I know, too. It's the altar.

VICTORIA: *(stands)* Let's go to the church.

MILDRED: *(stands)* Good idea.

*Song is sung as the **WOMEN EXIT**.*

SONG: "He Didn't Throw the Clay Away"

SCENE III

Restored

WOMEN *are seated at table.* ***VICTORIA*** *pours tea.* ***WOMAN*** *behind Teacup table pantomimes.*

TEACUP: *(reverb mike)* At Replacements Limited I did not sit still long. I was examined, categorized, and sent to the master craftsman. Burning acids removed my stains. Soft paint brightened my pattern. A soothing coat of glaze covered my cracks and the chip on my lip. I felt so good.

Then I was put into the furnace.

MILDRED: Oh, yes, the fire! I know about that!

TEACUP: The heat scorched my soul. It melted my pride.

MILDRED: Nothing can scorch your soul like a child on drugs. Nothing will melt your pride like bankruptcy.

TEACUP: The furnace reminded me of another fire—the time when I was born in the blaze of the fire. I remembered that the fire does not last forever, and I endured.

MILDRED: I remember other fires, too—fiery trials. I wonder why I let that little remark someone said that someone said that someone said become so big? I stained my soul with bitterness, and I can't even remember what they said!

I felt used, shoved aside, worthless, when all the time it was my attitude that was shutting me off from others.

Boy, when you get in the furnace, you see lots of things you don't want to see, don't you?

TEACUP: Finally, when I felt I could not stand another minute in the fire, the door opened. I was slowly removed and set on a rack to cool.

VICTORIA: There is hope, Mildred. The fire does not last forever.

TEACUP: I saw my reflection in the mirror on the wall. Was that me? That beautiful, delicate china teacup with the lovely flowers on its side and the gold trim around its lip? It was! I was like new, perfect, a rare piece of china. Oh, it felt so good to be whole.

MILDRED: Well, you're ahead of me, little Teacup. I haven't reached that place yet.

VICTORIA: You will. Believe me, Mildred, you will.

TEACUP: When I cooled, I was placed on a shelf with many other pieces like myself—restored vessels. We gloried in our beauty, reflected in one another. Were we in heaven?

No. We were in the waiting room . . . for while we rejoiced in our restored state, we were not content . . . sitting on a shelf. We were empty . . . waiting to be filled.

MILDRED: On a shelf in the waiting room? Wait a minute. I think that's where I got off track before. I couldn't wait.

When the living water leaked out of my vessel, instead of waiting before the Lord for Him to fill me, I filled my life with trinkets . . . shopping sprees, the Society for the Salvation of Crickets, the Committee to Restore Brick Streets to America . . . when I should have been attending prayer meeting, listening to my son, even teaching Bible studies.

TEACUP: The day came when I was lifted from the shelf, carefully wrapped (this time in clean tissue paper), and packed gently in a box. The trip was long and dark, but this time I was not afraid. I had confidence that he who had begun a good work in me would finish it.

VICTORIA: *"Being confident of this very thing, that he which hath begun a good work in you will perform it."*[1] Repeat that after me, ladies, please. *(Audience repeats.)* "*Being confident of this very thing, that he which hath begun a good work in you will perform it.*" What a promise!

TEACUP: The day came when the journey ended. Gentle hands lifted me from the box. I heard exclamations of joy and felt the warmth of love. I was washed and dried. A saucer just like the one I was parted from so long ago was placed under me. Hot, refreshing, fragrant tea was poured into me, and I was once again filled and pouring out to others.

There may be other chips and stains and hurts before my life ends. But I fear not, for I have been in the hands of the master craftsman who can restore scarred vessels and make them like new.

SONG: "Make Me What I Ought to Be"

[1]Philippians 1:6

Treasures of the Heart

CAST:

Narrator

President Nelda Jones—carries a gavel. She is sweet and patient.

Vice President Hilary Carter—walks with a cane to signify her age. Carries an ugly black box, containing an old, stained letter, a small broken toy, and a bank statement. She also carries a large purse with a scratch pad and pen in it.

Secretary Elsie Brown—carries a box stuffed with junk (whatnots, a cracked flowerpot, etc.) and a secretary's notebook and pen.

Treasurer Anna Anderson—carries a business-type box with ten diplomas and certificates in it. They are rolled up and tied with ribbons. She also carries a notebook with the treasurer's report in it.

All "hide" their scripts in their notebooks or treasure chests or on the podium.

PROPS:

Trash can
Podium
Table
3 chairs

STAGE SET-UP:

The podium is placed at an angle facing the three chairs. All are turned so the audience can see the characters' faces.

Programs for Ladies

NARRATOR: *"And the L<small>ORD</small> God formed man of the dust of the ground, and breathed into his nostrils the breath of life; and man became a living soul.*

And the L<small>ORD</small> God planted a garden eastward in Eden; and there he put the man whom he had formed."[1]

And God looked at man in his lovely home and said to the angels, "Hmmm, something is not quite right! I have given man this beautiful garden and told him to dress it, but what does man know about dressing?

"His color coordination is terrible. He planted those gorgeous American beauty roses. (Oops! No America yet.) Anyway, he planted those gorgeous red roses right in the middle of a patch of yellow zinnias! Can you imagine that?!"

The angels giggled, and God just shook His head. "If I didn't go down there every day and talk to him, he'd be content to play hide-n-seek with the dog and the deer all day, and, of course, he would never give the dog a bath.

"And he is so mopey! Look at him right now. He's down there with his shoulders slumped, looking like a man who has lost his best friend. What could he want that I haven't given him?"

Was it the angel standing closest to God who said, "I think I know what the problem is"?

Did the God, who knows everything, ask, "What?" No, probably not, but let's use our imagination. It makes a good story.

With twinkling eyes, the angel whispered, "He's lonely. He needs a woman."

God turned to the angel and asked, "What do you know about women?"

The angel chuckled and said, "Nothing."

God smiled and nodded. "That's what you will know one hundred years from now, too."

*"[So] the L*ORD *God caused a deep sleep to fall upon Adam, . . . and he took one of his ribs, and closed up the flesh. . . . And [with] the rib, which the L*ORD *God had taken from man, made he a woman."*[2]

And God brought the woman to the man, and Adam said, "Wow!" And his eyes grew big, and he straightened his shoulders and said, "I think I'll stay home today and transplant those roses and give the dog a bath . . . and uhhh . . . uhhh . . . get acquainted with my wife."

Right in the middle of woman's breast, God put a box—a special place for her treasures. He called it her "heart."

He said, "Fill it well, my child, *'for where your treasure is, there will your heart be also.'*"[3]

And ever since, women have been storing treasures in their chests.

ENTER FOUR WOMEN, *from different directions, each carrying a treasure chest. As they meet, they greet one another and ad-lib, asking excitedly, "Did you have a good week?" "What did you find?" "Oh, you'll be surprised at the treasure I found this week."*

THREE *take seats on the platform. The* **PRESIDENT** *stands behind the podium and bangs a gavel on it.*

PRESIDENT: The meeting of the Collectors' Club is called to order. Let us begin with a word of prayer. Anna, will you lead us, please?

TREASURER: *(stands)* Bow your heads, please. Dear heavenly Father, thank You for the treasures that You have so generously bestowed upon us. Bless our meeting as we share with one another the wonderful finds we have made. In Jesus' name. Amen. *(sits down)*

PRESIDENT: Thank you, Anna. Now we will have the reading of the

Programs for Ladies

minutes of the last meeting.

SECRETARY: *(stands and reads)* The meeting of the Collectors' Club was called to order by President Nelda Jones. She called for the reading of the minutes of the last meeting by Secretary Elsie Brown. The minutes were read and approved by three out of the four attending. *(everyone glares at the vice president)*

There was a brief discussion of changing the time of the meeting. By a 75% vote we decided not to change the meeting time.

New business included a discussion on having a garage sale to raise money for our charity project to aid the shelter for the homeless. Three out of four voted to have a garage sale *(everyone glares at the vice president)* the last Saturday of the month.

VICE PRESIDENT: The last time this Collectors' Club had a garage sale, I got stuck with the cleanup.

SECRETARY: The treasurer's report was given by Anna Anderson. She reported that three out of four members had paid their dues. *(everyone glares at the vice president)*

VICE PRESIDENT: *(defiantly)* I'll pay when I get good and ready!

SECRETARY: Everyone then shared the treasures they had found since the last meeting of the Collectors' Club. Hilary Carter, vice president, brought an article in the *Christian Weekly* that contained a typo. She said she planned to keep it because someday she was going to write a book about "bloopers in print." Secretary Elsie Brown showed us a collector's item she had found at a flea market—a Coca-Cola serving tray. Anna Anderson, treasurer, told about a rare copy of *Pilgrim's Progress* that she had found at a garage sale. President Nelda Jones brought a beautiful rose from her garden. She said it was the most perfect rose she had ever seen. She said she was going to take it to her friend in the hospital after the meeting.

We closed with prayer, worshiping our heavenly Father who has so bountifully blessed us, as we collect the things near and dear to our hearts. Refreshments were served by Elsie.

PRESIDENT: You have heard the reading of the minutes. Are there any corrections?

VICE PRESIDENT: *(laboriously gets to her feet)* Madam President, I have a correction.

SECRETARY: *(aside)* I never would have guessed!

VICE PRESIDENT: *(turns to the secretary)* Did you say something, Elsie?

SECRETARY: *(louder)* You're looking your best, Hilary.

VICE PRESIDENT: *(snorts loudly)* Nelda, I mean Madam President, I did not find that blooper in the *Christian Weekly*. I found it in the *Believers Monthly*. *(glares at the secretary as she sits down)*

PRESIDENT: Thank you, Hilary. Please note that correction, Elsie. Any other corrections? *(no response)* All who approve the minutes as corrected raise your right hand please.

EVERYONE, *but* **HILARY**, *raises her hand.*

PRESIDENT: Approved by a 75% vote. Thank you, Elsie, for that report. We will now hear the reading of the financial report.

VICE PRESIDENT *picks up her purse and digs in it, bringing out a pen and large scratch pad.*

TREASURER: *(stands)* Beginning balance at the first of the month $12.25. Paid to the newspaper for—

VICE PRESIDENT: Speak up. I can't hear you!

TREASURER: *(louder)* An ad for garage sale . . . $8.00.

VICE PRESIDENT: *(writes $8.00 on her pad)* What was the beginning balance?

Programs for Ladies

TREASURER: *(sighs heavily and shouts)* $12.25!

VICE PRESIDENT: *(mutters as she writes)* $12.25.

TREASURER: *(loudly)* We made $92.43 on the garage sale, leaving us an ending balance of $96.68.

VICE PRESIDENT: *(to self as she scratches on the paper)* $12.25 minus $8.00 equals $3.25—no, that's $4.25. How much did you say we made on the garage sale?

TREASURER: $92.43.

VICE PRESIDENT: $4.25 plus $92.43 equals $96.68. Humph! Guess she's right.

PRESIDENT: All in favor of accepting the treasurer's report, raise your right hand.

EVERYONE *raises her hand, except* **HILARY.**

VICE PRESIDENT: *(gets to her feet laboriously)* I have a question about the treasurer's report. How did we end up with three odd pennies from the garage sale? Everything was sold for a nickel, a dime, a quarter, or a dollar, right?

PRESIDENT: I suppose so. Is that right, Anna?

TREASURER: I think so.

VICE PRESIDENT: Then how did we end up with $.43?

PRESIDENT: *(sighs heavily)* Anna, do you know?

TREASURER: *(angrily)* No, I do not!

VICE PRESIDENT: *(snorts)* I thought not. Then I cannot vote to approve the report. Surely as little money as we have, someone in this club would count it correctly! *(sits down)*

PRESIDENT: The treasurer's report is approved by a 75% vote. Is there any old business to be discussed at this time?

VICE PRESIDENT *waits to see how the other two respond. They shake their heads "no." She vigorously nods her head "yes."*

PRESIDENT: Hilary, what old business would you like to discuss?

VICE PRESIDENT: *(laboriously gets to her feet)* Uhhh . . . I . . . uhhh . . . I remember . . . uhhhh . . . oh, at our last meeting we discussed changing our meeting time from 6:00 to 6:30.

SECRETARY: *(jumps up)* Ma'am President, I object. We have discussed this at every meeting for the last six months, and we have voted on it six times. Six times we have voted by a 75% majority not to change the time of our meeting. I think it is time to stop hashing this over and over and move on to new business.

PRESIDENT: Elsie is right. Hilary, please be seated.

HILARY *snorts but sits down.*

PRESIDENT: Now is there any new business?

VICE PRESIDENT *waits to see how the other two respond. They shake their heads "no." She vigorously nods her head "yes."*

PRESIDENT: *(very patiently)* Hilary, what new business do you have?

VICE PRESIDENT: A lot, but I am sure no one is interested. Go on with your meeting.

PRESIDENT: Who has added a treasure to your chest this month that you would like to share with us?

TREASURER: *(jumps to her feet)* I have. *(brings her treasure box to the front and pulls out a diploma)* Last week I received my diploma in computer programming from the Institute for Higher Learning.

SECRETARY: Congratulations, Anna. How many diplomas do you have in your treasure box now?

TREASURER: *(pulls out a rolled-up diploma as she names each one)* Here's my diploma for when I graduated from kindergarten. Here's one from elementary school, another from vacation Bible school, and middle school, and high school, and my bachelor's degree, and my master's degree. And here's an award for being on the National Honor Society—oh, there are three of these and—

VICE PRESIDENT: What good are those diplomas going to do you, if you can't even count odd pennies?

TREASURER: *(proudly)* I have interviewed for a good position with one of the top Fortune 500 corporations.

VICE PRESIDENT: Well, la-de-da, isn't that something!

PRESIDENT: We are proud of you, Anna. I am sure that you have dedicated your mind to God and will use your education wisely to serve Him and others.

TREASURER: *(gulps, looks blank)* Uhhh . . . of course. That's exactly what I plan to do. I'll pay my tithes and give big offerings and—

SECRETARY: And live in a big penthouse and drive a fancy car and pray for the missionaries when you think about it. Admirable, I'm sure.

TREASURER: Well, what else do you expect me to do? I've not been called to be a missionary to India.

PRESIDENT: *(to Elsie)* Perhaps God is calling Anna to be a missionary to the corporate world.

TREASURER: *(gulps loudly)* A missionary to the corporate world? *(softly)* I'd never thought about that. *(quickly stuffs her diplomas back in her box)* That's all I have for today.

PRESIDENT: Elsie, would you like to share your treasures with us?

SECRETARY: *(picks up her treasure box and comes to the front)* Oh, you won't believe all the wonderful things I have found this month. *(pulls two or three pieces of junk whatnots out of her box, gushing over each one, telling where she found it; finally pulls out a flowerpot with a large crack in it)* Just look at this flowerpot. I found it—

VICE PRESIDENT: And look at that crack in it. Whatever you paid for that cracked pot, Elsie, it was too much!

SECRETARY: Oh, dear, I didn't know it was cracked! Well, I'll just set it on the shelf with the crack to the back. *(sits the pot aside and takes out another item and begins to gush over it)*

PRESIDENT: Do you ever use any of these things, Elsie?

SECRETARY: Use them? Oh, no, they're just to look at and enjoy.

TREASURER: Is your house as crammed as your treasure chest, Elsie?

SECRETARY: It's pretty full. John threatened to move out if I didn't get rid of something. I finally persuaded him to rent a storage building. I just couldn't bear to get rid of anything.

VICE PRESIDENT: *(snorts)* Guess you can't do much looking at them if they're stuffed in a storage shed. Seems like there should be a better way to spend your money and time than collecting junk!

PRESIDENT: Hilary! One woman's trash is another woman's treasure. Thank you, Elsie, for sharing your treasures with us.

TREASURER *puts things back in her box and carries it back to her chair. It is evident that she is miffed.*

PRESIDENT: Now, Hilary, it's your turn. What treasure have you been collecting?

HILARY *picks up her chest and goes to the front. When she takes the lid off, the* **WOMEN** *gasp and hold their noses.*

PRESIDENT: Merciful day, Hilary! What is in your treasure chest?

Programs for Ladies

SECRETARY: *(grabs her stomach)* The smell is making me sick to my stomach.

VICE PRESIDENT: What's the matter with you girls? I don't smell anything.

TREASURER: Maybe you have lived with it so long, you have become accustomed to it. But something smells rotten.

ELSIE: What is it?

VICE PRESIDENT: *(pulls out a tattered and stained letter, angrily)* This is a letter from my daughter-in-law. She wrote it to me fourteen, no fifteen, years ago. She told me to quit sticking my nose in their business. Well, I stopped. I haven't spoken to her since.

SECRETARY: Hurry up and put that lid back on, Hilary!

VICE PRESIDENT: I'm not through telling you what's on my chest . . . I mean showing you what's in my box. *(pulls out a small broken trinket)* This is my toy, my favorite toy, that Buddy Wheeler broke when I was in the third grade! He never did say he was sorry.

SECRETARY: Hilary, I'm warning you. If you don't put that lid back on, I'm going to puke!

VICE PRESIDENT: I'm not through yet. *(pulls out a bank statement)* This is my bank statement. Would you believe that they made a mistake on my account? They failed to give me credit for a deposit, and then they charged me overdrafts on checks that they bounced. It was all their fault. I'm seriously thinking about suing them.

SECRETARY *jumps up, runs for the exit with hand over her mouth.*

VICE PRESIDENT: Well, what got into her?

TREASURER: *(holding nose)* I think the smell got to her.

PRESIDENT: Hilary, thank you for sharing your heart with us. I'll help you put these memories back in your treasure chest, or maybe you would rather just throw them away?

VICE PRESIDENT: Throw them away? You've got to be kidding. These are my memories . . . and I treasure every one of them!

PRESIDENT: I was afraid of that.

PRESIDENT and **VICE PRESIDENT** *put things back in the box.* **VICE PRESIDENT** *takes it back to her seat.* **SECRETARY** *returns, wiping her brow. She stops on edge of the stage and puts her hand over her nose.*

SECRETARY: Is it safe to come back in?

PRESIDENT: I think so. Are you okay, Elsie?

SECRETARY: I'm better now.

TREASURER: Now, Nelda, show us your treasures.

PRESIDENT: *(takes a deep breath)* Well, girls, I guess I might as well tell you, I gave my treasure chest away.

ALL: You gave it away?

Override each other. "Gave it away?" "But why?" "Who to?" "When?"

PRESIDENT: *(nods and holds up her hand for silence)* I gave it to a little boy, a foster child, who has come to live with us. He didn't have anything, and I have so much. I gave him my heart.

SECRETARY: But he won't appreciate it.

PRESIDENT: Maybe not. He's been hurt so many times that it's hard for him to be grateful for anything.

TREASURER: But what will he do with it? Probably just break it!

Programs for Ladies

PRESIDENT: *(puts her hand over her heart)* He already has cracked it, and it hurts. But it was the least I could give him.

VICE PRESIDENT: Nelda, are you telling us that you gave your heart to this kid, knowing that he would probably break it?

PRESIDENT *nods.*

TREASURER: It seems like a waste to me.

SECRETARY: It is just asking for pain.

PRESIDENT: But isn't that what Jesus did for us? He gave His love to mankind, knowing that we would break His heart. How can I give Him less?

SECRETARY: Oh, it's okay to give your treasure chest to Jesus, but to a bratty kid? No way!

VICE PRESIDENT: Elsie, do you think you can give your heart to the Lord and not give it to His children? You cannot worship God and ignore His little ones. I may be a cracked pot, but I know better than that. Worship is more than shouting, "Praise the Lord." It's breaking your treasure chest and pouring yourself out.

PRESIDENT: Before we dismiss this meeting of the Collectors' Club, does anyone else have anything to say?

VICE PRESIDENT *gets laboriously to her feet.* **SECRETARY** *and* **TREASURER** *groan loudly.*

VICE PRESIDENT: *(looks around)* Does anyone know where the trash can is? If Nelda can give away her treasures, I figure it won't hurt me any—in fact, it might help me—to throw mine away.

PRESIDENT *brings* **VICE PRESIDENT** *the trash can, and she throws her treasure box in it.*

SECRETARY *and* **TREASURER** *look at one another.*

TREASURER: *(picks up her treasure chest)* I wonder how you go about being a missionary in the corporate world?

SECRETARY: I'm sure the Lord will show you. *(picks up her treasure chest)* Meanwhile, I have some housecleaning to do. I have a lot of things that can go in the next garage sale . . . starting with this cracked pot. *(picks up the cracked pot)*

PRESIDENT: Elsie, will you dismiss this meeting with prayer, please?

WOMEN *bow their heads and* **FREEZE,** *as the* **NARRATOR** *speaks from the background.*

NARRATOR: So the ladies of the Collectors' Club have examined the treasures of their hearts, and some have been surprised at what they have found. Are you brave enough, dear ladies, to open your treasure chests and look at the things near and dear to you? Are you willing to hold them up in the light of eternity?

Listen to the words of our Master, *"Sell that ye have, and give alms; provide yourselves bags which wax not old, a treasure in the heavens that faileth not, where no thief approacheth, neither moth corrupteth. For where your treasure is, there will your heart be also."*[4]

PRESIDENT *hits the podium with her gavel.*

PRESIDENT: Lesson learned. Meeting adjourned.

---

[1] Genesis 2:7-8
[2] Genesis 2:21-22
[3] Matthew 6:21
[4] Luke 12:33-34

Dramas

Synopses of Dramas

A Wake-Up Call

The decisions and actions of Christine Saint, a selfish, materialistic-minded gal, are constantly challenged by her Conscience. Her wake-up calls come in strange ways. Searching for more "stuff," she is challenged by what she learns at Mary and Martha's garage sale and Jael's moving sale. The loudest wake-up call comes when she discovers in her home the pornography that her husband and son have been reading. On her knees in prayer, she envisions the Ten Virgins—another wake-up call. When Christine is confronted by her beloved but dreaded Aunt Pearl, she can no longer delay looking at herself. At the final wake-up call, she and her family . . . Well, you read the story.

Cast and audience laugh and cry together throughout this drama. Approximate time: ninety minutes.

The God of Hagar

This drama will shake your soul. It is the story of women in the real world practicing their parts in a ladies' retreat drama. Donna learns through unexpected hurts how to relate better to her role as Hagar. And Hagar learns that the God of Sarai, the rich, pampered mistress, is also the God of Hagar, the abused, rebellious maid.

As Sandy says in Act III, "Everyone has her hurts. Many have buried it deeply beneath a facade of smiles and surface relationships. Perhaps, we'd be better off to tear off the veneer and be real."

Many of the laughs in this drama dissolve into tears as a picture of life without the facade is painted by an ancient, timeless story from God's Word. Approximate time: ninety minutes.

Women of the Kingdom

The women who followed Jesus and ministered to Him were women just like us. They had their quirks, their personalities, their talents, and their fears. And they played a "waiting" role, not an easy role to fill. Often they chafed at the nitty-gritty of life while they waited and worked for a better day—just as we do.

In this drama the three years of Jesus' ministry are seen from the women's viewpoint, as they take the audience from the year of Christ's inauguration to the upper room.

Programs for Ladies

This is an emotional production. Expect to laugh a lot, sob heavily, and rejoice victoriously as the promise of the Father rains on the congregation. Approximate time: ninety minutes.

A Wake-Up Call

CAST:

Christine Saint
Voice of Conscience, in the background with a mike on reverb
Martha
Mary
Deborah
Jael
Wise Virgin
Foolish Virgin
Aunt Pearl
2 Readers (these parts can be pre-recorded)

PROPS:

Alarm clock
Telephone
Sound effects: alarm clock, telephone, doorbell
Packages
Classified section of newspaper
Magazine rack filled with paperback books and magazines
Baskets of stuff for garage sale, includes pretty vase
Garage sale sign
Labels for sale items
Pens
Broom
Telephone
Stack of mail, including *Redbook*
Brown paper covered magazine
Moving sale sign
Large tablecloth or sheet
Two lamps
Tape of call: "Behold, the bridegroom cometh; go ye out to meet Him."
Cardboard box

Programs for Ladies

    Lace tablecloth (long 8'-10')
    Crystal
    China
    Silver
    Candelabra with white candles
    Centerpiece
    Chairs
    Tape of reveille
    Tape of readers (optional)

STAGE SET-UP:

    The set-up is a simple living room scene on the right (facing the audience). On the left the set-up calls for tables and miscellaneous items. This changes slightly from act to act. Instructions are given with each act.

ACT I

Martha's Garage Sale

A Call to Worship

CAST:

    Christine Saint, dressed in modern bathrobe
    Voice of Conscience, on a reverb mike and out of sight
    Martha, dressed in biblical robe
    Mary, dressed in biblical robe
    Readers 1 and 2, in the background or on tape

PROPS:

    Alarm clock
    Telephone
    Sound effects: alarm clock, telephone, doorbell
    Packages
    Classified section of newspaper
    Magazine rack filled with paperback books and magazines
    Baskets of stuff for garage sale, includes pretty vase
    Garage sale sign
    Labels for sale items
    Pens
    Tape of readers (optional)

STAGE SET-UP:

On the right (facing audience) is a cluttered living room scene: chair, table, trash can, and lamp. A telephone and a Bible, hidden under newspaper, are on the table. A magazine rack beside the table is overflowing with paperback books and magazines. Copy of the script is on the table.

On the left is an 8' table.

Programs for Ladies

READER 1: "And take heed to yourselves, lest at any time your hearts be overcharged—"[1]

READER 2: *(on vibrato mike)* Be on your guard. Keep a watch on yourselves, lest you become loaded down, lest your minds become dulled and clouded—

READER 1: "With surfeiting, and drunkenness, and cares of this life—"[2]

READER 2: *(on vibrato mike)* With self-indulgence, with wasteful living, with excessive pleasure, intoxicated with materialism—

READER 1: "And so that day come upon you unawares."[3]

SOUND: ALARM CLOCK

SOUND: TELEPHONE *begins ringing a few seconds after the alarm starts. Both ring simultaneously.*

SOUND: DOORBELL *begins after telephone's second ring.*

***ENTER SAINT**, wearing a robe. Hair in curlers or scarf. Staggers around half-asleep.*

SAINT: *(grabs head)* Oh, my poor pounding, ringing head. *(jumps and screams)* What was that? A cockroach? How disgraceful! My aunt Pearl would die of humiliation if she knew there were cockroaches in my house! *(grabs head and moans)* Ohhhh, another sinus headache? This weather is terrible on my allergies. My aching head. *(tilts head, looks amazed)* Why, it's not my head. It's the alarm. Or is it the telephone? Or the doorbell? Or all three? Oh, wonderful! Most people get one wake-up call. I get three! Three wake-up calls. I have to do everything in excess . . . even wake-up calls.

(Staggers around) Now where is the clock? Must be here someplace. I hear it. And why is the alarm going off? I never set the alarm for me. It's just for Howard and the kids. They're old enough to get themselves up and off. No reason for me to get up with the chickens since the kids got to be teenagers.

(Alarm, phone, and doorbell ring insistently) All right! All right, I hear you.

Why in the world is that alarm going off at this time of day? And where is it? It's got to be here because I hear it. Ahhhhh, here it is. What time is it anyway? 7:30? *(turns off alarm)* 7:30? My lands! It's the middle of the night. Who in the world set the alarm for 7:30? What day is this? Thursday? Friday? Friday! It's garage sale day! Got to get dressed. Got to get there first to get all the bargains. Course, it is a problem, being first at sixteen garage sales . . . but I do what I can.

Oh, I forgot the telephone. It's still ringing. Oh, I pray it's not Aunt Pearl. She'd want to know how the revival was last night, and I didn't go. Now where is it? All these portable phones are good for is to play "hide and seek." Where is it? *(begins looking, muttering, "cold," "warm," "colder," "warm," finds the telephone, picks it up and shouts)* Hot! Uhhhh, I mean, hello.

Sorry, whoever you are, I've got to put you on hold. I have another call. *(pushes button)* Hello? Hello? Hello? *(holds the phone away and stares at it)* That's funny. There's no one there. They must have hung up. *(puts the phone down, stomps the floor, and shudders)* Another cockroach!

SOUND: DOORBELL

Oh, it's not the phone at all. It's the doorbell. Who would come at this disgraceful hour? I haven't even had time to get dressed. *(walks to edge of platform, pretends to "peer" out curtain)* Oh, it's the UPS man with my order from J. C. Penney's. They must work around the clock. Thankfully, he's left the packages and is getting back in his truck. If he saw me, he'd think Halloween came twice this year.

(Exits briefly and comes back staggering under packages) Howard's not going to be too happy about this. Maybe I'd better squeeze these into the guest closet and take them out now and then, one-at-a-time, so he won't be overwhelmed. Got enough clothes now to last me until the Resurrection. If I hang

Programs for Ladies

a dress in the closet for a couple of months before I wear it, when he asks, "Is that new?," I can say, "Oh, no. I've had it for ages. Haven't you noticed?"

CONSCIENCE: Now, Christine, is that honest?

SAINT: *(appears startled)* Who said that?

CONSCIENCE: I did . . . your conscience.

SAINT: Oh, no, don't tell me you're back on the job. Guess it's the revival that's got you stirred up. Didn't think I'd gone enough for that. But you're pretty touchy—one service and you're wide-awake. I wish you'd go back to sleep. Those wake-up calls were for me, not you.

(Pulls invoice off the top of the package and opens it) Wow! This can't be right. It says I've maxed out my Penney's credit card! I don't know how in the world I've done that. They must have made a mistake. I don't have a thing to show for it.

CONSCIENCE: Now, Christine—

SAINT: Don't you "now, Christine," me! I'll have to call Penney's and—

Call! That's reminds me. Somebody's on hold. *(picks up the phone)* Sorry to have kept you waiting . . . yes, this is Christine Saint . . . oh, really? You mean out of thousands of people I've been chosen for this wonderful offer? Of course I'd love to take a trip to the Holy Land. All I have to do is subscribe to the magazine of my choice, and my name will be put in the drawing for an all-expense-paid trip to Israel? Sure! Sure! Well, now let's see. I already take *True Confession* and *Ladies' Home Journal* and *Enquirer* and two or three others. My husband gets *Newsweek*, and he buys *Playboy* at the newsstand. Of course, he doesn't know that I know it. He hides them under the rug in the trunk of the car. You know, boys will be boys. And my son gets *Sports Illustrated* and *Field and Stream*, and the Lord only knows what else. You know, like father like son. So what else do you have to offer? *Redbook?* That sounds good.

CONSCIENCE: *Redbook?* Christine, remember the sermon Sunday night?

SAINT: You hush!—no, not you. I was talking to . . . uhhhh . . . one of my kids.

CONSCIENCE: Christine!

SAINT: Leave me alone! Oh, sorry. It was my kid again. *Redbook* has wonderful romance stories, almost as good as *True Confession*. Do you have my name and address? All you need is my VISA card number. I know it by memory. It's 478-0086-3428-06754-382. Expiration date eighth month of next year. Sure. Thank you . . . oh, say, when will I know if I've won the trip to the Holy Land? August *(two years from now)*. Thank you very much. *(hangs up the phone)* Just think I might get to go to Israel just because I subscribed to—August *(two years from now)*! Did she say *(two years from now)*?

Meanwhile, I get to pay for *Redbook*. Oh, well, when things get too stressful, I can always escape by reading another romance. That reminds me, I've got to get dressed. Maybe I can pick up some more Harlequin or Danielle Steel novels at the garage sales. I've read everything in the house.

CONSCIENCE: What about your Bible?

SAINT: Stop nagging me! Look at the clock! Now where's that paper? I've got to get moving if I'm going to be first at sixteen garage sales. *(sits down at the table, moves Bible)* I guess I really should read my Bible and pray, but I'll do that later—probably lots later. I've been so busy lately I haven't had much time for devotions. Oh, well, the Lord understands. We live in such a busy time. Life is so stressful.

Yeeks! Another cockroach. *(stomps the floor, trying to catch it)* I have got to clean house and call the exterminator soon. Might be easier just to move. In fact, if I don't stop buying things, we're going to have to move.

But I've got to be at these garage sales the minute they open.

Programs for Ladies

Guess I'm just a garage sale addict! *(picks up newspaper and pencil, yawns)* Where shall I start? Here's a big moving sale on South Thirty-first. "No early sales." *(yawns, head nods)* Or I could start at this three-family sale on Wilson; that's not far from here. Wonder who's selling three families? . . . I know one I'd like to sell . . . some days. *(rubs eyes, stretches)* This one . . . looks interesting . . . "lots of antiques" . . . 712 Olive Street . . . *(yawns)* in Bethany! Where . . . in the world . . . is Bethany? *(lays head down on table, goes to sleep)*

MUSIC: TRANSITION

ENTER MARY *and* ***MARTHA*** *from left, each carrying a basket of "goodies," which they start setting up on the table and pricing. One hangs up a garage sale sign.* ***SAINT*** *gets up as if sleepwalking and watches them.*

MARY: *(holds up item)* How much do you want for this, Martha?

MARTHA: Oh, I don't know, Mary. Do you think a couple of mites is too much?

MARY: Probably. It should have been junked years ago. I'll put one on it. *(prices it)*

MARTHA: *(holds up item)* What about this? How much is it worth?

MARY: Oh, are you sure you want to sell that, Martha? It was Great-aunt Elizabeth's.

MARTHA: I know, but I've got to get rid of things. I have too many things.

SAINT: *(sleepwalking)* This is too good to be true. I'm the first one at this garage sale! And look at the antiques. I must be dreaming! *(approaches Martha)* Pardon me, ladies. Would you mind if I browse around while you put things out?

MARY: Certainly not. Help yourself.

As soon as ***MARY*** *and* ***MARTHA*** *put items on table,* ***SAINT*** *snatches them up and piles them to one side.*

MARY: I never thought you'd turn loose of this, Martha. How much do you want for it?

MARTHA: One and a half farthings should be about right. I feel lighter already, Mary, getting rid of these things. I never realized how much of my energy was devoted to buying and paying for and taking care of things.

MARY: I hope you're not sorry tomorrow that you sold all these things today.

MARTHA: I won't be. Ninety percent of the things I have, I could live without.

MARY: I won't argue with that.

SAINT: *(to self)* No Harlequins or Danielle Steels around here.

MARTHA: This isn't a spur-of-the-moment decision, Mary. I've been thinking about it ever since that evening I fixed dinner for Jesus and His disciples. I finally made up my mind last week when we had dinner at Simon's, celebrating Lazarus's resurrection. That was a beautiful gesture of worship, Mary, when you anointed Jesus' feet with that costly ointment.

MARY: Not everybody approved. Most of the disciples were critical. Judas was very upset.

MARTHA: I know. There's a lot of "Judas" in me, Mary. That's why I have to get rid of some "things." Somewhere along the line I have tied my sense of self-worth to things.

MARY: But, Martha, it's not a sin to have things.

MARTHA: I know, Mary, but it's a sin for things to have me. I've been possessed by my possessions too long. I resented it when Jesus scolded me, ever so gently, because I was worried and anxious "about many things," when only "one thing is needful." Then to make matters worse He said you had

Programs for Ladies

chosen the "good part," and it wouldn't be taken away from you.

MARY: But He didn't tell you to sell all your possessions. *(holds up an item)* How much for this?

MARTHA: Put it in the "give away" basket. I know Jesus didn't tell me to sell all. And I'm not selling everything. Just enough to set me free from materialism.

SAINT: *(holds up a vase)* Pardon me, ladies. How much do you want for this?

MARTHA: Hmmm, that's very old and valuable. Our mother left it to our brother Lazarus. I think I'd better have two shekels. Do you think that's about right, Mary?

SAINT: Two shekels? Did you say shekels? How much is that?

MARTHA: Why, it's two shekels. Maybe that is a bit much. Would you give one and a half?

SAINT: I would if I had it. Do you take VISA?

MARTHA: Pardon me?

SAINT: Do you take VISA?

MARTHA: Mesa? Lisa? What did you say?

SAINT: I said VISA. You know, the credit card. Surely you know about VISA. Or do you use MasterCard?

MARTHA: *(shrugs)* Never heard of either. Look, lady, if you want that vase, you can have it for one shekel! But that's my bottom dollar . . . I mean, shekel.

MARY: Martha! You can't let her have that for one shekel. Why, that's highway robbery. What would Lazarus say?

MARTHA: He wouldn't care, Mary. When our brother died, he realized how unimportant things were.

SAINT: Oh, you lost your brother? I'm soooo sorry.

MARY: Don't be. It was a wonderful experience.

SAINT: Huh? Losing your brother was a wonderful experience?

MARTHA: You can't imagine how wonderful.

SAINT: *(looks at Martha as if she has lost her mind)* He was that bad, huh? Did you say this was his vase?

MARY: Yes, it's his. But he said it was okay to sell it.

SAINT: He said you could sell it? But I thought he was dead. Oh, I know. He told you before he died that it would be all right to sell it.

MARTHA: No, he told me after he died. In fact, he told me yesterday.

SAINT: *(shudders, eyes widened)* Don't tell me you're into the occult!

MARY: The o-what?

SAINT: The occult. You know, where you talk to the dead.

MARY and **MARTHA** laugh. **SAINT** is offended.

SAINT: I really don't see anything funny.

MARY: I'm sorry, my dear. It's not funny, but it is wonderful. You see, our brother was dead—

MARTHA: But now he's alive because Jesus came, and Jesus is "the resurrection and the life."

SAINT: He was dead, but now he's alive? Jesus is . . . wait a minute. Did you call her Martha?

MARY: Yes. She's my sister Martha.

Programs for Ladies

SAINT: And you called her Mary?

MARTHA: Yes.

SAINT: And your brother's name is Lazarus?

MARY and MARTHA nod.

SAINT: What is this address?

MARY: This is 712 Olive Street in Bethany.

SAINT: No wonder you don't know anything about VISA.

MARTHA: No, I don't know anything about VISA, but I do know that things won't make you happy. *(points at things Saint has stacked up)* Do you really need all that stuff?

SAINT: I . . . well . . . I thought . . . I . . . I mean, there are some valuable items here.

MARTHA: Valuable? Maybe so. I used to think so. Then I learned that the value of things depends upon where your heart is. When Jesus and His disciples came to my home, I fixed a gourmet meal. I set the table with my best linen, china, crystal, and silver. Everything was delicious and beautiful. My house was spotless.

SAINT: That was good. I'd do the same thing.

CONSCIENCE: Christine!

SAINT: I mean, I wish my house was spotless.

MARTHA: Yes. It was good. But I let the good cheat me out of the best.

SAINT: You what?

MARTHA: I let the good cheat me out of the best.

SAINT: The best? What was best?

MARTHA: Best was what Mary did. She sat at Jesus' feet and listened to His Word. I worked. That was good. But she worshiped. That was best. *(picks up another item)* How much do you think this is worth, Mary?

***SAINT** turns and sleepwalks back to chair, carrying with her the vase she had been bargaining for.*

MARY: Hey, wait. Come back, lady. You didn't pay for that vase. And don't you want all these other things? We'll take your Lisa or Mesa or VISA or whatever.

***SAINT** does not respond. Returns to her chair. Places the vase on the table. Sits down and lays head on the table.*

MARTHA: That's all right, Mary. Let her go.

MARY: But she didn't pay for that vase.

MARTHA: I don't think she realizes she has it. She has more important things on her mind.

MARY: Now look what you've done, Martha. You've given away one of your most valuable items. And it'll take us all day to sell the rest of this stuff that she was going to buy. You're acting like me.

MARTHA: That's okay, Mary. I have a feeling she doesn't really need any of this. She's been letting good take the place of best. I think she's about to realize that only one thing is needful.

***MARY** and **MARTHA** freeze.*

***SAINT** lifts her head, looks around in amazement, yawns, and stretches.*

SAINT: What was I doing? Oh, yes, looking for garage sales. Where was I? *(scans paper)* 712 Olive Street . . . in Bethany . . . I just had the strangest dream . . . I know it was a dream. Me the first one at a garage sale? It had to be a dream! Wait a minute. Where did I get this vase? *(sits in amazed silence for a few seconds, turning the vase around in her hand, then sets it down, folds the newspaper, and picks up the Bible)* What was it she said, "Only one thing is needful"? Where have I heard that before? *(turns to Luke 10:38 and reads) "Now it came to pass, as they went, that he entered into a certain village: and a certain woman named Martha received him into her house. And she had a sister called Mary, which also sat at Jesus' feet, and heard his word...."*[4]

SAINT EXITS, *reading.*

MARY *and* **MARTHA EXIT** *on opposite side.*

ACT II

Jael's Moving Sale

A Call to Stand Guard

CAST:

   Christine Saint, wearing apron and everyday clothes
   Voice of Conscience, on reverb mike, out of sight
   Deborah, dressed in biblical attire
   Jael, dressed in biblical attire

PROPS:

   Broom
   Telephone
   Stack of mail, including *Redbook*
   Brown paper-covered magazine
   Moving sale sign
   Large tablecloth or sheet

STAGE SET-UP:

   Same as for Act I, except items on sale table are covered with a cloth.

ENTER CHRISTINE SAINT, *wearing an apron, carrying a broom. Copy of script can be placed on table and in magazine.*

SAINT: What time is it? *(looks at watch)* Oh, dear me, I'm already six hours behind, and I've only been up two. *(starts sweeping)* I have got to stop buying things! That's all there is to it! This house looks like a war zone. And I'm battle fatigued. I sure do get tired of fighting the dirt and clutter. Sometimes I feel like running away from home. Say, that's a good idea. I could go to the ice cream shop. They have fifty-nine kinds of ice cream. Or I could go to the mall.

Programs for Ladies

CONSCIENCE: Remember Martha.

SAINT: Martha? Yes, I remember Mar . . . oh, no, not you again!

CONSCIENCE: Yep, it's me. Your conscience.

SAINT: My conscience? Oh, bother! I wish I could sweep you under the rug with the cockroaches. What I want to know is how much Howard pays you to follow me around and bug me. Okay! Okay, I won't go to the mall today. I don't have any money anyway and both J. C. Penney and VISA are maxed out! Does that make you happy?

CONSCIENCE: What? That the cards are maxed out or that you're not going to the mall?

SAINT: That I'm not going to the mall.

CONSCIENCE: Maybe. It depends on what you are going to do.

SAINT: I'll show you. Where's my list of things to do? *(rummages in apron pocket)* Ahhhh, here it is. *(pulls out crumpled paper and reads)* Pray. Read the Bible.

CONSCIENCE: Now you're living up to your name . . . Christine or Christian. You're really going to read your Bible and pray?

SAINT: Yes, I am . . . later.

CONSCIENCE: Oops! Remember Mary?

SAINT: I remember Mary! But if you want to know the truth, there's more of Martha in me than Mary. And may I remind you that we're in revival?

CONSCIENCE: Really? I thought you had forgotten.

SAINT: Just because I missed a night or two doesn't mean I've forgotten. I plan to go tonight. Now as I was saying, Brother Pastor asked us all to come early and pray. I'll do my praying then. I certainly don't have time to pray twice a day!

> *(Reads from list)* Go to dentist. Take dog to the groomer and Howard's suit to the cleaners. Call the exterminator. Scratch that one! I can't let anyone see this house until I clean it. Cash in aluminum cans. Write Aunt Pearl. That one's been on the list every day for two weeks. Bake a cake for the evangelist. *(louder)* Bake a cake for the evangelist! *(louder)* Bake a cake for the evangelist!

CONSCIENCE: I heard you the first time!

SAINT: Well, I thought it would make you happy!

> I don't know why we have to have a revival now when I have so many other things to do. Seems like all the pastor has to do is plan things for us to do.
>
> Oh, there's the mailman. *(goes out and comes back with handful of mail, including* Redbook *magazine)* I see my *Redbook* subscription has started. *(reads)* "Why I Chose to Have an Abortion," "The Day I Discovered My Daughter Was Gay," "How to Seduce a Child." *(clicks tongue)* My, my, it's a disgrace the shape this world is in. Hmmm, this condensed fiction book sounds interesting, "The Passionate Barber." I've got to read this right now.

CONSCIENCE: You're going to read that?

SAINT: Certainly. I have to keep up with what is happening in this world, don't I? How else am I going to know what to pray about? Abortion, child abuse, incest, homosexuality, AIDS, it's horrible.

CONSCIENCE: But you didn't have time to read your Bible.

***SAINT** ignores Conscience, sits down, thumbs through magazine, starts reading, sighing blissfully.*

SOUND: TELEPHONE

SAINT: *(keeping eyes glued on magazine, reaches for the phone)* Ohhhh, darling, kiss—oops! I mean, hello. *(mushy voice)* Oh,

Programs for Ladies

Howard sweetheart, I was just thinking about you. . . . What did I say when I answered the phone? I said . . . well, I said . . . uhhh—

CONSCIENCE: Tell the truth!

SAINT: You shut up!—No, not you, Honey. I was just talking to . . . to the dog. You didn't hear him? Well, he looked like he was about to bark—

CONSCIENCE: Uh-ho!

SAINT: *(takes a deep breath and looks angry)* I don't want to hear any more out of you!—No, Honey, not you, the dog. Certainly, you can call anytime you want to. It's just a bit unusual for you to call in the middle of the day. Do you have news? . . . What? . . . A promotion? A raise? That's wonderful. *(to self)* I might go to the mall after all.

CONSCIENCE: Remember Martha!

SAINT: I told you to hush!—No, not you, Darling, the dog. . . . We'll have to what? Move? Ohhhh . . . where? Middle Ground. But, Howard, there's not a church in Middle Ground. At least not a church that preaches the truth . . . Yes, I know it's a wonderful opportunity for you. And it would be nice to have a new house, a bigger house. . . . What? That vacation we've been planning? Sure, and better clothes for the kids and maybe even a swimming pool? Go out to dinner to celebrate? Tonight?

CONSCIENCE: *(weaker)* What about the revival?

SAINT: *(through clenched teeth)* I'd like to throttle you. *(mushy)* No, not you, Darling, the dog. Dinner for two at Jamil's. Wonderful. We can send the kids to church. *(mushy)* Congratulations, Sweetheart. I'll be waiting for you. *(hangs up the phone)*

(Dances a jig) We're moving! We're moving! *(squeals and stomps)* Yeek! Another cockroach. I won't even have to call the

exterminator. We'll just move away and leave the cockroaches. Or will we?

CONSCIENCE: *(weaker)* What about church?

SAINT: What did you say? I can't hear you.

CONSCIENCE: *(whispers)* I said, "What about church?"

SAINT: We'll find a church that Howard likes. You know he never has cared for the pastor here. That's why he misses so much. Why, we might even start our own church.

CONSCIENCE: *(chokes)*

SAINT: What's the matter with you?

CONSCIENCE: *(weakly)* Got choked on that bologna! You're killing me!

SAINT: You mean you're killing me. Well, I'm not listening to you any more today. I've got things to do. If we're moving, I have to have a moving sale. Think I'll start with this old chair. It was about worn out when Aunt Pearl gave it to us. I've wanted to pitch it for a long time. Now we'll be able to afford new furniture.

(Moves chair around, pulls up cushion, laughs) No telling what I'll find under here. Can't remember the last time I vacuumed— *(screams and stomps)* Cockroaches! *(finally settles down, looks again and holds up brown paper-wrapped magazine)* Why, what's this? *(opens and gasps)* It's pornography. Hard-core pornography! Oh, I never dreamed they published things like this! These pictures! This is trash! It's pure garbage! *(flips pages)* It's making me sick! *(holds stomach and moans)* Who put this here? How did this get into my home? Who's been reading this filth? Howard? John? Has my son been reading this? It could destroy him. This is hard-core stuff!

(Sinks into chair, drops magazine to floor, buries face in

Programs for Ladies

hands) Oh, dear Lord, what am I going to do? *(shoulders shake silently)*

ENTER JAEL, *removes cover from table and places "Moving Sale" sign where audience can see it.*

JAEL: It's a beautiful day for a sale. I should do well. Ahhh, here comes my first customer.

ENTER DEBORAH. SAINT *stands and moves nearer to watch.*

JAEL: Why, it is Deborah, the eloquent prophetess and judge of Israel. Welcome, Deborah, to my humble tent. What can I sell you?

DEBORAH: Nothing, Jael. I hear that you and Heber are moving south, and I came to say, "Good-bye and thank you."

JAEL: Heber says we never should have moved away from our people, the Kenites. He realizes now the danger he placed his family in by moving near Jabin, king of Canaan.

DEBORAH: Why did you move?

JAEL: *(hangs head in shame, wrings hands, whispers)* I . . . I . . . I'm ashamed to say.

DEBORAH: *(places hand on Jael's shoulder)* I apologize for asking. I have a pretty good idea why you moved near the capital of Canaan. It had to do with your husband's profession, didn't it?

JAEL: Yes. Heber felt he could make a better living if he was in league with the Canaanites. He's always been socially minded. Why, even his name means "society or fellowship." And he is a metalsmith and the Canaanites have—they had—nine hundred chariots of iron. The Israelites didn't even have shields and spears. He didn't see much future in working for the Israelites. And King Jabin did make him an attractive offer.

DEBORAH: Oh, but how we needed him! He could have been such a blessing to God's people.

JAEL: I know. I know, and I am so ashamed. I feel like a traitor, a compromiser.

DEBORAH: Not you, Jael. You are a courageous woman. It was through you that God gave a great victory to Israel.

JAEL: Oh, not me, Deborah. You are the one who led Israel to a great victory over the Canaanites. I heard that the mighty captain Barak refused to go into battle unless you were by his side.

DEBORAH: *(laughs)* God seldom uses women to lead the army, but He often uses them to start the battle. I was just the prick He used to wake up Israel. It was God who gave us the victory. My, what a hail and sleet storm we had! It came right into the face of the enemy but was behind us.

JAEL: And the river flooded?

DEBORAH: Talk about a flash flood! The chariots of the Canaanites got stuck in the mud and many of their army drowned.

JAEL: So that is why the commander of the Canaanite army, Sisera, was on foot when he ran to my tent?

DEBORAH: That's why. Did you know that Sisera means "field of battle"?

JAEL: No, I didn't know. "Field of battle" . . . the field of battle came right into my home.

SAINT *gasps loudly and moves in closer, drawing attention of audience to herself.*

SAINT: Pardon me. I couldn't help but overhear your conversation. That must have been a frightening experience . . . to have the enemy in your home.

JAEL: Yes and no. Sisera had been in our tent before. Since my husband Heber fellowshiped with the enemy, Sisera was often in our home. I never did like him, but I wanted to keep peace in my marriage and be submissive to my husband, so I tolerated him.

Programs for Ladies

> But this time when Sisera came seeking, even demanding, my protection, I'd had enough! I knew I could no longer give him shelter in my home.

DEBORAH: Tell us about it.

JAEL: He asked for a drink of water. Instead I gave him warm milk. *(chuckles)* He thought I was being hospitable. Actually, I was giving him a sedative—putting him to sleep! I covered him with a warm rug. He was chilled to the bone. Just before he went to sleep, he asked me to stand guard at the door. If anyone came looking for him, I was to say he wasn't in my tent.

Sisera wanted me to believe the enemy was outside. Actually, the enemy was inside my home! *(shivers)* It scares me half to death now when I think about it. He could have destroyed my family! Thank God he didn't.

DEBORAH: That's because you had the courage to destroy him first.

SAINT: Please, tell me what you did? How did you get rid of him? I must know.

JAEL: I took a hammer and drove a tent peg through his temple. I nailed him to the floor!

SAINT: *(aghast)* You didn't?

JAEL: I did.

SAINT: But that was tacky! Gruesome, too.

DEBORAH: It was brave!

JAEL: What else could I do? He would have destroyed my family. I couldn't stand there and let him. Every woman I know would have done the same thing.

SAINT: I know my aunt Pearl would have. She has fought the devil single-handedly for years.

DEBORAH: While the army was fighting the enemy without, Jael defeated him within. We can never have complete victory over the enemy in our nation until he has been defeated in our homes! We women have to wake up and stand guard!

JAEL: Say that again.

DEBORAH: We can never have complete victory over the enemy in our nation until he has been defeated in our homes! We women have to wake up and stand guard!

SAINT: Say it again.

DEBORAH: We can never have complete victory over the enemy in our nation until he has been defeated in our homes! Women of God, wake up! Stand guard!

SAINT: *(in despair)* But how do I stand guard? The enemy has invaded my home. How can I defeat the enemy?

DEBORAH: The same way Jael defeated him in her home. First, you must wake up.

SAINT: I am awake. What I just found has shaken every bit of sleep from me. I am awake . . . believe me, I am wide awake!

DEBORAH: Then you must be sure that the enemy has no hold on you. You must drive his influence out of your life. You must gird up the loins of your mind.

SAINT: His influence out my life? My mind? But I don't read that garbage. I don't—

CONSCIENCE: You don't?

SAINT: *(snaps)* I told you to hus . . . *(soberly)* wait. Wait. Let me think. Maybe I have fellowshiped with the enemy more than I realized.

DEBORAH: Then you must nail him!

SAINT: Nail him? How can I nail the devil? How can I defeat the spirit

Programs for Ladies

of lust that threatens to destroy my family?

DEBORAH: Clean house. Then use the hammer of God's Word and the nail of prayer to break his influence in your home.

JAEL: It's not a pleasant task! Nor an easy one.

SAINT: But it's something I have to do. *(turns and starts to walk away)* It's something I have to do.

JAEL: Wait! Wait! Come back. Don't you want to buy something?

SAINT: *(turns to Jael)* No. I have too many things now. Besides you probably don't take VISA.

DEBORAH: VISA? What in the world is VISA?

ALL EXIT.

ACT III

Not for Sale

A Call to Prepare

CAST:

    Christine Saint, dressed as in Act II.
    Wise Virgin, dressed in white
    Foolish Virgin, dressed in white
    Aunt Pearl, dressed in exaggerated "old lady" attire

PROPS:

    Two lamps
    Tape of call: "Behold, the bridegroom cometh; go ye out to meet Him."
    Cardboard box

STAGE SET-UP:

Same as in other acts, except another chair is added beside the table and a cardboard box is behind the chair.

READER: *"Be ye also ready: for in such an hour as ye think not the Son of man cometh."*[5]

SOUND: TELEPHONE

ENTER SAINT, *in robe and curlers, half-awake, groping for the phone.*

SAINT: Now where is that phone? Like I said, "Who needs an alarm clock when you have a telephone?" There goes a cockroach. Oh, well, no need bending myself all out of shape to kill it. What's one among so many? What time is it anyway? *(peers at watch)* 9:15? 9:15! How'd it get so late so early? I never get enough sleep.

Programs for Ladies

CONSCIENCE: You could if you'd do what I'm telling you to do.

SAINT: Don't you ever sleep? You prodded and poked me all night.

CONSCIENCE: Remember Jael?

SAINT: Yes, yes, I remember Jael.

CONSCIENCE: And Deborah?

SAINT: And Deborah. And I know I'm supposed to stand guard. I know I need to clean house. I know all that! Why do I always have to be the strong one? Howard's supposed to be the watchman of our family. In fact, that's what his name means, "watchman." I wish he'd live up to his name!

CONSCIENCE: Do you?

SAINT: Do I what?

CONSCIENCE: Live up to your name . . . Christine, Christian, Christ-like?

SAINT: Oh, go back to sleep. All I need is you nagging me to make this a perfectly wonderful day. Please go back to sleep.

> Where is that phone? Ahhhh, here it is. Hello . . . who? Great-aunt Pearl? . . . It's so good to hear from my favorite aunt. Where are you? . . . At Denny's! Denny's down the street? Oh, in the city. Thank heaven . . . No, I just said that's living.

CONSCIENCE: Christine!

SAINT: You'll be here when? Some time today? Oh, wonderful! Just wonderful! . . . Of course, I mean it.

CONSCIENCE: *(weaker)* Christine!

SAINT: How long will you be staying? . . . What? Until you get your next check? But that's the first and this is only the fourth! . . . I mean, of course, we'll be glad to have you—only we might be moving. Howard's getting this wonderful promotion, and we may move to Middle Ground . . . I know, I know, Aunt Pearl. But you know Howard. Church is not very important to him. And it will be lots more money.

CONSCIENCE: *(weakly)* Remember Jael? Remember—

SAINT: We can talk about all this later. . . . This is costing you. . . . Sure. You know you're always welcome. Bye. *(hangs up)*

Twenty-seven days with Aunt Pearl! What did I do to deserve that?

CONSCIENCE: *(weakly)* You know you love her. Remember when you were growing up, she was your role model. Remember how lovingly she led you to the Lord.

SAINT: *(wails)* I know! I know. There never was a godlier woman on this earth than Aunt Pearl. She lived for God even when Uncle Albert didn't, and she raised her children to live for God, too. That's the problem . . . Aunt Pearl is so . . . so . . . so perfect!

CONSCIENCE: *(weakly, gasping for breath)* If Aunt Pearl came to your house to spend a day or two—if she came unexpectedly—I wonder what you'd do.

SAINT: Oh, I wish I could choke you.

CONSCIENCE: *(whispers weakly)* You can. You are . . . you are. . . . *(gasps)*

SOUND: TELEPHONE

SAINT: Now what? *(picks up phone)* Hello . . . Aunt Pearl, is something wrong? . . . You just called to tell me not to worry about cleaning house. You'll help me when you get here. . . . That's what I was afraid of. . . . No, no. I just mean I don't want you working while you're here. I've got everything under control. . . . Okay, Aunt Pearl . . . Good-bye. I love you, too. *(hangs up phone)*

Now to clean house. But what am I going to do about the cockroaches? It's too late to call the exterminator.

(Puckers brow) Something is strange. What is it? It's too quiet . . . in my head . . . or is it my heart? I know what's wrong. Not one time during that last phone call did my conscience interrupt. And I didn't exactly tell the truth either. *(mimics self)* "I've got everything under control." Ha! I didn't tell the truth. So where's my conscience? Probably catnapping. *(yawns)* That's what I'd like to do. *(looks at watch)* But first I've got to clean house. I can't let Aunt Pearl find me this way. It would break her heart to see me living such a sloppy life . . . in house and heart!

Where shall I start? With these books and magazines. I'll just box them up and sell them at my next garage sale. *(piles about half of the books and magazines into box)* I could take them down to the used bookstore and trade them in.

No! No! No! If I want my family to be saved, I've got to start by saving myself. I have to stand guard over my mind. I have to "gird up the loins of my mind." But these aren't nearly as bad as that garbage Harold and John have been reading and watching.

(Stops and looks around) Well, say something! . . . I said, "Say something!" Hellloooo . . . *(louder)* Hellllloooo? Wake up, sleepyhead. Wake up! *(yells)* This is a wake-up call! Can't you hear me?

(Looks horrified) My conscience! What has happened to my conscience? Surely I haven't destroyed it! I didn't intend to destroy my conscience. I meant to destroy the enemy, not my conscience. Oh, what have I done? Without my conscience I can't be saved!

(Falls to knees) Oh, dear God, forgive me. I didn't use to be like this. I wasn't consumed by materialism. I went to prayer meetings and on visitation instead of spending all my time shopping at garage sales and the mall. I used to pray and read my Bible. I had a clean mind—I even had a clean house. Oh,

God, cleanse me. Help me gird up the loins of my mind. Help me! Help me! Help me! I want to stand guard for my family. I really do. *(shoulders shake silently)*

ENTER WISE and FOOLISH VIRGINS, *dressed alike, carrying lighted lamps.*

FOOLISH: *(yawns)* What time is it anyway?

WISE: Close to midnight. Been a long night.

FOOLISH: I don't think he's coming. Who does he think he is to keep everybody waiting so long? His watch must be broken.

WISE: I don't think he wears a watch.

FOOLISH: *(swats at arm)* These bugs are driving me crazy! My dress is getting wrinkled. The night air is bad for my asthma.

WISE: Just relax. Surely, he'll be here soon.

FOOLISH: Relax! That's easy for you to say. You're not allergic to the night air. *(grabs the hem of her dress)* Oh, great! That carriage just splashed mud on my dress. I thought this was going to be a joyous occasion, or I never would have agreed to be a bridesmaid.

WISE: It will be when the bridegroom comes.

FOOLISH: And if he doesn't come?

WISE: Oh, but he will.

FOOLISH: But if he doesn't come, we've spent all this money in vain . . . new dress . . . new shoes . . . a lamp and oil.

WISE: He'll come, I'm sure. He loves the bride.

FOOLISH: Well, I hope so. In the meantime, I'm going to take a nap. Wake me, if he shows up. *(sits down, lays head on the table, and immediately starts snoring)*

WISE: Well, that was quick. *(yawns)* I'm getting sleepy myself. I don't suppose it would hurt if I took a little nap. First, I'd better check my lamp. *(does so)* Good. Now for a little shuteye. *(sits down, lays head on the table, and goes to sleep)*

Several seconds of silence. The only sound is an occasional snore from the Foolish Virgin.

CALL (on tape): "*Behold, the bridegroom cometh; go ye out to meet him.*"[6]

VIRGINS *jump up.*

FOOLISH: Oh, uh? What? What's going on?

WISE: It's the bridegroom. He's coming. Are you ready?

FOOLISH: Of course I'm ready. I've been ready for hours.

WISE: Then grab your lamp and come on. It's dark out there, but I see some lights ahead of us. The other virgins are lighting the way for the bridegroom.

FOOLISH: My lamp? Oh, uh-oh, wait a minute.

WISE: We don't have time to wait. Come on.

FOOLISH: But my lamp is about out of oil.

WISE: What? You mean you sat here all evening unprepared?

FOOLISH: But I was prepared. I had oil in my lamp. I just forgot to bring extra in my vessel. I didn't expect to have to wait so long. Sell me some of yours. You've got plenty.

WISE: Plenty for myself, but not any to sell.

FOOLISH: Don't be like that. You wouldn't miss it.

WISE: Oh, yes, I would. If I sold some to you, there might not be enough for either of us. My oil is not for sale. You'll have to go buy for yourself.

FOOLISH: Please, sell me some of your oil.

WISE: I'm very sorry, but my oil is not for sale! Go buy for yourself.

FOOLISH: Buy for myself? At this time of night? Are you foolish?

WISE: No, I'd say I'm wise. It looks like some of the others are going to buy. You'd better go with them. Hurry!

WISE EXITS *one way.* ***FOOLISH EXITS*** *the other.*

As they do so, ***AUNT PEARL*** *moves to the "door."*

SAINT: *(still on knees, moans)* Oh, God, have I sold out? Have I sold my oil? Oh, God—

SOUND: DOORBELL

SAINT: (jumps to her feet) Oh, no! There's Aunt Pearl. And I'm not ready! I'm not ready! *(rushes around trying to straighten house; shoves a few more books and magazines into box)*

SOUND: DOORBELL

SAINT *opens door.*

SAINT: *(hugs Aunt Pearl, sincerely)* Oh, Aunt Pearl, I'm so glad to see you. I really am.

AUNT PEARL: And I'm glad to see you, child. *(peers through bifocals)* You're looking good—a bit harried perhaps, but good. Now you didn't go to a lot of work to prepare for me, did you?

SAINT: No, no, not a bit . . . well, a li . . . well, not enough. I can't tell you how glad I am to see you. I didn't know . . . I needed . . . you . . . so much. *(puts head in hands and begins to cry)* Oh, Aunt Pearl, help me!

AUNT PEARL: I had a feeling you needed me, Christine. That's why

Programs for Ladies

I'm here. Let's sit down. My feet ain't as firm a foundation as they used to be.

BOTH sit down.

AUNT PEARL: Now tell me all about it.

SAINT: Oh, everything's wrong! And I do mean every thing!

> *While* **SAINT** *is talking,* **AUNT PEARL** *is peering over, under and through her glasses at a cockroach crawling across the floor.* **SAINT** *who is wringing her hands and looking at them does not notice.*

SAINT: *(pours everything out breathlessly)* This house is a mess. I'm sick of it! Howard's got an offer of a promotion—lots more money, but we have to move to Middle Ground and there's no church there, but we really do need a bigger house. I've maxed out the credit cards, and we're head-over-heels in debt—and don't have anything to show for it. Well, we really do have lots of things, but they're just cluttery things. And I just found out that Howard and John are into pornography! Pornography, Aunt Pearl! It's gross! And I've killed my conscience and—

AUNT PEARL: What's that black spot on the floor, Christine?

SAINT: What? *(gasps as she sees the cockroach)* Oh, it's . . . it's just . . . it's just an oil spot. John's been working on his cycle and he track—

AUNT PEARL: Hmmm . . . that's strange. That's the first oil spot I ever saw that crawled!

SAINT: Oh! Well, maybe you've spots before your eyes, Aunt Pearl. Sometimes that happens as you get older and the retina pulls away—

AUNT PEARL: Christine! My eyes ain't what they used to be. But my spiritual perception is sharp as ever!

SAINT: Yes, ma'am. I was afraid of that.

AUNT PEARL: You've got some problems, young lady, and cockroaches is the least of 'em.

SAINT: Yes, ma'am.

AUNT PEARL: Now I've been talking to the Lord about you, child, and He's been talkin' to me.

SAINT: I was afraid of that, too.

AUNT PEARL: We'll start with the little things first.

SAINT: Yes, ma'am.

AUNT PEARL: The cockroaches.

SAINT: But, Aunt Pearl, we haven't had the money to pay an exterminator. They're so expensive.

AUNT PEARL: Honey, you don't have to call a 'term-i-nator. Just clean house! Then buy a can of Roach-Pruf, only $8.00. Sprinkle it in corners and drawers and poof! The cockroaches disappear. All it takes is a little time and energy.

SAINT: Why, Aunt Pearl, how'd you know that? About the Roach-Pruf, I mean.

AUNT PEARL: You don't think I've lived this long without fightin' a few cockroaches, do you? And we've always had to pinch pennies . . . never could afford them expensive 'term-i-nators. Now let's talk about what's buggin' you spiritually.

SAINT: *(takes deep breath)* Well, it's Howard. He's not really interested in church and he—

AUNT PEARL: Hey, wait a minute! Howard ain't your problem, Christine. Christine is.

SAINT: But, Aunt Pearl—

AUNT PEARL: Don't you go "Aunt Pearling" me. Don't you think I've

Programs for Ladies

learned a few things in eighty-six years? Your biggest problem, Christy Sue, is you're not honest.

SAINT: Aunt Pearl! How can you say that?

AUNT PEARL: Easy enough. I just said it. "Your biggest problem, Christy Sue, is you're not honest." Take fer instance, you say to me on the phone that you'll be glad to have me come fer a visit. And then you say that you don't want me workin' while I'm here. Now that's not honest.

SAINT: *(weakly)* But I am glad you're here.

AUNT PEARL: Now you are. On the phone you were lyin'. Then you say that cockroach is an oil spot! Christy Sue, that's lyin'.

SAINT: Aunt Pearl!

AUNT PEARL: You've got this bad habit of stretching the truth. Some calls it "being tactful." Others call it "exaggerating." Some even call it "evangelistically speaking." I call it "lyin'."

SAINT: But, Aunt Pearl.

AUNT PEARL: You'd like to say that Howard's your problem. He's the one wanting that money. Maybe he wants it because he thinks you want it. Goodness knows you spend it fast enough! Be honest, Christine.

SAINT: *(weakly)* Aunt Pearl!

AUNT PEARL: Gotta quit lying to yerself . . . and others, child. Don't you know Howard's smart enough to know when you're being real and when you're puttin' on?

SAINT: Oh, Aunt Pearl.

AUNT PEARL: Listen to me, child. I ain't lived eighty-six years in vain. I've learned a few things, and I'd like to keep you from fallin' in the same mud holes I've fell in. Your Uncle Albert weren't interested in church neither. And I learned the hard way—

almost lost my soul 'fore I learned it—that I had to have my own walk with God. I couldn't make it with a sloppy off-and-on spirituality.

SAINT: I know.

AUNT PEARL: Which brings us to problem number two. Discipline ain't a pretty word, but you can't live for God without it.

SAINT: Oooohhh, discipline—prayer, Bible reading, fasting, diet, exercise—discipline! I hate it!

AUNT PEARL: And it shows! Discipline can be your friend or your enemy. You decide. But I'll tell you this, child, when you live an undisciplined life, you open your heart and your home to all kinds of spirits.

SAINT: All kinds of spirits? What are you talking about, Aunt Pearl?

AUNT PEARL: I'm talkin' about discontentment, rebellion, lust—

SAINT: Lust? What does discipline have to do with lust?

AUNT PEARL: Everything. If you can't discipline yourself, you lose control of your mind—and lust moves in. And goodness knows, it doesn't have far to go. Lustful thought seeds are everywhere. Lose control of your mind and in moves lust.

SAINT: Into my heart and into my home.

AUNT PEARL: It's kinda strange . . . but I've found that dirty spirits like dirty houses.

SAINT: Aunt Pearl! Ooooh, that hurt! Don't say it again.

AUNT PEARL: Just statin' facts . . . just statin' facts. You're the only one that can take care of the bugs in your spiritual life, Christine. What are you going to do about it?

SAINT: *(stands up)* I'm going to clean house! I'm not going to sell out. *(louder)* My oil is not for sale! Not for a bigger house . . .

not for a fancy vacation . . . not for better clothes for my children . . . not for a swimming pool . . . not for anything! Not for any thing! No thing is going to separate me from the love of God. No thing. Nothing!

Oh, Aunt Pearl, I'm so tired of sloppy living—in house and heart. I'm sick of being drunk on materialism. I'm through with excesses . . . too much of everything. Who needs fifty-nine kinds of ice cream? I won't sell out my experience with God for anything.

SAINT *gathers up magazines, (leaving one) and dumps them in trash.*

SAINT: Step one in standing guard over my family and destroying the enemy—girding up the loins of my mind.

Fight the filth! Clean house!

Women of God, be wise. Wake up! Stand guard! Go home and clean house! Prepare for the coming of the Lord.

SAINT *starts to* **EXIT** *carrying the trash can.*

CONSCIENCE: Hey, wait a minute. You missed one.

SAINT: Oh, thank the Lord, you're alive and well.

CONSCIENCE: You did give me a rough time. I'm a bit battered . . . and tired. While Aunt Pearl's here, you won't need me, so I'm going to catch up on my sleep.

SAINT *returns to "house," throws overlooked magazine into trash can.*

SAINT EXITS *carrying trash can and singing,* "I'm Getting Ready to Leave This World." **AUNT PEARL** *follows.*

ACT IV

Moving Day

The Final Call

CAST:

>Christine Saint
>Martha
>Mary
>Jael
>Deborah
>Wise Virgin
>Aunt Pearl
>All wear white robes and crowns
>Conscience

PROPS:

>Lace tablecloth (long 8'-10')
>Crystal
>China
>Silver
>Candelabra with white candles
>Centerpiece
>Chairs
>Tape of reveille

STAGE SET-UP:

>Table and chairs set up for Marriage Supper of the Lamb.

SOUND: REVEILLE (on tape)

*During reveille **ALL ENTER**, except **SAINT** and **FOOLISH VIRGIN**. **WOMEN** are yawning and stretching as if just waking up.*

Programs for Ladies

MARTHA: *(shouts)* Time to get up! Wake up, saints of God. It's the final wake-up call!

MARY: *(laughs)* Martha! Martha! You always were the first to get up.

JAEL: I feel so rested, so refreshed, so alive!

DEBORAH: I never felt this alive on earth.

AUNT PEARL: And I feel so young! *(kicks up her heels)* Look, girls, no arthritis. *(feels face)* No glasses! And better yet, no wrinkles! What a facelift!

MARY: Ooohhh, girls, look at this table! Isn't it beautiful?

MARTHA: And just think . . . I didn't set it, and I don't have to wash the dishes.

VIRGIN: And we can eat all we want to! No diet. No counting calories. No Weight Watchers. Girls, this is heaven.

ALL *stand behind their places at the table.*

VIRGIN: I knew He would come. I knew it. Oh, it was worth the wait. I'm so glad I didn't sell out.

MARTHA: And I'm glad I sold out! Nothing on earth could compare to this!

DEBORAH: It was worth the battle.

MARY: We can spend eternity doing what I love to do most . . . worshiping.

AUNT PEARL: *(looks around sadly)* But where is Christine? I was so sure she would get her life strai—

ENTER SAINT. *Comes running breathlessly, making a big commotion. Crown is lopsided, and she looks thrown-together.*

SAINT: Whoopee! I made it! I made it! What a trip! Talk about a plane ride! Nothing plain about that ride!

AUNT PEARL: *(runs to meet her, gives her a big hug)* Oh, Christine, I'm so glad to see you.

MARTHA: You had us worried.

SAINT: Worried? In heaven?

MARTHA: *(laughs)* Well, old habits are hard to break.

SAINT: *(dances around)* Yeah, I know. There was a garage sale on Mars. I stopped by to look. I just can't believe I made it. There were times when I doubted that I ever would.

DEBORAH: You look like you've been running.

SAINT: Life on earth is one big rat race. It's run, run, run! The stress is almost unbearable. I'm sure it got me here ten years early.

AUNT PEARL: Christine! Are you still exaggerating? We all got here at the same time—it was the last wake-up call, the Resurrection.

SAINT: But, Aunt Pearl, I wasn't resurrected. I came up in the Rapture. And the dead in Christ—all you girls—got a head start.

AUNT PEARL: So that's why you were a little late. Where's Howard and John, Christine?

SAINT: They're here, Aunt Pearl. They're here! We made it. My family made it! Oh, Aunt Pearl, I'm so happy I could cry.

VIRGIN: No, no, none of that. No tears in heaven.

AUNT PEARL: Did you move to Middle Ground?

SAINT: No, we didn't. When I stripped off the veneer and got real—and cut up the credit cards—Howard changed, too. It didn't happen overnight. But you were right, Aunt Pearl, he wasn't nearly as interested in money as I was.

Programs for Ladies

MARTHA: I had a battle with materialism, too.

SAINT: Really? I thought my day had a monopoly on materialism.

MARTHA: Not at all. Not at all. Human nature has always been greedy.

SAINT: Say, don't I know you? You look familiar.

MARTHA: You came to my garage sale one time.

SAINT: I did? Ooooohhhh, now I remember. I owe you for a vase. Do you take VISA?

AUNT PEARL: Christine!

SAINT: *(laughs)* Just kiddin', Aunt Pearl. Actually, when I discovered I had walked off with your vase, I didn't know how to get the money to you. So I gave twice what I thought it was worth to missions. The Lord seemed satisfied with that. I hope you are.

MARTHA: Fine with me. I just marked it off as a contribution to your cause.

SAINT: My cause?

MARTHA: Learning an important lesson.

SAINT: I remember. "Only one thing is needful."

JAEL: You came to my moving sale.

SAINT: Really? What did I buy?

JAEL: You didn't buy—or take—anything.

SAINT: Really? Now, I remember. Must have been the only sale in my life I went to and didn't buy anything, except this last one on Mars. I figured I wouldn't need any of that stuff in heaven.

AUNT PEARL: Christine!

SAINT: *(laughs)* Believe it or not, Aunt Pearl. That's the truth . . . almost.

(To Jael) I didn't buy anything from you, but I got something from you. I got the courage to go home and stand guard. I cleaned house after I met you and Deborah. And in time, my husband and son cleaned house, too. We got rid of the filth that was polluting our minds.

(To Virgin) And I learned something from you, too.

VIRGIN: You did?

SAINT: I did. I learned not to sell out—not for anything!

DEBORAH: I guess whatever generation we lived in, we had our battles. Mine was an army with nine hundred chariots of iron.

JAEL: And mine was a man with a sneaking, dirty spirit who invaded my home.

MARY: Mine was criticism. People didn't understand the way I worshiped.

MARTHA: I said mine was materialism, but I guess it really was my poor-little-me attitude.

VIRGIN: And mine was weariness. I got so tired of waiting.

AUNT PEARL: And mine was loneliness . . . living for God, going to church by myself for years.

SAINT: And mine was Christine! But I won the victory over her! With the help of God and Aunt Pearl, I won—

CONSCIENCE: Hey, what about me?

SAINT: And my conscience, I woke up! I stood guard! I prepared! I won! Hallelujah!

ALL: We won! We won! Hallelujah, we won!

Programs for Ladies

SONG OF VICTORY *such as "We're Gonna Make It" by the* **CONGREGATION** *as the* **CAST EXITS**.

---

[1]Luke 21:34
[2]Ibid.
[3]Ibid.
[4]Luke 10:38-39
[5]Matthew 24:44
[6]Matthew 25:6

The God of Hagar

CAST:

DONNA, raised in church, cynical and selfish.
TINA, new convert, enthusiastic, warm and compassionate.
SANDY, "religious right," all's well with me and mine.
JEANNIE, single, pregnant, working on JTPA (Job Training Partnership Act) grant.
SISTER MCAULEY, director of the drama.

PROPS:

Coffee mugs
2- or 3-liter Diet Coke
Box of donuts
Bananas
7-Up
Card table
Tablecloth
Chairs
Magazines
Copies of script
Telephone
Telephone ringer

Sunglasses
Biblical costumes
Bean bags
Oriental throw rug
Candles and holder
Pottery
Ragged cloak
Rocks
Logs
Whip
Fountain
Bowl of grapes

STAGE SET-UP:

The set-up is given with each act.

DRAMAS

ACT I

Coffee Break

"Whosoever drinketh of this water shall thirst again: but whosoever drinketh of the water that I shall give him shall never thirst."[1]

CAST:

>Donna
>Tina
>Sandy
>Jeannie

PROPS:

>Diet Coke
>Coffee mugs
>Box of donuts
>Bananas

STAGE SET-UP:

>Break room on the right (facing the audience): a card table, tablecloth, chairs, magazines on table. On left: a couple of chairs.

CAST *is dressed in office clothes.*

ENTER DONNA and TINA. DONNA *is carrying a large Diet Coke, box of donuts, and bunch of bananas.* ***TINA*** *carries a coffee mug.*

DONNA: *(angrily)* Glorious Monday morning! So I'm three minutes late! I had to stop at the donut shop. You'd think I'd missed the Rapture the way Ms. Denison glared at me.

Programs for Ladies

TINA: I doubt if she knows what the Rapture is. I didn't three months ago. *(motions at Donna's "snacks")* All that for morning coffee break? Are you planning to starve before lunch?

DONNA: *(defensively)* I didn't have time for breakfast. It's wild at my house in the mornings with one in Webster High, one in preschool, one in OU post-graduate school and one in P.I.T.S.

TINA: Who's at P.I.T.S.?

DONNA: I am.

TINA: I didn't know you were going to school. I don't see how you have the time. *(looks thoughtfully)* I've never heard of PITS. P-I-T-S? Is that a technical school?

DONNA: It's the "pits." I'm in training there every morning, Monday through Friday. *(puts food on table)* Want a donut?

TINA: No, thanks. Coffee's enough for me this time of day.

BOTH *sit down at the table.*

DONNA: I make a couple little mistakes and Ms. Denison acts like I'd bankrupt the company! She expects me to balance the books to the penny! If I could do that Don would let me carry the checkbook. Tell me, Tina, what did I do to deserve a perfectionist for a supervisor?

TINA: Don't be too hard on her.

DONNA: Me? Hard on her? Honey, it's the other way around.

TINA: Maybe she had a bad weekend.

DONNA: Probably did. She acts like she's still hung-over from it. Somebody must have put an olive pit in her martini and ruined her happy hour. But she doesn't have to take it out on me. No wonder her husband left her! Was that husband number two or three?

190

TINA: *(laughs uncertainly)* Oh, Donna, you're a scream.

DONNA: Do you know what I think? I think Ms. Denison—by the way, how do you pronounce Ms. Mssss? You know she insists she is not a Miss M-i-s-s or a Mrs. M-r-s. She is a Ms. M-s.

TINA: I guess you just say "mss."

DONNA: Anyway . . . what I was going to say before I said what I said was . . . *(frowns)* was uhhhh . . . what I was going to say before I said what I said was . . . *(frowns again)* what I was going to say was . . . let's see . . . what did I say?

TINA: You asked me how to pronounce Ms.

DONNA: Oh, yeah. How do you pronounce it?

TINA: I don't know.

DONNA: I don't either. But ever since Ms. Denison got her last divorce she has—oh, now I remember what I was going to say. I think she's a candidate for AA.

TINA: Or L.W.

DONNA: L.W. What's that?

TINA: Living water. I think she is a candidate for living water, like I found at your church three months ago. Have you already forgotten that I was quite a party gal before I received the Holy Ghost?

DONNA: I guess I had.

TINA: I didn't run in the same social circle as Ms. Denison, but I had the same habits. I read something a couple years ago that has really stuck with me. It was an old Swedish or Scottish proverb: "You often talk about my drinking but never my thirst."

DONNA: *(slowly, as if trying to decipher it)* "You often talk about my drinking but never my thirst." My drinking—but not my thirst. Oh, I get it.

TINA: Ms. Denison drinks because she is thirsty, Donna. She has a spiritual thirst that liquor can't satisfy. I know because I had the same thirst. Then you invited me to church. Have you ever witnessed to her?

DONNA: Witnessed to her! Ms. Denison? Tina, apparently you don't know that she is head of the state N.O.W. chapter (National Organization of Women), deeply involved in the pro-choice movement, and on the board of P.P. (Planned Parenthood). She is a feminist-deluxe.

TINA: So? *(pauses)* Have you ever invited her to church?

There is another pause. **TINA** *looks straight at Donna.* **DONNA** *looks at the floor.*

TINA: Well, I'm going to.

DONNA: *(shrugs)* More power to you.

TINA: Ms. Denison needs to drink at the springs of living water. Didn't we have a glorious service last night? I sang in tongues all the way home. I still feel the joy bubbling up inside me.

DONNA: Ha! You wouldn't have if you'd gone home with my family. If I keep the spring bubbling till we get out of the parking lot, it's a major accomplishment.

TINA: Why, Donna, what do you mean?

DONNA: Little Donnie whined all the way home. Crystal pouted because church lasted so late she couldn't go to the Pizza Hut with Byron. I declare that girl thinks she has to be with that boy every waking minute. It's the worse case of puppy love I ever saw. Then Don threw a fit because I'd forgotten to buy milk and bread. We had to stop at the Get-N-Go and pay two prices.

TINA: Well, Joe wasn't exactly happy about me getting in so late. He can't understand church lasting until eleven o'clock. But he says I'm so much easier to live with than I was three months ago it's worth the inconvenience. He's promised to come with me next Sunday. Isn't that wonderful?

DONNA: *(yawns)* Sure is. Man, am I drug out! I didn't get to bed until after midnight. This morning my feet had an argument about which one had to hit the floor first. I wish we'd start service on Sunday evening at 6:00 like the church across town. I'm trying to get Don to change churches.

TINA: Change churches? Donna, you're not serious?

DONNA: Well, I certainly am. They are Pentecostal, too. That's where Sandy and her family go. They believe the doctrine just like we do, but they're not nearly as radical about the side issues. At the church across town they—

ENTER SANDY, *carrying coffee cup.*

SANDY: What about the church across town?

DONNA: Oh, hi, Sandy. I was telling Tina that you start church at 6:00 on Sunday evenings.

SANDY: *(laughs)* Not anymore we don't. We don't have church on Sunday evenings.

DONNA: Say, that might not be a bad idea.

TINA: *(shocked)* Donna! Oh, you're just kidding. I wouldn't miss Sunday night service for the world.

DONNA: *(mutters to herself)* Baby, that's because you haven't been going all your life.

TINA: What did you say, Donna?

DONNA: *(clears throat)* Uhhh, I said, "Neither would I. Not on your life."

SANDY: We do have a youth social on Sunday evenings. My son is the president of the youth group, and my daughter is the treasurer. These Youth Alive meetings give the teens something to do while we parents catch our breath.

DONNA: Somewhere I've got to find time to catch mine. Work five days a week, clean house on Saturday, church all day Sunday. It's a vicious cycle. There's no end to it!

SANDY: I've noticed you do have church a lot. That's rather outdated, don't you think? In these busy times with jobs and school and social obligations, once on Sunday is sufficient. That's what our pastor says. *(picks up a magazine and sits down on the side of room opposite the table, and hides behind magazine)*

DONNA: *(rolls eyes at Tina, says aside)* La-tee-da! If ever there was a "religious right," it's Sandy. She's religious and she's right—about everything! Perfect husband. Perfect kids. Perfectly lovely home.

TINA: I like Sandy.

DONNA: *(shrugs)* To each his own. I wonder why she works? Her husband has a big position at IBM.

TINA: Maybe she likes to work.

DONNA: She's not that crazy! Maybe she likes money!

TINA: Why do you work?

DONNA: Because I have to! To pay the bills. To put clothes on the kids' backs. Do you know how much a pair of Doc Marten boots cost?

TINA: No, I don't. I wouldn't know a pair of Doc Marten boots if they walked by with blinking lights.

DONNA: You can be sure the teens know them. And they cost about $110.00! Isn't that ridiculous? And we have two kids to boot up! Do you know how much a new Lincoln costs?

TINA: No. We drive an old Chevy.

DONNA: Ours was almost $45,000. Isn't that highway robbery? And now we are paying on our kidney-shaped, in-ground deck and swimming pool.

TINA: In-ground deck? Is that something new?

DONNA: No, silly. The pool's in the ground. The deck's around the pool. And, of course, we had to have deck furnishings and landscaping. After all, we had to have something to keep the kids home in the summer while I work.

TINA: Oh, of course, you do. This is changing the subject, but are you in the drama at the ladies' retreat this year, Donna?

DONNA: *(sighs heavily)* Yes. I don't know why I said I'd be in it. I really don't have the time, but Sister McAuley needs me so desperately, so I just didn't have the heart to tell her no. Are you in it?

TINA: She asked me to be, but I don't know if I can do it. The thought of getting up in front of nine hundred women scares me to death. I just know I'll forget my lines.

DONNA: It's no big deal if you do. We ad-lib quite a bit. When did Sister McAuley say the read-through is?

TINA: Tonight at seven o'clock.

DONNA: Tonight? Oh, dear, I promised Crystal we'd find time for a little mother-daughter chat this evening. She's been wanting to talk to me for a couple days, and I can't seem to find time. Oh, well, maybe tomorrow night.

TINA: Who's the new file clerk?

DONNA: Some gal they hired through JTPA or something like that.

TINA: J-T-P-A?

Programs for Ladies

DONNA: Job Training Program something-or-another. It's designed to get these people off welfare and into the work force. I think the employer pays part of the wages and the government—that's us, in case you don't know—we pay the difference.

TINA: She seems rather reserved and quiet. I admire her for working and trying to better her life. *(as if telling a secret)* I think she's pregnant. She looked a little green this morning, and once she made a wild dash for the restroom.

DONNA: *(sarcastically)* She probably is.

TINA: *(sorrowfully)* I'm beginning to wonder if Joe and I will ever have a family. We've been married eight years and still no little Joes. We're thinking about adopting.

ENTER JEANNIE, *carrying a 7-Up.*

TINA: Hi. Come and join us. *(looks at watch)* We've got a few more minutes. My name is Tina. This is Donna.

JEANNIE *sits down at the table.*

JEANNIE: *(dully)* Hi. I'm Jeannie . . . Jeannie Winters.

TINA: Welcome to the wonderful world of working women. If there's anything I can do to help you learn your job, just ask. I worked that position when I started here.

JEANNIE: Thanks.

There is a brief silence as girls sip their drinks. **JEANNIE** *stares markedly at Donna's donuts.*

DONNA: Would you like a donut, Jeannie?

JEANNIE: No! No thanks! *(starts to take a drink, looks sick, and puts her 7-Up down)*

TINA: Are you sick, Jeannie?

JEANNIE: Yeah, kinda.

DONNA: Pregnant?

JEANNIE: Yeah.

TINA: Oh, that's wonderful. Aren't you excited?

JEANNIE nods half-heartedly.

TINA: Joe and I want a family so badly. Is this your first baby?

JEANNIE: Yeah.

TINA: Oh, that's wonderful. I know your husband must really be— *(Donna gives her a big poke in the ribs.)* Ouch! Do you want something, Donna?

DONNA: Isn't it about time to get back to work, Tina?

TINA: *(looks at watch)* We've got five minutes yet. Does your husband want a boy, Jeannie? Most men— *(Donna gives her another poke in the ribs.)*

TINA: Donna, what is the matter?

DONNA: Oh, nothing. Nothing. I've just got a slippery elbow and *(rolls eyes)* you've got a slippery tongue. Better watch it.

JEANNIE jumps up, holding her hand over her mouth.

JEANNIE: Excuse me.

JEANNIE EXITS on the run.

TINA: Poor girl.

DONNA: Yeah, poor girl. By the way, Tina, she's not married.

TINA: Not . . . not married? Oh . . . poor girl.

Programs for Ladies

DONNA: *(snorts)* Yeah, poor girl.

TINA: Another candidate for L.W.

DONNA: What? Oh, yeah, living water. I guess so. Let's get back to work before Ms. Denison sends out the troopers. *(calls)* Sandy! Wake up! Break's over. Back to the real world.

ALL EXIT.

ACT II

Just Practicing

"Therefore with joy shall ye draw water out of the wells of salvation."[2]

CAST:

>Donna (Hagar)
>Tina (Sarai)
>Sister McAuley (Director)
>Sandy (Angel)

PROPS:

>Copies of script

STAGE SET-UP:

>Four chairs—three on the right and one on the left, facing each other.

CAST *wears casual or church clothes.*

ENTER DIRECTOR, TINA, *and* ***SANDY.***

DIRECTOR: *(looks at watch)* I wonder where Donna is? She is coming, isn't she?

TINA: I'm sure she is. She's usually a few minutes late . . . at least, she is for work and church. I hope I can do this, Sister McAuley. I've got butterflies in my stomach, and this is just the read-through.

SANDY: This is my first year, too. I've got bullfrogs in my stomach.

Programs for Ladies

(sings) "Bullfrogs and butterflies . . ."

DIRECTOR: Relax, girls. It's really lots of fun. Sandy, you are the angel of the Lord, and you don't have many lines to memorize.

SANDY: *(sighs)* That's good.

TINA: You shouldn't have any trouble playing an angel. Just act your normal self.

SANDY: Why, Tina, what a sweet thing—

ENTER DONNA, *huffing and puffing.*

DONNA: Am I late, girls?

SANDY: No more than normal.

DONNA: *(flatly)* Oh, hi, Sandy. I didn't know you were going to be in the drama this year.

SANDY: I was just telling the girls that I sure am nervous.

DONNA: No! Surely not. Not you.

DIRECTOR: Let's get started.

DONNA: Sorry I was late. You know how it is in a house with a teenager. At the last minute, the phone. . .

GIRLS *are seated.*

DIRECTOR: That's okay, Donna. We understand. Tonight is a simple read-through to help you get the feel of your character. *(hands out scripts)* The title of our play is "The God of Hagar." Donna, you are Hagar. Tina, you are Sarai. Sandy is the angel of the Lord. Notice that we are calling Abraham and Sarah "Abram and Sarai" because this scene happened before God changed their names. Let's get started. First Sarai enters. That's you, Tina.

TINA: *(in "reading" voice)* Ten years! It's been ten years since we left

Haran. For ten years we have been following a call—a promise. How long must we wait? Abram and I are old enough to be grandparents, and we still do not have a child. *(reads with feeling)* My arms are so empty. My heart is so broken. My womb is so barren. Oh, Lord God, how long must we wait?

DIRECTOR: At this point Hagar enters. Donna, that's you. You are the Egyptian slave who was given to Sarai by Pharaoh when Abram and Sarai went to Egypt. Read.

DONNA: *(reads)* Mistress Sarai, why is your face so long? *(looks up with raised eyebrows)* Perhaps it was made that way?

TINA: Is that in the script?

DIRECTOR: *(in warning voice)* Donna! Please stick with your lines.

DONNA: *(reads)* Mistress Sarai, why is your face so long? Why are you troubled?

DIRECTOR: Tina, your turn.

TINA: *(reads)* Oh, Hagar, I am so weary of wishing and waiting for a baby. I am seventy-five years old! I feel so old and helpless and hopeless.

DONNA: *(reads)* Oh, but Mistress Sarai, you don't look . . . *(looks up and grins)* a day over seventy-two.

DIRECTOR: Donna!

DONNA: *(reads)* Oh, but Mistress Sarai, you don't look it. You are still a beautiful lady.

TINA: *(reads with feeling)* Perhaps, but I am so empty, so lonely. Only one who is childless can feel my pain.

DONNA: It's a little late to be moaning about that. According to my calculations, lady, your biological clock stopped a long time ago.

DIRECTOR: Donna! Please stop ad-libbing. Continue, Tina.

Programs for Ladies

TINA: *(reads)* If only there was some way to fast-forward the plan of God.

DONNA: *(to Director)* Fast-forward the plan of God? Sister McAuley, what did Sarai know about fast-forwarding recorders?

DIRECTOR: *(smiles)* Nothing, but it is a picturesque way of expressing her impatience. Tina, read please.

TINA: *(reads)* If only . . . . looks at Hagar thoughtfully.

DIRECTOR: No, Tina, you don't read the parts that are in parentheses. That's what you do, not say. You look thoughtfully at Hagar and say, "If only." Rewind, Tina.

TINA: *(reads)* If only *(looks thoughtfully at Hagar)* we could adopt . . . if only . . . Hagar! Of course, that's it!

DONNA: *(reads)* What's it, Mistress Sarah . . . uhhhh, Sarai?

TINA: *(reads)* Clears throat and straightens shoulders as if making a big decision . . . *(looks up)* oh, no, I'm not supposed to read that; I'm supposed to do it. *(clears throat and straightens shoulders, reads)* Hagar, don't you think Master Abram is a handsome man?

DONNA: *(sneers)* That old man? Handsome? Look, according to my figures, he's eighty-five years old!

DIRECTOR: Donna, that is not in the script at all!

DONNA: I know, but I also know what *(points at Tina)* she's planning. And there's no way I'm going to agree to being a substitute wife to that old man, or any man for that matter, even in a skit.

DIRECTOR: Donna, you have to forget yourself and become Hagar. Remember you are a bondwoman—a slave. You have no say-so whatsoever about what happens to you. You are a victim of circumstance.

DONNA: I'd call it a victim of Sarai's selfish scheming.

DRAMAS

TINA: But I don't mean to be selfish, Donna, I mean Hagar. I am—I mean Sarai is just so empty and hopeless. Have you ever felt hopeless, Donna? I mean, Hagar.

DONNA: Well . . . sure I have. I felt hopeless when . . . *(pauses a moment)* when . . . when the dishwasher broke down and the repairman said he couldn't get to it for a week.

TINA: That's not what I mean. I mean really hopeless . . . no hope of things ever getting better.

DONNA: Well . . . I felt pretty hopeless when Crystal was five and got bubble gum in her long hair.

TINA: Donna, I mean really hopeless, like there is no reason to live.

DONNA: Well . . . I guess I've never felt that bad.

TINA: That's because you were raised in church. Ever since you can remember you have known God, so you have had hope. You've always had access to that fountain of living water.

DONNA: Well, Sarai is supposed to know God, too, so why is she so hopeless? After all, God promised Abram a family. Doesn't she believe God's Word? She has no right to use me to satisfy her whims!

DIRECTOR: Yes, I mean, no, she doesn't. But remember up to that point, God had not necessarily promised Sarai a family. He had promised Abram a family.

DONNA: But she's his wife. Oh, I see what you mean. Sarai was beginning to wonder if she was part of the plan after all. Perhaps, I would make a better Sarai than Hagar.

DIRECTOR: We can't all be Sarais, Donna. Someone has to be Hagar.

TINA: I know how Hagar felt. I know what it feels like to be used and abused by someone you trust. It's an ugly, ugly feeling.

DIRECTOR: Let's get back to the script. Tina, read your last lines again.

Programs for Ladies

TINA: *(reads)* Hagar, don't you think Master Abram is a handsome man?

DONNA: *(reads)* Mistress Sarai, I don't understand. *(reads sneeringly)* Of course, Master Abram is a handsome man and very kind, but why? What does it matter what I—

TINA: *(reads)* You can be Abram's . . . uhhhh . . . his uhhhh . . . you can have a child for me by Abram.

DONNA: *(jumps to her feet and throws down her script)* I knew that was coming, and I think the plan stinks!

DIRECTOR: Donna, read your lines, please.

DONNA: *(points at Tina)* She wants me to be a surrogate mother for her, and you say, "Donna, read your lines please." Everybody thinks this surrogate mother business is a modern-day issue! Tell that to Hagar. I'm not about to have a baby and give it up to another woman.

DIRECTOR: Donna, remember you are a bondwoman. You have no say-so in the matter.

DONNA: Oh, but I do. No one is going to use me like that—not even in a drama—without me having my say-so.

TINA: Look, Donna, can't you understand my feelings? I mean Sarai's? I can. I know how it feels to want a baby so bad you feel like your heart is being shredded by a salad maker.

DONNA: I will admit my life would be awfully empty without Crystal and little Donnie.

DIRECTOR: Then try to put yourself in Sarai's place.

DONNA: Look, I'm having a hard enough time putting myself in Hagar's place. What do you want me to do, develop a split personality? At this rate, I'm going to become a triple-brained conglomeration of Hari, Sagar, and . . . I mean *(pronounces slowly and distinctly)* Hagar, Sarai, and Donna.

DIRECTOR: Donna, please—

DONNA: Talk about finding yourself, I'm about to lose me!

DIRECTOR: Okay! Okay! Just concentrate on Hagar.

DONNA: I am. That's why I refused to become Abram's concubine and have a baby and give it to her! *(points at Tina)*

DIRECTOR: *(sighs heavily)* Perhaps, I have made a mistake in assigning the roles. Maybe you would be a better angel, Donna, and Sandy could be Hagar.

SANDY: I'd like that.

DONNA: No, no, wait a minute. Ahhh . . . what's the name of this play?

DIRECTOR: "The God of Hagar."

DONNA: So Hagar is the star—the leading role—right?

DIRECTOR: Right.

DONNA: Well then, in that case, I think I'm beginning to feel the part more and more. *(picks up the script and sits down)*

DIRECTOR: Then let's proceed. Tina, read your last lines again.

TINA: *(reads)* You can be Abram's . . . uhhhh . . . his uhhhh . . . you can have a child for me by Abram. Sarai stands up. Oh, no, I don't read that. I do it. *(stands up)* Yes, that is what we shall do. You will have a baby, Hagar. A baby for me.

DONNA: Stands up. Now I'm reading the action lines. *(stands up)* But, Mistress Sarai, I can't. I can't. Don't make me do that. Please, Mistress Sarai.

DIRECTOR: At this point Sarai and Hagar exit with Hagar pleading and Sarai arrogantly ignoring her. Then there is a brief musical interlude.

Programs for Ladies

DONNA: *(very pronounced and full of significance)* A very well placed musical interlude, I'd say.

DIRECTOR *gives Donna a withering look.*

DIRECTOR: The next scene opens with Hagar entering and arrogantly sitting in Sarai's chair. Sarai enters and shows astonishment at what she sees. Read, Tina.

TINA: *(reads)* Hagar! What are you doing in my chair?

DONNA: *(reads)* Sneeringly submissive. Oops, I'm not supposed to read that. *(clears throat)* Why, what does it look like, Mistress Sarai? I am sitting in it.

TINA: *(reads)* So I see. Please remove yourself promptly.

DONNA: *(reads)* Oh, I think not. You see I am feeling poorly this morning. I think for the baby's sake, I should stay off my feet.

TINA: *(reads)* You forget yourself! You are nothing but an Egyptian slave—a bondwoman. I can have you beaten.

DONNA: *(reads)* Oh, I think not. Remember . . . the baby—

TINA: *(reads)* I've had it! I've had it! I tell you I've had it! Ever since you learned you were expecting, you have been arrogant and rebellious. I am reporting your behavior to Master Abram immediately.

DONNA: *(reads)* Help yourself, Mistress Sarai. Help yourself. Just remember that this whole program was your idea.

DIRECTOR: *(looks at watch)* Look at the time! We've got to stop right here.

SANDY: You mean I have wasted this entire evening? I haven't read one line yet.

DIRECTOR: I'm sorry, Sandy. It shouldn't take nearly this long to read through the script. *(looks meaningfully at Donna)* There have been too many interruptions. Donna, are you going to be able to play the part of Hagar? Or would you rather be the angel? It's not too late to switch.

DONNA: Oh, I can handle Hagar. It'll take a lot of "acting," but I can do it. After all, that's my specialty.

ALL EXIT.

Programs for Ladies

ACT III

The Valley of Baca

"Who passing through the valley of Baca make it a well; the rain also filleth the pools."[3]

CAST:

> Sandy
> Donna
> Tina
> Jeannie

PROPS:

> Coffee mugs
> Cokes
> Sunglasses
> Telephone
> Telephone sound effect

STAGE SET-UP:

> Office break room, same as Act I on right side of stage. On far left is a table with a phone.

CAST wears office attire.

SOUND: TELEPHONE

ENTER SANDY, *just as the phone rings. Hurries to answer it.*

SANDY: Good morning. Johnson and Company . . . Ms. Denison? I'm sorry, but she isn't in yet. Would you like to leave a message? . . . Donna? You don't sound like yourself. We missed you yesterday. Are you still sick? Have you been to the doctor? . . . Sure, I'll tell her. Do you think you'll be back tomorrow? Maybe? I hope so. The work is really piling up on your desk. Take care. Good-bye.

ENTER TINA, *from office side.*

SANDY: Donna just called to say she is still sick and won't be in today. She sounded terrible. She wasn't sick Monday night at play practice, was she?

TINA: Not that I know of.

SANDY: I hope she doesn't have something contagious. My schedule doesn't leave room for sickness.

ENTER JEANNIE.

TINA: Are you feeling better, Jeannie?

JEANNIE: Much better, thank you. You know, I think it helps me to have a job. I don't have as much time to lie around, feeling sorry for myself.

TINA: I've been meaning to ask you something, Jeannie. Would you like to go to church with me? I have found the most refreshing church and living water that satisfies my spiritual thirst.

JEANNIE: What? I don't understand that religious garble, but I . . . well . . . I . . . I would like to go to church with you . . . but don't you go to the same church as Donna?

TINA: Yes. Why?

JEANNIE: *(coolly)* Then thanks for the invitation, but no thanks.

TINA: But, Jeannie, I don't understand. What does Donna have to do with this?

JEANNIE: Well, since you asked, I just don't feel like going to her church. I don't think I'd be comfortable there. Thanks anyway.

Programs for Ladies

TINA: But, Jeannie—

JEANNIE: We'd better get to work before Ms. Denison shows up.

GIRLS EXIT *in different directions.*

MUSIC: TRANSITION

ENTER TINA AND DONNA, *from right, carrying Cokes or coffee mugs.* **DONNA** *is wearing dark glasses. They take seats at the table as they talk.*

TINA: I haven't had a chance to say a word to you all morning, Donna. What? No donuts?

DONNA: I'm not hungry.

TINA: Are you feeling better?

DONNA: Some.

TINA: What was wrong? It's not like you to miss work.

DONNA: Oh, I just had . . . I just had some . . . some problems, some personal problems.

TINA: Do you have an eye infection?

DONNA *shakes her head, takes a sip of coffee, and stares straight ahead.* **TINA** *looks puzzled.*

TINA: Well, we're glad you're back. *(a few seconds of silence)* While you were gone, I invited Jeannie to church. She asked if it was where you went. When I said, "Yes," she said, "Thanks, but no thanks." Do you know what's bothering her?

DONNA: *(dully)* No.

TINA: Donna, are you okay?

DONNA: I'm okay. *(determinedly, through clenched teeth)* There's nothing in the world wrong with me.

TINA: Do you suppose Jeannie thinks you don't want her to come to our church? You do, don't you?

DONNA: *(chokes back a sob)* Of course, I do. Now I do. *(breaks down, buries head in hands on table, shoulders shaking)* Oh, Tina, I've been such a fool, such a fool!

TINA: *(touches Donna gently)* I don't understand, Donna. What are you talking about?

DONNA: *(takes a deep, ragged breath and lifts head, takes off sunglasses)* I guess I may as well tell you. Soon the whole world will know. Crys . . . *(voice catches in a sob)* Crystal . . . my Crystal . . . my beautiful baby . . . my baby is pregnant.

TINA: Your Crystal? But I didn't know she was married.

DONNA: *(angrily)* She's *not* married.

ENTER SANDY, *carrying a Coke or coffee.*

SANDY: Who's not married?

TINA and DONNA FREEZE. *Silence of several seconds.*

SANDY: *(flippantly)* I gather I asked the wrong question. Erase the tape. Sorry, girls.

TINA: Uhhh . . . Uhhhh . . .

ENTER JEANNIE, *who stands silently and listens.*

DONNA: It's okay, Tina. *(turns to Sandy)* Sandy, Crystal is not married.

SANDY: Crystal? Your daughter? Oh, I know she's not married. She's just seventeen, same age as my Tara. What's the big deal about that?

DONNA: *(slaps hand on table, jumps up and shouts)* She's pregnant! My baby is going to have a baby! Now you know! Now

Programs for Ladies

    the whole world knows! *(falls back into chair, puts head down on table sobbing)*

TINA: Maybe she can get marr—

SANDY *shakes her head violently at Tina and sits down beside Donna.*

SANDY: *(puts her hand on Donna's shoulder)* I'm sorry, Donna. *(a few seconds of silence)* Donna, I understand your pain.

DONNA: *(shakes her head that is still down on her arms)* No, you don't. No one does.

SANDY: But I do, Donna. I do!

DONNA: *(raises her head to look in shock at Sandy)* Tara? Is your Tara pregnant?

SANDY: *(shakes head)* No. It's not Tara. It was me. When I was sixteen, I had an abortion.

DONNA: *(raises her head to look in shock at Sandy)* You? You, Sandy? You had an abortion? How could you . . . Oh, I'm sorry. I shouldn't have asked that. I just can't believe that you had an abortion!

SANDY: But I did. No one ever knew but my parents and Bill. I told him before we got married. *(takes a deep breath)* This is the first time in nineteen years that I have told anyone. But there has not been one day in that nineteen years that I have not thought about . . . about my baby.

DONNA: I . . . I can't believe it. Everything about you, your family, is so perfect.

SANDY: *(shakes her head)* No, Donna. I'm not perfect; my family's not perfect. No one is. Everyone has her hurts. Many of us have buried it deeply beneath a facade of smiles and surface relationships. Perhaps, we'd be better off to tear off the veneer and be real. I don't know. I just don't know.

JEANNIE walks over to Donna's side.

JEANNIE: And I understand your pain, Donna. My mother understands your pain.

DONNA: But . . . but this is different. It's not supposed to happen to my family. We've always gone to church. Ever since I was a little girl, I've gone to church. We, Don and I, raised our children in church.

SANDY: Anything that touches the world, eventually touches the church, Donna. We're not immune from life's hurts.

DONNA: But why? Why would my Crystal . . . who has always had everything she ever wanted . . . do such a thing?

TINA: Maybe she was thirsty.

DONNA: Thirsty?

TINA: "You often talk about my drinking but never my thirst." Remember?

DONNA: What does that have to do with my Crystal? She's not an alcoholic.

TINA: Inside everyone is a deep, spiritual thirst. Many try to satisfy that thirst with material things or alcohol and drugs or sex. But these things are only broken cisterns filled with polluted water. Lust is never satisfied. Lust is never satisfied, but it takes some people a lifetime to learn that.

SANDY: We only see the drinking. We forget about the thirst . . . until it comes home to our family.

DONNA: But Crystal? She's been in church all her life.

SANDY: In church? Or around the church? There's a difference, a big difference.

TINA: You can lead your children to the well, Donna, but you can't force them to drink.

DONNA: Oh, I've made so many mistakes . . . so many mistakes.

SANDY: We all have. But remember the name of the drama for the ladies' retreat?

DONNA: "The God of Hagar"?

SANDY: Yes. He's not just the God of Sarah and Ruth and Mary of Nazareth. Our God is the God of Hagar and Rahab and the Samaritan woman at the well.

DONNA: And the God of Sandy and Crystal and Jeannie . . . and Donna?

SANDY: Yes. Sometimes we have to be reminded of that.

JEANNIE: Break time is over, ladies.

ALL STAND.

SANDY: *(hugs Donna)* The next few months, even years, are not going to be easy for Crystal or for you, Donna. But you can make it, because you can always go back to the fountain.

DONNA: Oh, Sandy, I'm so sorry. I misjudged you terribly.

SANDY: Probably not. You judged what you saw, and I did my best to make sure that no one saw the real Sandy. I realize now that was a mistake.

JEANNIE: Tina, I've changed my mind. If that invitation is still open, I'd like to go to church with you.

TINA: Oh, I'm so glad, Jeannie.

DONNA: And so am I.

***DONNA** hugs Jeannie.*

SANDY: Now let's get back to work before Ms. Denison comes to see what we're drinking on break.

SONG: "Come to the Waters" (written by Marsha J. Stevens)

Programs for Ladies

ACT IV

Water in the Wilderness

"I will open rivers in high places, and fountains in the midst of the valleys: I will make the wilderness a pool of water, and the dry land springs of water."[4]

CAST:

>Donna (Hagar)
>Tina (Sarai)
>Sandy (Angel)
>Sister McAuley (Director)

PROPS:

>Whip
>Biblical costumes, including worn cloak for Hagar

STAGE SET-UP:

>Right side—inside of Abram's tent, bean bags, Oriental-type throw rug, table, candle, pottery, and a bowl of grapes. Left side—barren land of rocks, logs, an electric fountain is hidden under a log or behind a rock. Place it so the electric cord to the fountain does not show. Arrange for someone behind the scene to secretly plug it in while Hagar is running around the audience.

CAST *is dressed in biblical attire, according to position.*

ENTER SARAI, *walks the floor.*

>SARAI: Ten years! It's been ten years since we left Haran. For ten long years we have been following a call, a promise. How long must we wait? Abram and I are old enough to be grandparents . . .

and we still do have not a child. *(with strong feeling)* My arms are so empty. My heart is so broken. My womb is so barren. Oh, Lord God, how long must we wait?

ENTER HAGAR.

HAGAR: Mistress Sarai, why is your face so long? Why are you troubled?

SARAI: Oh, Hagar, I am weary of wishing and waiting for a baby. I am seventy-five years old! I feel so old and helpless and hopeless.

HAGAR: Oh, but Mistress Sarai, you don't look it. You are still a beautiful lady.

SARAI: Perhaps, but I am so empty, so lonely. Only one who has never had a child can feel my pain. If only there was some way to fast-forward the plan of God . . . If only . . . *(looks at Hagar thoughtfully)* we could adopt. If only . . . Hagar! Of course, that's it!

HAGAR: What's it, Mistress Sarai?

SARAI: *(clears throat and straightens shoulders as if making a big decision)* Hagar, don't you think Master Abram is a handsome man?

HAGAR: Mistress Sarai, I don't understand. Of course, Master Abram is a handsome man and very kind, but why? What does it matter what I—

SARAI: *(takes deep breath)* You can be Abram's . . . uhhhh . . . his uhhhh . . . you can have a child for me by Abram. *(stands up)* Yes, that is what we shall do. You will have a baby, Hagar. A baby for Master Abram . . . and for me.

SARAI *stands up and starts to* ***EXIT.***

HAGAR: *(follows, pleading)* But, Mistress Sarai, I can't. I can't. Don't make me do that. Please, Mistress Sarai.

Programs for Ladies

***THEY EXIT** with **HAGAR** pleading and **SARAI** arrogantly ignoring her.*

MUSIC: TRANSITION

***ENTER HAGAR**, humming, arrogantly takes a seat on Sarai's bean bag. She sings snatches of a lullaby as she plops grapes into her mouth.*

***ENTER SARAI**, looks at Hagar in astonishment.*

SARAI: Hagar! What are you doing in my chair?

HAGAR: *(sneeringly submissive)* Why, what does it look like, Mistress Sarai? I am sitting in it.

SARAI: So I see. Please remove yourself promptly.

HAGAR: Oh, I think not. You see I am feeling poorly this morning. I think for the baby's sake, I should stay off my feet.

SARAI: *(voice raises to a shout)* You forget yourself! You are nothing but an Egyptian slave—a bondwoman. I can have you beaten.

HAGAR: Oh, I think not. Remember . . . the baby—

SARAI: *(screams)* I've had it! I've had it! I tell you I've had it! Ever since you learned you were expecting, you have been arrogant and rebellious. I am reporting your behavior to Master Abram immediately.

HAGAR: *(shrugs)* Help yourself, Mistress Sarai. Help yourself. Just remember that this whole program was . . . your idea.

***SARAI EXITS** in hysterics. **HAGAR** stands and watches her with an ugly smile on her face. When Sarai is out of sight, **HAGAR EXITS** slowly and arrogantly.*

SOUND: LASHING OF WHIP

***HAGAR SCREAMS** from off stage. "Stop! Stop! Ooohh! Please, stop!"*

ENTER HAGAR, *a ragged cloak around her stooped shoulders.*

HAGAR: *(in angry tears)* She can't do this to me! How could he let her? How could he? She hates me . . . but he shouldn't.

Doesn't he care anything about the baby? What about the baby? They said they wanted it. And I'm the sacrifice . . . the victim of her selfish scheming . . . I am the means of satisfying her whims.

(Sarcastically) "If Sarai wants it, Sarai must have it." No matter what it costs anyone else. No matter what it does to me. And to think . . . I trusted her. I respected her. I even loved her. *(angrily)* What a fool I've been. I should have known better.

(Occasionally she shrugs, then winces as if in pain from the beating.)

(Louder) All my life I've been used and abused. A slave in Egypt, given by the Pharaoh to the woman from Canaan, just like a piece of furniture.

But I didn't mind because I expected life to be better. *(laughs bitterly)* Master Abram seemed such a kind man . . . and Mistress Sarai was a beautiful lady. They loved one another . . . and I just expected my life to get better, even though I would be living in tents instead of the Pharaoh's palace.

And things were better . . . for a while.

They talked about their God . . . "the one true God," they call Him. When we left Egypt, the first place we traveled to was Bethel, "the house of the Lord." I watched as Master Abram built an altar. I listened as they talked about their God and the promise He had given them. They spoke of a city—a city not built with hands.

I longed to meet their God and see that city. But I'm just a slave . . . a concubine—a means to their end.

Now I don't belong anywhere. I don't fit with the servants

Programs for Ladies

> . . . and I don't fit with the family. I'm a misfit, hated, used, abused . . .
>
> All my life I've been "expecting." Expecting things to get better. And now I'm "expecting" again. *(laughs hard, bitterly)* I'm expecting a baby, and I'm expecting things to get worse.
>
> Mistress Sarai fears me. She is afraid I am going to take from her what she has. She hates me because I have what she wants. *(places hands on stomach as if cradling the baby)* A baby! It's my baby! My baby! I'll never give it to her. Never! Never!

HAGAR *runs off the stage, screaming.*

> I'll never give up my baby! She cannot have my baby!

HAGAR *runs down the aisle, screaming. As everyone's attention is riveted on her, someone backstage plugs in the fountain.*

> I'll go back to Egypt! Back to Egypt before I'll give up my baby! Back to Egypt . . . my baby . . . back to Egypt . . . back to Egypt . . . she'll never get my baby . . . never!

HAGAR *slows down, as she seems to tire. She goes around back of the congregation and comes up the center aisle. Her pace gradually slows to barely a crawl as she climbs stairs on left side of stage. Her scream has been reduced to a gasping whisper.*

> I'll never give up my baby . . . never . . .

HAGAR *slumps down on log or rock on stage. She looks up to heaven with tears streaming down her face.*

> Oh, God of the heavens . . . God of the sun, the moon, the stars, God, whoever You are and wherever You are, do You see me? I am so tired . . . and so lonely . . . and so thirsty. Do You see me? *(listens)* What do I hear? *(looks behind her)* Ahhh, what is this? A fountain? Water in the wilderness? A spring in the desert. A fountain just for me. *(scoops up water from the fountain and washes her face)*

ENTER ANGEL, *from left.*

DIRECTOR *moves silently to front to be ready to go on stage as angel exits.*

ANGEL: Hagar!

HAGAR *turns in astonishment. Her face is wet. She falls to her knees and looks up at the angel.*

HAGAR: I . . . I . . . who—

ANGEL: Hagar, Sarai's maid, where are you coming from? And where are you going?

HAGAR: I . . . I . . . I am running away from my mistress Sarai.

ANGEL: Go back home and humble yourself. Submit to your mistress.

HAGAR: But . . . I . . . I . . . *(bows head and nods)*

ANGEL: I will multiply your seed exceedingly, that it shall not be numbered for multitude.

HAGAR: *(looks up)* But that sounds like the promise the Lord God of my master gave to him.

ANGEL: You are expecting a baby, Hagar. You will have a son. Call him Ishmael . . . because the Lord has heard your affliction.

HAGAR: *(repeats)* The Lord has heard my affliction?

ANGEL: Yes, the Lord God has heard your affliction. He has heard the pain, the tears, the anguish. He has heard.

HAGAR: The Lord God of Abram has heard the cry of Hagar? The bondwoman?

ANGEL: Yes, Hagar, the Lord God of Abram has seen you and heard your affliction.

Programs for Ladies

EXIT ANGEL.

HAGAR: *(stands)* The Lord God has heard me. He has seen me. Now I can return and humble myself, for I have met the God of Abram and Sarai, and He is the God of Hagar! *(starts to exit, pauses)* Who knows? Maybe someday I will come "back to the fountain." Perhaps someday I will bring my son to the fountain where I met God.

HAGAR EXITS.

DIRECTOR: It's not hard to play the part of Hagar . . . when you have been humbled and hurt . . . when you have suffered abuse and rejection . . . when you have been a misfit and an outcast.

Not everyone is a Sarah or a Ruth or a Mary of Nazareth. Among us are Hagar . . . and Rahab . . . and the Samaritan woman.

Some of us have known the bitter taste of polluted water drank from broken cisterns. We have tried to satisfy our thirst with alcohol and drugs, sex, material things, and even education and success. Our expectations only deepened our thirst, and our drinking polluted our souls.

Some of us have known the trauma of divorce and rejection; some have been abused sexually, emotionally; some have had a baby out of wedlock; some have had abortions; some have been addicted to drugs and alcohol; some have attempted suicide.

No . . . we are not all Sarahs. We are not all princesses. Some of us have been slaves—bound by sin.

But one day . . . at the low point in our life . . . when we were on the road back to Egypt, the God of Hagar met us at the fountain of life. And He said, "Let her that is athirst come. Come and take of the water of life freely."

For us . . . for you . . . for me, He opened rivers in high places and fountains in the midst of the valley. For you . . . for me . . .

He made the wilderness a pool of water, and He put springs in the desert. And He said, "In your valley of Baca, the valley of weeping, I have dug a well. Drink deeply, my daughter, and you will never thirst again."

Let us go to the fountain of living water and meet the God of Hagar. He waits for us. Let us stand and give Him praise.

MUSIC: FINALE

---

[1] John 4:13-14
[2] Isaiah 12:3
[3] Psalm 84:6
[4] Isaiah 41:18

Women of the Kingdom

"There were also women looking on afar off: among whom was Mary Magdalene, and Mary the mother of James the less and of Joses, and Salome; (who also, when he was in Galilee, followed him, and ministered unto him;) and many other women which came up with him unto Jerusalem."[1]

NOTE from the author:

Whatever the era or the generation, women have always played a "waiting" role, and it is not easy. Women in Jesus' day were basically just like we are. They dealt with—sometimes chafed at—the nitty-gritty of life while they waited for a better day.

This drama is biblically correct to the best of my ability. We do not know that the "Susanna" mentioned in the Bible was Peter's mother-in-law, but we do not know that she was not. Many Bible commentators believe that Salome was the sister of Mary of Nazareth. The personality ascribed to each character is based on the few facts I found about each lady in Scripture and history. If when "we all get to heaven," I find I have portrayed anyone incorrectly, I will apologize to her.

Meanwhile, let's relax and accept these ladies as our "sisters," just as human as we are, yet Jesus welcomed them as part of His special following. May we learn from their mistakes and their victories and take heart—for the King is coming.

CAST:

> SUSANNA, Peter's mother-in-law, good heart.
> MARY C, mother of James the Less and of Joses—wife of Cleopas: weak-hearted, fearful, but as she waits on the Lord, she gains courage.
> SALOME, mother of James and John, aunt of Jesus—power hungry, has allergies, does not like to wait [serve], expects

to be waited on. Vacillates between seeing Jesus as her nephew and the King of the Jews.

MARY M—of Magdala goes from an extremely evil to a pure heart of love, the singer.

JOANNA, wife of Chuza, steward of Herod, elegant, thankful heart, giving.

MARY B—of Bethany, kind hearted, a bit absent-minded, daydreamer.

MARTHA—wrong priorities, high blood pressure, impatient; learns to wait, but not easily—always complains about being exhausted, but never stops to rest.

7 EXTRAS—These ladies are dressed in simple biblical robes. Only one (the lady with the infirmity, referred to as Extra 1 in Act IV) has anything to say.

INSTRUCTIONS:

Directions are given from stage facing audience. Stage set-up directions and props are given with each act.

Make a tape of market noise—sheep, cattle, birds, and the general hubbub of a crowd. Animal sounds can be found on children's sound effects books or check at the public library. This part of the tape should be about five minutes long.

The second portion of the tape is a man's voice shouting, "Get these things out of here. Do not make my Father's house a house of merchandise! My Father's house is a house of prayer. You have made it a den of thieves . . . a den of thieves . . . den of thieves." In the background is a loud, crashing, shouting noise mingled with animal squeals.

After the first portion of the tape plays, put the tape on "pause" until time for the cleansing of the Temple.

The third portion of the tape is a man's voice: "Daughters of Jerusalem, weep not for me, but weep for yourselves and for your children. Weep for yourselves and your children . . . *(fades)* weep for yourselves and your children . . . weep for your children . . . weep for your children."

The final portion of the tape is the sound of the wind. Or someone behind the scene can simply blow into a microphone.

COSTUMES:

Biblical attire. Dress defines character. Joanna, elegant. Martha and

Susanna, workers. Mary B, gentle and kind. Salome, style-conscious. Mary M, possessed then delivered—from ragged and filthy to clean, modest, and beautiful. Mary C, mousy.

Programs for Ladies

ACT I

Waiting for the Kingdom

The Court of Women, the Temple in Jerusalem
The Year of Christ's Inauguration

CAST:

- Susanna
- Mary C
- Joanna
- Mary B
- Martha
- Salome
- Mary M
- 6 extras

PROPS:

- Suitcases
- Miscellaneous bundles, containing copies of scripts
- Table
- Chair
- Lamp
- Scroll
- Pen
- Tape
- Tape Player

INSTRUCTIONS:

Salome is seated on far right, about halfway back in the audience. Mary C and Susanna are seated far left, about one quarter of the way back in the audience. Mary Magdalene is seated far left front. She is dressed in dirty, ragged clothes, hair matted, wearing a cloak to cover her costume. Mary and Martha enter from the back, come up the center. Everyone, except Mary Magdalene and Joanna, carry suitcases and bundles with scripts.

STAGE SET-UP:

Table with lamp, scroll, and pen is on far right. Joanna sits at the table, registering the ladies.

ENTER SUSANNA and MARY C *from left and "get in line," with Mary C in back. A line of* ***six EXTRAS***, *all but the lady with the infirmity, forms in front of Susanna and Mary C.* ***JOANNA*** *moves them through slowly.*

ENTER MARY B *and* ***MARTHA,*** *from the back, pushing their way through the crowd, ad-libbing. Martha grumbles about the crowd, the dirt, the noise, etc. Mary enjoys the sights, calling out to people in the audience. Calls ladies in the audience by their names. "I haven't seen you in a year. How's your family? How about the kids? My, you look great!" etc. As they near the front, they begin using the script, which is hidden in the bundles they carry.*

MARTHA: Hurry up, Mary. You've been dawdling ever since we left Bethany. Lazarus is away ahead of us. *(louder)* Mary! Hurry up!

MARY B: *(notices Martha)* What did you say, Martha?

MARTHA: I said, "Hurry up." You're dawdling.

MARY B: I'm sorry, Martha. But there are such interesting sites between Bethany and Jerusalem and so many people to stop and chat with.

MARTHA: *(scolding)* You're just like a child, Mary. Things never lose their wonder to you.

MARY B: I hope they never do. It's a wonder-full world the Lord God has created.

MARTHA: Right now I'm wondering how long we are going to have to stand in line to register. I've been on my feet since dawn. My luggage weighs a ton. I am exhausted. I would like to sit down.

Programs for Ladies

MARY B: Poor Martha. Why don't you stop and rest?

MARTHA: *(screams)* Stop and rest? Mary, are you out of your head? If we stop and rest, we'll never get there.

MARY B: Your blood pressure must be up again, Martha. Maybe you should see Dr. Luke while we are in the city.

MARTHA: And sit in his waiting room for half a day when I have so much to do? No, thank you.

MARY B: I really wish you would. *(stops and points to her right, says painfully)* Ooohhh, do you see that woman over there? *(seen only by Mary)*

MARTHA: *(disgusted)* I see nine hundred women over there! *(peers into the distance)* We must be getting close to the Temple. Listen at the noise! Phew, it stinks!

MARY B: *(still looking to her right)* She's all bent over.

MARTHA: *(stops and looks back at Mary in exasperation)* Mary! Hurry up! *(starts again, then stops)* Who's all bent over?

MARY B: That poor woman over there. She'll never be able to get through this crowd. Perhaps, I should go help. *(sits down suitcase)* Watch my luggage.

MARTHA: *(grabs Mary's arm and stops her)* Mary! Don't go wandering off to help someone you don't even know. If we get separated in this mob, I'll never find you. Your heart's in the right place, but I declare I don't know where your brain is!

MARY B: But, Martha—

MARTHA: Don't you go butting me. This crowd gets worse every year. We should have stayed home.

MARY B: And miss the Passover? Martha, you don't mean it. The Passover is the highlight of the year. Besides the spiritual atmosphere of the holy city, we get to visit with our friends from all over Palestine.

SALOME *stands up, sneezes loudly two or three times, fusses with her luggage.*

MARTHA: I know, but it is such a hassle getting ready—when we get here, we still have to stand in line to register, then we—rather—I have to try to find lodging, and—

MARY B: Oh, look, Martha. There's our friend, Salome. *(calls)* Salome! Salome! Over here.

MARTHA: *(pulls on Mary, but she adamantly stands her ground)* Mary, we're already late. You can catch her later.

SALOME *looks around.*

MARY B: *(calls)* Over here, Salome. We're over here.

MARTHA: For goodness' sake, Mary, do you have to make a spectacle of us?

MARY B: She sees us. Wait, Martha.

MARTHA: *(mimics)* Wait, Martha, wait!

MARY B: *(mimics)* Hurry, Mary, hurry!

SALOME *pushes her way through the crowd, carrying her luggage, sneezing.*

SALOME: *(huffing and puffing)* Greetings, Mary. What a mob! Worse than last year. Zebedee had all the servants doing jobs for him, and I have to carry my own luggage. I'm so exhausted!

MARTHA: *(clicks tongue)* Ta-ta-ta. You're exhausted? That's so sad. This is probably the first time since you married Zebedee you've had to carry your luggage.

SALOME: *(ignores Martha)* And I am also mad!

Programs for Ladies

MARY B: Mad? Because you have to carry your luggage?

MARTHA: If we don't hurry up, we'll be the last in line to register, and then *I'll* be mad.

SALOME: *(seems to notice Martha for the first time)* Oh, greetings, Martha. Seems like the last time I saw you, you were in a hurry. How's your blood pressure?

MARTHA: Not as high as yours. And the last time I saw you, you were mad.

MARY B: Girls! Girls! Come with us, Salome. I'll help you with your luggage. *(tries shifting her load to take on more)*

SALOME: *(clings to her luggage)* No! No, Mary, I can manage. It's not carrying my luggage that makes me so angry. At least, that's not the main thing.

MARY B: Then why are you so upset?

WOMEN *move up the aisle.* **MARTHA** *hurries ahead, followed by the other two at a leisurely pace, talking as they go.* **SALOME** *sneezes often and* **MARY B** *always responds, "God bless you." They cross in front to left side of stage and slowly work their way onto the stage where they stand in the back of the line.*

SALOME: Those Roman soldiers! Fresh upstarts! They think they own the streets.

MARTHA: *(slowing her pace so she can hear, talks over her shoulder)* They think they own the whole city!

SALOME: They push us around like second-class citizens—us, the Jews, God's chosen people! Why, my family is descended from King David. We are members of the royal family. Sometimes I wish I was a man. I'd lead a revolu—

MARY B: *(loud whisper)* Salome, hush! Do you want someone to hear you?

SALOME: *(looks about furtively and lowers voice)* I don't care if they do. *(gets louder)* Just the other day one of those disgusting Roman soldiers made James carry his load for a mile. Imagine my son doing a slave's job for a Roman!

MARY B: *(finger over mouth, in loud whisper)* Shhhhh. Remember, the streets have ears.

SALOME: *(lowers voice)* I don't care! I wish the King of the Jews would come and deliver us. How long must we wait for the Messiah?

TAPE: <u>market noise of sheep, cattle, and birds fades in—becomes louder as women near the Temple.</u>

*As the **WOMEN** near the Temple, **SALOME'S** sneezing gets worse. She has to stop occasionally to rest, showing she is not accustomed to carrying her own bags.*

MARTHA: I don't know, but I'm beginning to wonder if He is ever coming. All my life I've been hearing "The Messiah is coming," and my mother heard it all her life, and my grandmother heard it all her life, and my great-grandmother—

MARY B: Yes, yes, Martha, we know.

SALOME: I am tired of waiting for the King of the Jews. I am sick of the Romans treating us like dirt!

MARTHA: Talk about dirt! Look at this Temple courtyard! It's disgusting.

MARY B: It does stink!

SALOME: Business must go on. We do need the animals for sacrifices, you know. But it really aggravates my allergies.

MARTHA: I wonder how much the moneychangers cheated Lazarus out of this year. He's such a softy!

SALOME: *(proudly)* I doubt they cheated Zebedee or my boys. They're much too smart for these scoundrels. My men are businessmen.

MARY B: It seems sacrilegious for this to be going on in the house of the Lord.

MARTHA: Well, hurry, girls, let's get through this stinking mess! At least, in the Court of the Women there's no blood or dirt—

SALOME: Or Romans! I think I'm more allergic to them than I am to the dirt! Maybe that's because they are dirt!

MARTHA: Would you look at the Court of the Women? I've never seen it so crowded. *(points at the line)* Look at that line. I told you, Mary.

MARY B: I know. We're the last in line, and it's all my fault. *(looks dreamily in distance)*

MARTHA: Mary, did you remember to pack your . . . *(Mary is not listening, staring at the Temple)* Mary? Mary!

MARY B: *(starts)* Oh! What, Martha? What did you say?

MARTHA: Never mind.

MARY B: Have you ever wished you could go in there, Salome?

SALOME: Go in where, Mary?

MARTHA: She's talking about going into the Temple. Mary's a dreamer. She dreams of the day women will be allowed into the Temple. Mary's philosophy is, "If you're going to dream, might as well dream big!"

SALOME: I would like to see the furnishings—the golden candlestick, the magnificent veil. Think how much they are worth. They're priceless.

MARY B: That's not why I want to go in there, Salome. *(with deep hunger)* Something in me longs to be in the presence of the Creator of all this beauty.

MARTHA: *(looks around and snorts)* All this beauty? Mary, open your eyes. We are in the Court of the Women; behind us is the Court of the Gentiles—nothing more than the stockyards!

MARY B: Oh, Martha, must you always be so practical? *(turns to Salome)* How are the boys and Zebedee, Salome?

SALOME: *(speaks in a gushy rush of words)* Just wonderful! The boys are so handsome and intelligent—half the girls in Galilee are chasing them.

MARTHA: Ha!

SALOME: The fishing business is booming. But the Roman taxes are eating us up. I don't see why we Jews have to pay tribute to Caesar.

MARTHA: Your mouth is going to get you in trouble someday, Salome.

SALOME: *(ignores Martha)* Zebedee and I had planned to move from Capernaum into our second home here in Jerusalem when he retired—and that reminds me. Do you girls have a room yet?

MARTHA: No. And thanks to Mary's dawdling, probably all the rooms are taken.

SALOME: Why don't you and Lazarus stay with us? We have plenty of room, even though it is just our vacation cabin. We also have a number of servants, although no one had time for me today!

MARY B: That's very kind of you, Salome.

MARTHA: *(grudgingly)* We could go home, but it is much more convenient to stay in the city.

SALOME: Well, hospitality is one of my gifts. As I was saying, we had planned to retire here, but something has happened lately that has our family in turmoil. I am so upset.

MARTHA: Upset? You, Salome? I can't believe it!

Programs for Ladies

SALOME: *(ignores Martha; sadly)* We may never be the same.

MARY B: I hope no one is ill.

SALOME: No, it's not that. My boys have decided to change professions—and I wasn't even consulted. They were doing so well in the fishing business—in spite of Roman taxes. Now they have lost interest in fishing—at least, fishing for fish.

MARTHA: *(sarcastically)* What else would you fish for?

SALOME: They are talking about "fishing for men."

ENTER MARY MAGDALENE *from left front, quietly as possible.*

MARTHA: Come on, Salome. I've heard of women fishing for men. Have your boys gone off their rockers?

SALOME: *(haughtily)* Certainly not. Not my boys! Talking about rockers, how is Lazarus?

MARY B: Not too well. I worry about him.

MARTHA: You worry about everybody, even crippled old ladies you don't know. There's nothing wrong with Lazarus—or his rocker. He just needs to stick to his diet and get more exercise.

SALOME: Talking about being off your rocker, look who's coming. What is she doing here?

ALL *look at* **MARY MAGDALENE**. *She walks slowly in front of them. Her eyes are glassy, and she walks like a zombie. As she passes the women, they—except for* **MARY B**—*turn from her and pull their robes closer to them. As she passes,* **MARY B** *reaches out and touches her softly.* **MARTHA** *grabs Mary's hand and jerks it back, whispers loudly, "Mary, don't touch her!"* **MARY M** *seems not to notice. No one else speaks until* **MARY M** *is off stage. She walks all the way across the front and sits down on far right. All eyes are on her.*

MARY B: *(loud whisper)* Poor thing. Who is she?

SALOME: Mary of Magdala. They say she's possessed. And I believe it! She is sooooo sinful! It's disgusting!

MARY B: Ohhh, poor thing.

MARTHA: Watch Mary. She'll be taking this outcast home with us.

MARY B: *(ignores Martha)* Can no one help her? No one at all? *(no one answers)* Maybe I could help her. *(starts to leave)*

MARTHA: *(grabs Mary and holds her)* No, you don't. Where's your brain? And it's a strange thing you have time to help everyone but me.

MARY B: But, Martha, you don't need me to help you.

MARTHA: Let's get in line.

SALOME: Who is that at the registration desk?

MARY B: That's Joanna, the wife of Chuza, Herod's steward. She's a sweet lady. We met her in Dr. Luke's office last year.

MARTHA: *(sighs)* You think everyone's sweet, Mary. Personally, I think she's a little highbrow. Just because her husband works in the palace doesn't mean she's anybody special.

MARY B: She's been sick for a long time. Some strange disease. Dr. Luke has sent her to physicians all over the country, but they can't help her. I'm surprised she's able to be here. Must be one of her good days.

SALOME: *(sees Mary C and Susanna)* Oh, no. There's Susanna and Mary, wife of Cleopas. They are from Galilee, too. Let's get in another line.

MARTHA: Why should we? This is the shortest line.

MARY B: Don't you like them, Salome?

SALOME: *(shrugs)* Oh, they're okay, I guess. The younger woman is

Programs for Ladies

Mary, the mother of James and Joses. She's a mousy little thing, afraid of her own shadow. Her boys grew up with mine.

MARTHA: So?

SALOME: So—she and I just never did hit it off. Personality conflict, I guess. She thinks her boys are the smartest, the best looking, the politest, the—

MARTHA: *(raises eyebrows)* I'm beginning to see why you didn't hit it off.

SALOME: And the older woman is our business partner's mother-in-law.

MARTHA: Which partner, Simon Peter or Andrew?

SALOME: Simon Peter. She's always bragging about how important Peter is to our business, and . . . wait a minute, I just remembered something—maybe I do want to stand there, after all.

THEY stand behind **SUSANNA** and **MARY C,** who have not noticed them. **SALOME** taps Mary C on the shoulder.

MARY C: *(jumps wildly, grabs heart)* Oooh! Oooh! Oh, it's only you, Salome. You gave me such a fright. You shouldn't do that. I have a weak heart.

SALOME: Greetings, Mary. Sorry about your heart. I forgot. Greetings, Susanna.

SUSANNA: *(nods at Salome)* Greetings, Salome.

SALOME: These are my friends, Martha and Mary of Bethany.

SUSANNA: Greetings, Mary. Greetings, Martha. This is my friend, Mary.

MARY C: *(still has hand over heart, taking deep breaths, laughs timidly)* Greetings, ladies. *(looks around)* I wonder if there is any place where I could . . . sit down. I feel . . . rather weak.

WOMEN, *except for Salome, help her into a chair.* **SALOME** *stands aside, looks down her nose, and watches.* **MARY B** *frets over Mary C.* **SALOME** *sneezes.*

MARY C: *(puts hands over face)* Oh, don't do that!

SALOME: Do what?

MARY C: Sneeze in my face. What if I got a virus around my weak heart? I heard the other day about—

MARTHA: If you'd shut your mouth, fewer germs could get to your heart.

MARY B: Martha! *(pats Mary C on the shoulder)* If you need anything, Mary, just let me know.

MARY C: *(breathlessly, whiny)* I'll be all right in a few minutes. Don't worry about me, Mary.

MARY B: Mary must have been the most popular name in the country about the time we were born.

SALOME: Must have been. I have a sister named Mary, too—Mary of Nazareth.

SUSANNA: Mary of Nazareth? I didn't know she was your sister.

SALOME: Not many people know it.

SUSANNA: Is she here?

SALOME: I think so. She usually comes to the Passover.

MARTHA: Move up, everybody.

WOMEN *move up as if the line is shortening.*

MARY B: *(to Mary C)* Don't try to stand up yet. We'll hold your place in line.

MARY C: *(joins them, says weakly)* No, I wouldn't want you to have to do that. I'm fine now. You mustn't worry about me.

*As the **WOMEN** talk, **SALOME** occasionally sneezes, usually in Mary C's direction. When she does, **MARY C** gasps, covers her face with her hands, and moves farther away from Salome.*

SALOME: Susanna, I hear your son-in-law, Peter, has taken up a new profession—joined his brother, Andrew, and my sons as disciples of Jesus, my nephew.

SUSANNA: Yes. It came as quite a shock to us. Peter's always loved the fishing business, and he has been so good at it. I'm really not sure what got into him. It may just be a phase—but he seems quite adamant that he's through fishing—at least, for fish.

MARY B: What does this Jesus do?

SUSANNA: He's a teacher of some kind—speaks very authoritatively, I understand. At least, that's what Peter says. A strange thing happened the other day. He turned water into wine!

MARTHA: Peter turned water into wine?

SUSANNA: No, not Peter—Jesus.

MARTHA: Now, Susanna—

SUSANNA: Whether you believe it or not, it happened. I was there. It was at that big wedding in Cana. I'm surprised you weren't there, Salome.

SALOME: I wasn't invi . . . *(slaps hand over mouth and shrugs)* I had more important things to do.

MARY C: Jesus turned water into wine? My boys have been talking about Him. They have known Him for years.

SALOME: My boys have known Him all their lives. It's only natural that He should choose them to be His disciples.

MARY C: *(apologetically)* Oh, of course, He would. But my boys have known Him for years, too, and they are quite surprised at what they are seeing and hearing these days.

SUSANNA: Peter said that John the Baptist called Jesus "the Lamb of God" when he baptized Him.

SALOME: *(proudly)* John the Baptist is another relative of mine. We are descendants of King David.

MARY C: He's *(shakes head in wonder)* . . . He's ahhhh . . . a little strange, to say the least—rather frightening.

SALOME: *(defensively)* I'm certainly not scared of him. I think he's pretty smart. He knows how to get a crowd.

MARY C: Yes, but I hear his message isn't all that popular. *(shudders)* Imagine calling the Pharisees "snakes."

SUSANNA: Peter said that John said the "kingdom is at hand."

MARTHA: The kingdom? Our kingdom? Do you mean we will soon be free from the Romans?

MARY C: I'm surprised the Romans haven't locked him up for saying such things. *(shudders)* They say the Roman jails are horrid!

MARY B: Wouldn't it be wonderful if the King of the Jews would come?

SALOME: I can't think of anything that would make me happier. I'd love to see those Roman soldiers carrying our loads.

MARY C: *(looks around fearfully)* Hush, Salome! What if a Roman soldier heard you?

SALOME: Get real, Mary. There are no Roman soldiers in the Court of the Women.

MARY B: Do you suppose . . . . *(hesitates)*

MARTHA: *(impatiently)* Move up, everybody. *(Everyone moves up*

Programs for Ladies

as if line is moving.) Suppose what, Mary?

MARY: Do you suppose this Jesus is . . . that this Jesus is the *(reverently)* King of the Jews?

SALOME: *(scoffs)* The King? The Messiah? My sister's son, Jesus of Nazareth?

SUSANNA: Oh, I wouldn't think so. He's probably just a prophet—certainly not the Messiah. You know the saying, "Can anything good come out of Nazareth"?

SALOME: I resent that remark, Susanna! Just because you live in Capernaum—

SUSANNA: You live in Capernaum, too, Salome.

SALOME: I know, but my sister Mary lives in Nazareth. And who are you to say whether Jesus is the Messiah or not? After all, my family is descended from King David. I remember Mary telling us something strange about His birth. We—

<u>TAPE:</u> <u>Loud crashing, shouting, animals, confusion (Man's voice) "Get these things out of here. Do not make my Father's house a house of merchandise! My Father's house is a house of prayer. You have made it a den of thieves . . . den of thieves . . . den of thieves . . ."</u>

WOMEN ad-lib. *"What in the world?" "What is going on?" "Watch out! The animals are loose."*

WOMEN *scatter everywhere, hands raised in horror, hiding from animals. When the tape has completely faded, there is a few seconds of silence. The women come out from hiding and stand in shock.*

SALOME: *(awestruck)* That was Jesus! I'd recognize His voice anywhere. He sounded so powerful!

MARTHA: Do you suppose . . . do you suppose the kingdom is at hand?

MARY B: Do you suppose the King has come?

ALL FREEZE *until middle of the first verse of the song, then* ***EXIT.***

SONG: "I'm Glad I Know Who Jesus Is"

Programs for Ladies

ACT II

Working for the Kingdom

Susanna's House in Capernaum
The Year of Jesus' Popularity

"(Who also, when he was in Galilee, followed him, and ministered unto him;) and many other women . . . ."[2]

"And it came to pass afterward, that he went throughout every city and village, preaching and shewing the glad tidings of the kingdom of God: and the twelve were with him, and certain women, which had been healed of evil spirits and infirmities, Mary called Magdalene, out of whom went seven devils, and Joanna the wife of Chuza Herod's steward, and Susanna, and many others, which ministered unto him of their substance."[3]

CAST:

      SUSANNA, Peter's mother-in-law
      MARY C, mother of James the Less and Joses
      SALOME, mother of James and John, aunt of Jesus
      MARY MAGDALENE
      JOANNA, wife of Chuza the steward of Herod

PROPS:

      Table
      Tablecloth
      Lamp
      Chairs
      Greenery
      Miscellaneous trash from "roof"
      Two covered dishes
      Miscellaneous baskets
      Large trash can

STAGE SET-UP:

Right side is set up like living room of Susanna's house. Trash from roof is scattered everywhere. A basket is on the front row right for Mary C. Luggage for Mary M and Joanna is on the front row left.

ENTER SUSANNA, *straightening things, picking up trash.*

SUSANNA: I love having Jesus and the boys here, but . . . *(laughs)* it sure is hard on the house.

MARY C ENTERS *from right, carrying a covered dish. Knocks on "door."* ***SUSANNA*** *goes to the door.*

SUSANNA: Greetings, Mary. Come in. Come in.

MARY C: *(hand over face, backs away)* No, no, no. I heard you were sick, Susanna.

SUSANNA: That was yesterday. I had a terrible fever. Won't you come in?

MARY C: *(holds dish toward Susanna at arm's length, puts hands over nose and mouth)* Oh, no. You might be contag . . . I mean, I have a lot to do. I'll just leave this dish for your dinner. Good-bye.

MARY C EXITS, *sits on front row.*

SUSANNA: Well, thank you. I wish you didn't have to rush . . . *(laughs)* poor Mary. She's afraid of everything, soldiers and germs and her shadow. *(sets dish on the table and continues straightening the room)*

ENTER SALOME, *carrying a dish, knocks on door.*

SUSANNA: Now who could that be? It's as busy around here as the Dallas/Fort Worth terminal. Oops, wrong dispensation. It's as busy around here as the Court of the Gentiles.

SUSANNA *goes to the door.*

Programs for Ladies

SUSANNA: Greetings, Salome. Come in.

SALOME: *(hands dish to Susanna, says with a touch of envy)* Greetings, Susanna. Since Jesus and the disciples have made Capernaum their headquarters, I notice they spend most of their spare time at your house. So I had my cook prepare something for their dinner.

SUSANNA: Thank you, Salome. I love having Jesus and the boys here.

SALOME: Apparently. But you could share. After all, two of them are my sons. I would enjoy having them, too. And I do have lots of help to wait on them. You can at least tell them that I made this meat dish for their dinner.

SUSANNA: You made it?

SALOME: Well, I had my cook make it. Tell them it came from my kitchen.

SUSANNA: I'll be happy to, Salome. How are your allergies?

SALOME: Much better since I got away from that filthy courtyard. How are you, Susanna? I heard that you were awfully sick with a high fever.

SUSANNA: My, word gets around fast.

SALOME: You know what they say, "Telephone, telegram, and tell-a-woman."

SUSANNA: Wrong dispensation, Salome! No telephone. No telegraph.

SALOME: Sorry. I forgot! *(sneezes three times violently)*

SUSANNA: Back to my fever. I was terribly ill. I don't know whenever I have been so sick.

SALOME: *(lightly)* Probably just some bug. I had it a couple of weeks ago.

SUSANNA: Well, whatever it was, Jesus healed me, and I feel wonderful.

SALOME: *(sneezes again, looks around)* My goodness! Look at the dirt and trash! What happened? It looks like a tornado hit—or do we have tornadoes in Galilee?

SUSANNA: It wasn't a tornado, but pretty close to it. Jesus held a healing service here yesterday.

SALOME: So? *(looks up)* What does that have to do with a hole in the roof? *(sneezes often, at the most inappropriate times; looks around)* Don't you have any Kleenex around here?

SUSANNA: Wrong dispensation, Salome.

SALOME: Oops! Forgot. Sorry. Back to the script.

SUSANNA: *(moves around clearing a chair for her guest as she talks)* There were so many people packed in here that not one more person could get in. Some friends of that man who has had palsy for years . . . what's his name?

SALOME: I can't remember, but I know who you are talking about.

SUSANNA: Four of his friends wanted to get him to Jesus, but they couldn't get in the house. So they tore a hole in the roof and let him down with ropes right in front of Jesus.

SALOME: Talk about dropping in for a visit! What happened?

SUSANNA: Jesus told the man his sins were forgiven.

SALOME: His sins were forgiven? Jesus said his sins were forgiven? *(in wonder, no sneezing during this serious portion of conversation)* Susanna, only God can forgive sins.

SUSANNA: *(hushed tones)* I know.

SALOME: Susanna, do you believe the man's sins were forgiven?

SUSANNA: Have you ever known Jesus to tell a lie, Salome?

Programs for Ladies

SALOME: *(slowly)* No—but do you realize what that means?

SUSANNA: Yes, I know what that means. It means that Jesus is God.

SALOME: Mary said the angel told her that her son would be called, "Emmanuel, God with us." My nephew—the Messiah? *(thoughtfully)* We are descendants of King David. It's overwhelming.

SUSANNA: I know. After Jesus forgave the man's sin, He healed him.

SALOME: *(thinks a few seconds, mouth falls open as if a light has come in her head, jumps to her feet, dances around)* Susanna, our God—the King of the Jews—has come to save us from the Romans. And we are in on the action from the ground floor. Remember what the prophet Isaiah wrote: *"For since the beginning of the world men have not heard, nor perceived by the ear, neither hath the eye seen, O God, beside thee, what he hath prepared for him that waiteth for him!"*[4] The kingdom has come! The kingdom has come! *(sneezing begins again)*

SUSANNA: Sit down, Salome, before you trip over this mess and break your neck.

SALOME: *(sits down)* Where are Jesus and the disciples now?

SUSANNA: Somewhere in the area. I'm not sure they will be in tonight. Sometimes Jesus prays all night. Peter says that they are bringing the sick from as far away as Syria. Demons are being cast out, lepers healed, the blind see—

SALOME: And the Romans are on their way down! Oh, I can hardly wait to see the day we Jews can spit in the Romans' eyes.

SUSANNA: Salome! Can you see Jesus spitting in anyone's eye?

SALOME: Well, maybe we won't spit in their eyes, but we can make them lick our boots. We certainly won't have to bow and scrape to them. We'll have our own kingdom—a kingdom of power and prosperity. *(jumps up again)* We'll be rich! Rich beyond our wildest imagination!

SUSANNA: I wonder—

SALOME: You wonder what?

SUSANNA: I wonder if there isn't more to the kingdom of God than prosperity and power—

SALOME: What more could you want?

SUSANNA: How about peace? Or maybe . . . righteousness?

SALOME: *(shrugs)* Doesn't sound very exciting to me. Do you know what Jesus did the other day? The boys had been fishing all night and had not caught one thing—

SUSANNA: Yes, Peter told us about that. Jesus told them to let down the nets again—

SALOME: And they caught so many fish that both boats almost sank. I tell you, Susanna, if Jesus would do that just once a week, we'd all be rich! It wouldn't matter that the boys had left the fishing business. Zebedee could retire, and we could move to Jerusalem. I'm sure Jesus will set up His headquarters in Jerusalem. In fact, the prophets prophesied that the King would reign on the throne of His father David. We'll be right where the action is.

SUSANNA: Perhaps, Salome.

SALOME: Perhaps? Where's your faith, Susanna? Don't you believe that Jesus, my sister's son, is Emmanuel, the Messiah?

SUSANNA: It's not that I don't believe, Salome. I remember that Isaiah also wrote that God's ways are far above our ways.

SALOME: *(stands to leave)* Well, I'm sure wonderful things are happening, and this is just the beginning. I'm glad Jesus had enough sense to choose my boys as His disciples . . . I mean, I'm glad my boys had sense enough to leave the fishing business and follow Jesus.

Now, I've got to go to the market and pick up some fresh fruit.

Programs for Ladies

> If the men come in tonight, why don't you send some of them over to my house? The servants will be happy to wait on them . . . *(looks pointedly at the mess)* ahhhh, I mean, you don't suppose Jesus has another healing service planned for tonight, do you?

SUSANNA: I really don't know, Salome. I never cease to be amazed at what Jesus does. *(picks up basket)* I think I'll go with you to the market.

BOTH *go down right-hand steps and walk around front of the stage.* **MARY C**, *carrying a basket, joins them. From left side,* **JOANNA** *and* **MARY M**, *on front row, pick up luggage, and go on stage. Set down luggage and look around as if searching for someone.*

MARY C: Wait, Susanna—Salome. Wait and I'll go to market with you.

SALOME and SUSANNA *stop and wait for her.*

SUSANNA: Aren't you afraid you'll catch something from me, Mary?

MARY C: I'll walk beside Salome.

SALOME *sneezes.*

MARY C: Never mind. I'll just walk behind. I was waiting for someone to go to market with. You know it just isn't safe for a woman to go anywhere alone these days.

SUSANNA: Oh, Mary, you are afraid of everything. Why can't you shake off that fear?

MARY C: *(cries out)* I don't know, but it torments me. I wish I was strong like you and Salome.

WOMEN *notice Mary M and Joanna.*

SUSANNA: Who are those women?

MARY C: They look strangely familiar.

SALOME: They certainly are elegant. They must be from the city. They don't look like typical Galilean women. Look at those expensive robes.

SUSANNA, SALOME, and **MARY C** *continue across the front and up the left steps onto the stage.*

JOANNA: *(fades in)* He can't be far away. Let's ask someone. *(turns toward approaching women)*

MARY M: *(reaches out in panic to stop her)* No! No! Don't . . . *(laughs self-consciously)* Go ahead. It's okay. I forgot.

JOANNA: You forgot what?

MARY M: I've forgotten what it's like to speak to people and not have them scorn me. I have trouble remembering that I'm not different anymore.

JOANNA: I know. I have trouble remembering that I can do the normal things of life now that I'm well. *(turns to other women)* Greetings, ladies.

WOMEN: Greetings to you.

SUSANNA: Welcome to Capernaum. I am Susanna. These are my friends, Salome wife of Zebedee and Mary wife of Cleopas.

JOANNA: I am Joanna wife of Chuza—

SALOME: Chuza? King Herod's steward?

JOANNA: Yes.

SUSANNA: That's why you look familiar. We saw you in the Court of the Women at the last Passover. But somehow you look different.

JOANNA: *(joyfully)* That's because I feel different. *(turns to Mary M)* This is my friend, Mary Magdalene.

SALOME: Welcome to Capern— *(stops in shock, slowly)* Did you say

Programs for Ladies

    Mary Magdalene . . . Mary of Magdala?

JOANNA: Yes.

SALOME: But she . . . then there are two Marys of Magdala?

JOANNA: No, only one.

SALOME: Uhhh . . . *(aside)* now how do I say this? *(to Joanna)* Uhhh . . . uhhhh . . . uhhh—

SUSANNA: *(pokes Salome, says aside)* Salome, don't be rude.

SALOME: *(aside to Susanna)* I'm not, but I've got to know who she is.

JOANNA: We are looking for Jesus of Nazareth. Have you seen Him?

SALOME: Oh, yes. He's my nephew.

JOANNA: Do you mind telling us where He is?

SALOME: Well, I wouldn't mind to tell you, but . . . I don't think it would be good for His reputation for her—

SUSANNA: *(pokes Salome forcefully)* Salome! I am ashamed of you! *(to Joanna)* Jesus and His disciples are out somewhere ministering to the people. They will probably be back later this evening.

JOANNA: Do you know any place where we might wait for Him?

SUSANNA: Certainly. You are welcome to wait at my— *(Salome pokes Susanna in the ribs)* oh!

SALOME: Pardon me, Susanna. I just . . . I just slipped. Hadn't we better be going?

MARY C: Mary Magdalene, what has happened to you? You are not the same woman we saw in Jerusalem.

SUSANNA: *(aside to Salome)* That's how you say it. You just ask.

MARY M: I know I'm not. And to God be the glory. You see, I met Jesus.

SALOME: You? You met Jesus?

MARY M: Yes, and He delivered me. I'm not the same woman you saw in Jerusalem.

JOANNA: Neither am I. You see, I met Jesus, too. And He healed me.

SALOME: Wow!

JOANNA: Everyone who meets Jesus is changed.

SALOME: *(looks on self-questioningly)* They are? Funny, I don't feel any different than I've always felt.

JOANNA: You don't? You've met Jesus and you aren't changed?

SALOME: Of course, I've met Jesus. I told you He's my nephew.

JOANNA: That's odd.

SALOME: Odd? What's odd about Jesus being my nephew?

JOANNA: Nothing. It's just strange that you haven't been changed.

SALOME: *(haughtily)* Perhaps, I don't want to be changed!

MARY M: Well, all I know is He changed me! We have come looking for Him because we want to follow Him and minister to Him and His disciples.

SALOME: You want to minister? Do you mean go around the country being in the spotlight, speaking to the multitudes, and giving your burning testimony?

SUSANNA: Or do you mean you want to "minister to" them: wash clothes, cook meals, do dishes, pick up after them, run errands, wait on them?

MARY M: We want to serve in any way we can.

Programs for Ladies

JOANNA: We have come to give our energy, our time, our money to His cause. He has done so much for us, we owe Him everything.

SUSANNA: All right. Follow me, ladies. I know just the place for you to begin your ministry.

WOMEN *follow Susanna across stage to "her house" on right side in this order: Susanna, Joanna, Mary M, Mary C, and Salome.*

SUSANNA: *(waves at mess around her)* Right here!

SALOME: *(aside to Mary C)* Leave it to Susanna. She found someone to clean her house.

EVERYONE, *but* **SALOME,** *starts to pick up trash and straighten the stage.* **SALOME** *just watches, occasionally pointing out something someone has missed. When the stage is almost clean,* **MARY M** *turns to the audience and sings.*

SONG: "I Will Serve Thee"

WOMEN EXIT *as* **MARY M** *sings.*

ACT III

Weeping for the Kingdom

Salome's Home in Jerusalem
Passover Feast A.D. 29

CAST:

> Mary B
> Martha
> Salome
> Mary C
> Joanna
> Susanna
> Mary M

STAGE SET-UP:

> Room set up similar to Susanna's house in Act II. Change position of furniture and tablecloths. Perhaps add brass ornaments and small items to give appearance of a more elegant home. Ceramic pot and cups on the table.

ENTER MARY B, MARTHA, *and* ***SALOME.***

MARTHA: Thanks, Salome, for letting us stay with you again this year.

SALOME: Zebedee and I are happy to have you.

MARY B: It's getting to be a tradition. I believe this is our third year to be your Passover guests.

MARTHA: *(yawns)* It's getting late and I am—

ALL: Exhausted!

Programs for Ladies

MARTHA: *(looks puzzled)* How did you know?

MARY B: You have only told us a dozen times in the last hour.

MARTHA: *(yawns again)* Oh, well, I didn't think you were listening. Old habits are hard to break.

SALOME: Have a seat. Let's have juice before we go to bed.

WOMEN *sit down and Salome pours juice for each. They sip their drinks as they talk.*

MARY B: You aren't sneezing, Salome. Are your allergies better?

SALOME: Of course. I am home where it is clean.

MARY B: Remember the lady who was bent over that we see every year when we come to the Passover?

MARTHA: Yes. What about her?

MARY B: I saw her today, and she's walking straight and tall. She told me Jesus healed her. She had been so weighted down and depressed, and then Jesus came. It's wonderful what happens when Jesus comes. People change.

MARTHA: Some of us take longer than others, but no one can sit in His presence and not be changed!

SALOME: *(yawns)* That's what I hear. What a week!

MARTHA: Yes, and it's not over yet. I have a list this long of "things to do while in the city." *(measures with hands)*

SALOME: I'm rather disappointed. I thought Jesus was going to set up His kingdom Sunday when He rode into the city and the crowd proclaimed Him King of the Jews.

MARTHA: We all did. I don't know why He didn't. The first part of the week, He stayed at our house in Bethany and walked back and forth into the city. That's one reason I am so—

ALL: Exhausted.

MARTHA: I'm trying, girls. I'm trying. Ever since Jesus reprimanded me for wrong priorities, I'm trying to do better. I even left a bed unmade all day so I could have time to pray.

SALOME: Amazing!

MARTHA: You're a fine one to talk. You haven't made a bed since you married Zebedee. If I had the servants you have . . . I'm sorry, Salome. I guess I'm just jealous.

SALOME: *(surprised)* You're sorry? You, Martha? You have been with Jesus, haven't you?

MARTHA *nods.*

MARY B: *(to Salome)* It's such an honor to have Jesus in our home. Somehow when I sit at His feet, I don't mind that I cannot enter the Temple. It's as if I am in the presence of the Almighty.

MARTHA: He's the resurrection and life, that's for sure. Lazarus is a walking testimony of that.

MARY B: The disciples were so excited when they came home Sunday evening after Jesus' triumphant entry into Jerusalem. They believe that Jesus is going to set up His kingdom before the week is over.

SALOME: Yes, but—

MARTHA: But? But what? You are the one who has been so excited about the kingdom of the Jews, Salome.

SALOME: I know, and I still am, but—

MARY B: But what?

SALOME: My sister Mary is so worried, she is almost distraught! I'm puzzled. Something is not quite right.

Programs for Ladies

MARY B: You feel it, too?

SALOME: Yes, it's a heaviness—a tenseness in the air. *(takes a deep breath)* Ohhh, maybe it's not in the air. Maybe it's just in me. I . . . I did something so foolish. *(puts head in hands)* Zebedee and the boys are disgusted with me!

MARY B: Would it make you feel better to tell us?

SALOME: Maybe. It couldn't make me feel any worse. I . . . I asked Jesus to . . . to give my boys positions of honor in His kingdom. After all, they are His cousins, and they're well qualified for any position.

MARTHA: So, that's not too surprising. A lot of mothers would do the same thing.

SALOME: But it wasn't right. It was pushy and selfish and . . . just not right.

MARY B: What did Jesus say?

SALOME: That's what bothers me. He turned to James and John and asked them if they were able to drink of the cup He was about to drink of and be baptized with the baptism that He was about to be baptized with.

MARTHA: That's a strange question. Wasn't Jesus bapized by John the Baptist? He's surely not going to be baptized again.

SALOME: I don't understand about them drinking out of His cup either. Do you?

MARTHA: No . . . but Jesus doesn't waste words. It must be important.

MARY B: What did the boys say?

SALOME: Oh, they assured Him that they could. They didn't like my making the request, but they weren't about to refuse the positions either. *(puts head in hands and shudders)* I'm scared, girls. I'm scared for my boys. I'm scared of the cup.

MARY B: *(puts hand on Salome's shoulder)* Don't be afraid, Salome. You can trust Jesus.

SALOME: *(looks up and wipes eyes)* Yes, I can trust Jesus. Sometimes I forget that He's . . . He's more than Mary's Son—a mere man. It's hard for me to grasp His deity. Maybe I take His presence for granted. *(goes to "window" and peers out)* I didn't realize it was so late. I wonder what's keeping the boys. There is such unrest in the city tonight. I wish they were home.

MARTHA: *(laughs)* Spoken like the typical mother, Salome. Remember your boys are grown men.

SALOME: I know, but once a mother, always a mother. And my spirit is so restless.

MARY B: Mine, too. I feel the same thing. It's as if something is about to happen . . . something—

MARY C, SUSANNA, JOANNA, *and* ***MARY M*** *come bursting in from right front. They are gasping for breath. They "pound" on Salome's door.* ***SALOME, MARY B,*** *and* ***MARTHA*** *rush to the door.*

SALOME: Come in. Come in. What has happened? Where are my boys? Where are James and John?

SUSANNA: *(gasping)* Oh, it's horrible. Too horrible for words.

SALOME: Where are my boys? Where are James and John?

JOANNA: *(gasping)* I don't know. I suppose they went with the soldiers—

SALOME: The soldiers! The Roman soldiers?

JOANNA: *(catching her breath)* Yes. The Roman soldiers came to the garden where Jesus was praying. They have arrested Him.

WOMEN *are thrown into a panic. Their words fall over each other.*

SALOME: Oh, I knew it! I knew something terrible was going to happen.

Programs for Ladies

JOANNA: But it's not the Romans that hate Jesus. It's the Jews—our own people—the high priest, the Pharisees, the scribes. They want to kill Him!

MARY M: How could they be so blind?

MARY B: *(holds up hand)* But wait! *(women hush)* Perhaps this is how Jesus will reveal His power and set up His kingdom.

*As the **WOMEN** react to Mary's words, the momentum builds, each gets louder and more emphatic than the one before.*

SUSANNA: You're right. He can stop them.

MARTHA: They can't hurt Him. After all, He raised Lazarus from the dead.

MARY M: He can conquer the demons of hell. He drove out the demons in me.

MARY C: Remember? He said the kingdom of God was coming with great power and glory. We don't have to be afraid.

JOANNA: He can call for legions of angels.

MARY B: Then it has come! The time has come for the King of the Jews to set up His kingdom.

SALOME: Down with the Romans.

JOANNA: All hail, King Jesus, King of the Jews!

SALOME: Up with the kingdom of the Jews—a reign of prosperity and power!

MARTHA: Tomorrow is sure to be a big day—the day Jesus will be crowned King of the Jews!

ALL EXIT, *talking excitedly.*

MUSIC: "The Old Rugged Cross"

READER: *"And when [Pilate] had scourged Jesus, he delivered him to be crucified.*

Then the soldiers of the governor took Jesus into the common hall, and gathered unto him the whole band of soldiers.

And they stripped him, and put on him a scarlet robe.

And when they had platted a crown of thorns, they put it upon his head, and a reed in his right hand: and they bowed the knee before him, and mocked him, saying, Hail, King of the Jews!

And they spit upon him, and took the reed, and smote him on the head.

And after that they had mocked him, they took the robe off from him, and put his own raiment on him, and led him away to crucify him."[5]

"And there followed him a great company of people, and of women, which also bewailed and lamented him."[6]

ENTER WOMEN *from right, gather on stage, and look into distance.*

SALOME: Where are my boys? Surely James and John have not forsaken Jesus.

MARY C: I can't believe this is happening. It has to be a nightmare.

SALOME: Why doesn't He stop them? Why?

MARY M: I can't look. I can't look. It's too horrible. It makes me sick.

SALOME: I would never have thought He'd let it go this far. When is He going to stop them?

SUSANNA: Maybe He isn't.

MARY M: Susanna, don't say that!

Programs for Ladies

SUSANNA: But I remember what the prophet wrote, *"He is brought as a lamb to the slaughter."*[7]

SALOME: John the Baptist called Him "the Lamb of God."

MARY B: *"He was wounded for our transgressions, he was bruised for our iniquities: the chastisement of our peace was upon him; and with his stripes we are healed."*[8]

MARY M: *(covers ears)* Stop! I don't want to hear any more.

JOANNA: The prophecies have been there—being fulfilled right before our eyes, but we saw only what we wanted to see, heard only what we wanted to hear.

SALOME: The crown—not the cup.

JOANNA: The glory—not the suffering.

SUSANNA: The throne—not the cross.

MARY C: We looked for a King, but we needed a Savior.

MARY M: Don't say any more! Don't say any more! I can't bear it.

MARY C: I don't understand what is happening, girls, but I'm not afraid! I'm not afraid anymore! Everything's going to be okay.

MARY M: If only I could believe that! If only I could take His beating, carry His cross, die in His place.

MARY C: But, Mary Magdalene, don't you see? That's what He's doing, taking our beating, bearing our cross, dying in our place. *"The LORD hath laid on him the iniquity of us all."*[9]

TAPE: *"Daughters of Jerusalem, weep not for me, but weep for yourselves, and for your children. Weep for yourselves and your children . . . [fades] weep for yourselves and your children . . . weep for your children . . . weep for your children."*[10]

WOMEN EXIT *as song is sung.*

SONG: "Where Are the Children?"

ACT IV

Welcome to the Kingdom

The Upper Room in Jerusalem

"Thy kingdom come. . . . For thine is the kingdom, and the power, and the glory, for ever."[11]

"And I heard a loud voice saying in heaven, Now is come salvation, and strength, and the kingdom of our God, and the power of his Christ."[12]

"For the kingdom of God is not meat and drink; but righteousness, and peace, and joy in the Holy Ghost."[13]

CAST:

>7 women
>7 extras, including the woman who had the infirmity

STAGE SET-UP:

>14 chairs set up in the upper room

INSTRUCTIONS:

>The seven extras are dressed in biblical robes and sit among the audience until the other women come up the aisle on their way to the upper room. They fall in behind them and take their places on the stage.

WOMEN, *led by* **MARY M,** *burst out from door on right side.*

MARY M: *(to audience)* He has risen! He has risen! I have seen Him. My Savior and my Lord. He lives! *(to women)* Come, we must go tell the disciples. We must tell the world!

WOMEN *spread out, running through the congregation, telling the audience.* "He's alive." "He's risen. We saw the angel." "The tomb is empty." "The veil has been torn in two. We can go into the presence of God. We can go into His presence." "He lives. He lives!" "Surely now He will set up His kingdom. Everyone will have to believe. Everyone will know He is the King of the Jews." *As* ***THEY EXIT*** *out the back, the song is sung.*

SONG: "Rise Again"

ENTER WOMEN, *from the back. They ad-lib as they make their way to the front.* ***SEVEN EXTRA WOMEN*** *fall in behind them.* ***ALL*** *take their seats on the stage.*

MARY B: I feel like I have been on an emotional roller coaster.

MARY C: I know exactly what you mean. Jesus was alive. Then He was dead. Then He arose, and He was here. Now He's gone again.

SALOME: And we're back where we started.

MARY C: What do you mean, Salome?

SALOME: We're waiting again. Waiting for "who knows what." I wonder if the kingdom will ever come—if we'll ever be free from the Romans.

JOANNA: How many days have we been here?

THREE OR FOUR EXTRAS *start wiggling, whispering, expressing boredom.*

MARTHA: I've lost count. It's either ten or fourteen days. Long enough for whatever is going to happen to have happened.

MARY B: Patience has never been your strongest virtue, Martha.

MARTHA: *(sighs)* But waiting is so hard. I can wait on the Lord easier than I can wait for Him. I don't know how much longer I can take this "tarrying" business.

THREE OR FOUR EXTRAS *seem to be agreeing with Martha.*

JOANNA: Surely you aren't going to leave before the "promise of the Father" comes.

MARTHA: What is the "promise of the Father"?

JOANNA: I don't know, but I'm going to wait for it.

SALOME: I'm like Martha. I am tired of tarrying. Come on, Martha. Let's go.

MARTHA and SALOME, *along with* ***3-4 EXTRAS****, start to leave.*

MARY B: *(jumps up and grabs Salome and Martha)* Please, Martha. Please, Salome. Wait, girls. Don't leave now. Please, don't leave.

MARTHA: Well, I—

MARY B: Please, Martha, wait. Wait on the Lord.

MARTHA: *(resignedly)* Wait, Martha, wait.

MARY C: What do you have to lose, Martha? You've waited this long, wait a little longer. Don't leave now.

ALL sit down.

MARTHA: All right, I'll wait. I'll wait for the promise.

SUSANNA: Let's sing.

SONG: "They That Wait upon the Lord"

As they sing, ***TWO EXTRAS*** *stand up. They seem to be trying to get others to join them. Then they leave. A little later, another leaves, then another.*

SUSANNA: Let's have a testimony service.

MARY C: A testimony service?

SALOME: *(stands)* I'm leaving. Nothing is happening here. It's as dry as the First Church Uptown.

MARY B: *(begs on the verge of tears)* Salome, please stay for testimony service! Please don't leave. Don't leave.

SALOME: Oh, very well.

THEY *sit down.*

SUSANNA: Who wants to be first to tell what the Lord has done for you?

MARY M *jumps up.*

MARY M: I do. You know what He did for me, but I must thank Him again. I was dirty and rotten and tormented by spirits that I couldn't control. They possessed my thoughts, my actions, and life. Everyone, even you—everyone but Mary of Bethany—drew your robes about you and refused to touch me. I was so alone. Then Jesus came—and He reached out to me. Now I'm clean and free. Oh, how I love Him. *(sits down)*

SALOME: *(thinks aloud—reverb on mike)* I love Him, too. More than I realized.

EXTRA 1: *(stands)* I don't know you ladies, but I know Jesus. For eighteen years I was bent over and could not lift up myself. Depression, bitterness, anger pushed me down, down, down. Then Jesus came. It was on the Sabbath in the Court of the Women. Jesus came and He lifted me. I stand straight and tall—a whole person, body, soul, and spirit because Jesus touched me. *(sits down)*

SALOME: *(thinks aloud—reverb on mike)* Jesus touched her, and she was changed. Everyone's been changed but me. I didn't think I needed to be changed—but now . . . now I want to be changed. I want Jesus to touch me, but it's too late. He's gone. I was so close to Him, yet so far away. I want Him to touch me, but it's too late. Oh, I'm sorry . . . I'm so sorry . . .

MARY C: *(stands)* I was tormented by fear—afraid of everything and everyone. Then Jesus came and the more I sat in His presence, and the more I served and ministered to Him, the less I feared. *(sits down)*

JOANNA: *(stands)* I was sick with a fatal disease. The physicians could not help . . .

TAPE: WIND BLOWING

JOANNA: me. I was weak and discouraged, about ready to give up . . .

TAPE: *"And when the day of Pentecost was fully come, they were all with one accord in one place. And suddenly there came a sound from heaven as of a rushing mighty wind, and it filled all the house where they were sitting. And there appeared unto them cloven tongues like as of fire, and it sat upon each of them. And they were all filled with the Holy Ghost, and began to speak with other tongues, as the Spirit gave them utterance."*[14]

WOMEN *stand to their feet and begin to praise the Lord during the Scripture reading.*

SONG: "Rain on Us"

The End

[1]Mark 15:40-41
[2]Mark 15:41
[3]Luke 8:1-3
[4]Isaiah 64:4
[5]Matthew 27:26-31
[6]Luke 23:27
[7]Isaiah 53:7
[8]Isaiah 53:5
[9]Isaiah 53:6
[10]Luke 23:28
[11]Matthew 6:10, 13
[12]Revelation 12:10
[13]Romans 14:17
[14]Acts 2:1-4

Miscellaneous

A Daughter's Day

Lots of body language and movement is needed. There are no props; everything is imaginary.

DAUGHTER ENTERS.

Hi, Mom. I'm home.

Nothing. It was just another boring day.

I'll get it. It's for me.

Oh, hi, Amy. Guess what happened to me today? The most exciting thing . . .

But, Mom, I'm busy.

What? What?! WHAT? I CAN'T HEAR YOU!

TURN MY MUSIC DOWN?

BUT IT'S NOT LOUD!

Who's been in my room?

Mom, make everybody stay out of my room!

Why didn't someone make my bed?

I'm bored!

But, Mom, I'm busy.

I'll get it. It's for me!

Programs for Ladies

I don't have a thing to wear.

I can't find my green sweater. I wish I had a bigger closet.

I can't do a thing with my hair.

What do you mean, "Fix my hair"? It's fixed!

But, Mom, I'm busy.

Not chicken casserole again! Why don't we ever have pizza?

Sorry, I can't do the dishes. I've got a ton of homework.

I'll get it. It's for me.

Oh, hi, Candace. I don't have a thing in the world to do. I'll be right over.

But, Mom, I've got my driving permit.

There's a button off my blue skirt.

But I can't find a needle.

I don't have a thing to wear.

But, Mom, everybody's got one.

No, there's nothing wrong with me.

No, I don't have fever.

No, I'm not mad.

No, nobody hurt my feelings.

Oh, Mom, my whole world just fell apart. I don't have a friend in the . . .

I'll get it! It's for me.

But, Mom, I just got on. I've got to tell Stacy one more thing.

I'll call you back, Stacy.

I wish you'd fix something that is low calorie.

What? Do you expect me to eat this rabbit's food?

Dad said to ask you, Mom.

Why didn't you remind me to do my homework?

I'm bored.

But, Mom, I'm busy.

Wait for me.

Leave me alone.

Get out of here.

Why is everyone ignoring me?

I'll get it. It's for me.

I'm not arguing. I'm just presenting the facts!

I'll get up early and do my homework before school.

Did you sew that button on my blue skirt?

Mom, I love you. Good night.

The Party Line

CAST:

    Sarah
    Operator
    Bertha Snodgrass
    Bertha Jones
    Bertha Wilson

PROPS:

    4 telephones (at least one should be the old-fashioned ringer kind)
    Telephone sound effect
    Headphone set for operator

INSTRUCTIONS:

Phone sits on table, front center. The operator is in opposite corner, wearing a headphone. Three other phones are scattered around the room, preferably toward the front where everyone can see. Women who will talk on the phones are seated at the banquet table, as if they were not even in the skit.

*Enter **SARAH** and **OPERATOR**.*

SARAH: Oh, I've got to call Bertha and tell her the news. She'll be so excited. I declare she'll be tickled plumb pink. Just wait till she hears my news. *(Picks up the phone and rings it)* Operator? Operator? Minnie? Where is that operator? Minnie?

OPERATOR: Operator. Number please.

SARAH: Minnie, this is Sarah . . . Sarah Jane. Would you ring Bertha? I cain't remember her number, but you know it. You know the number of ever'body in Payne County.

Programs for Ladies

OPERATOR: Bertha? Bertha Jones? Bertha Wilson? Bertha Snodgrass?

SARAH: Minnie, you know that I ain't talked to Bertha Jones in two months, ever since she listened in on my phone call to Clara. She says she ain't talkin' to me. But really it's the other way around—I ain't talkin' to her.

OPERATOR: Well, it's a good thing you're not. Her daughter just won the state 4-H dress contest, and I tell you her head's so big, her brain got lost on the way to her mouth. She's been callin' ever'body in the county.

SARAH: Well, she ain't called me, and I'm right glad she ain't 'cause I wouldn't talk to her if'n she did. And I couldn't care less what her kids is doin'. What'd you say her daughter won?

OPERATOR: The state 4-H dress contest.

SARAH: Oh, hoitty-toiddy! Now she'll never shut up. But her news ain't nothin' compared to mine. Would you ring for Bertha, Minnie?

OPERATOR: Bertha?

SARAH: Sure. That's who I asked fer, ain't it?

OPERATOR: But you said you weren't talkin' to her.

SARAH: I ain't talkin' to Bertha Jones.

OPERATOR: Well, who do you want, Bertha Wilson or Bertha Snodgrass?

SARAH: Well it sure ain't Bertha Wilson. She's so hard-hearing she never gets the message right. Last time I called her she thought I was the preacher's wife and she like ta never shut up. Told me ever'thing that she thought ever'body on the party line had said about the preacher's last sermon. Was pretty interestin', but probably not a word of truth in the whole thing.

OPERATOR: What'd she say?

SARAH: Well, fer one thing she said that Deacon Nelson's wife said that the preacher was gettin' so evangelistic that he couldn't tell fact from fiction.

OPERATOR: You have to admit that it sure makes the sermons a lot more interestin'. You must be wantin' to talk to Bertha Snodgrass—only Bertha left in Payne County.

SARAH: Yep! That's the one. Ring her up right away. I've got some mighty interestin' news fer her.

OPERATOR *rings phone, two long and one short.* **THREE BERTHAS** *jump to their feet. Operator rings the phone again, two long and one short.*

BERTHA W: *(puts her hand behind her ear and count loudly)* One . . . two . . . one . . . two long and one short. That's Bertha Snodgrass's ring. Wonder who could be callin' her?

BERTHA J: *(puts hands on hip)* Two long . . . one short. Oh, no! Somebody's callin' Bertha Snodgrass. Now it'll be an hour before I can finish my calls to tell the rest of Payne County about Mary Bell's winnin' that contest. Wonder who'd be callin' Bertha Snodgrass?

BERTHA S: Yep! Two long and one short. That's my ring. Wonder who's callin' me? *(totters to the phone and picks it up)* Hello? Who's a callin'?

As **BERTHA S** *picks up the phone,* **BERTHA W** *and* **BERTHA J** *rush to pick up theirs. As* **BERTHA W** *picks up the phone, she trips over her own feet and makes a big commotion.*

SARAH: My lands, Bertha, ya breakin' your neck or something?

BERTHA S: *(speaks at the same time as Bertha W)* No, that weren't me.

BERTHA W: Speak up, I cain't hear ya.

SARAH: *(yells)* I said, did ya break your neck?

Programs for Ladies

BERTHA S: No.

BERTHA W: Just about.

SARAH: Well, make up your mind. Did ya or didn't ya?

BERTHA S: I didn't.

BERTHA W: I did.

SARAH: Is this you, Bertha?

ALL BERTHAS *answer in echo effect: "Yes."*

SARAH: Lands sake, this phone's got an echo. Did you hear that?

ALL BERTHAS *answer in echo effect: "Yes."*

BERTHA S: Is this you, Sarah Jane?

SARAH: I reckon it is.

BERTHA J: *(covers up receiver with her hand)* Boy, this'll be interestin'. Sarah Jane's the biggest gossip in Payne County.

SARAH: What did you say, Bertha?

BERTHA W: Speak up! I cain't hear ya.

BERTHA S: *(yells)* I didn't say nothin'.

SARAH: Sure sounded like somethin' ta me. Somethin' 'bout a gossip.

BERTHA S: Did you say ya got some gossip?

SARAH: I reckon I do.

BERTHA J: *(hand still over the receiver)* Yep, I told ya.

BERTHA W: Speak up! I cain't hear ya.

SARAH: *(yells)* Just wait till ya hear my news.

BERHTA S: Well, ya don't have to yell. I ain't hard-hearin'.

SARAH: And ya don't have to get snappy. Do ya wanta hear my news or not?

ALL BERTHAS *answer eagerly in echo effect: "Yes."*

SARAH: Well, it's like this. Awhile ago when I was down at the general store, I heard Clara say that . . . that—

ALL BERTHAS *answer in echo effect: "Yes? What?"*

SARAH: That . . . she . . . that she heard that . . . that . . . my lands sakes, I done fergot what Clara said that she heard. Don't that just take the cake?

ALL BERTHAS *groan loudly and slam down the phones.*

SARAH: *(grins)* Let's see, that was one, two, three—three eavesdroppers. Reckon I gave them somethin' to stew about.

SARAH *hangs up phone and* ***EXITS.***

Just for Fun Games

Door Prizes
As each lady arrives, she signs in on a pad with numbered lines. Drop corresponding numbers into a basket.

Set timers to go off at various times throughout the banquet. When a timer sounds, draw a number from the basket. The name written by the corresponding number receives a door prize.

Let's Get Acquainted
As the ladies enter, give each one a slip of paper with the following instructions.

Find someone who fits each statement. Have her initial that statement. The same lady cannot initial your paper twice.
1. Someone whose birthday is in the same month as yours.
2. Someone who has a child (or sibling) in college.
3. Someone who has been out of the state in the last week.
4. Someone who has a living great-grandparent.
5. Someone who has read the Bible through.
6. Someone who can quote the books of the Bible.
7. Someone who wears contacts.

What Is It?
Place white ingredients (flour, powdered sugar, baking soda, baby powder, etc.) in zipper baggies. Number each baggie and place them on a table. The ladies look at each item and try to guess what is in each bag. Each records her answers on a numbered paper.

Taste Test
Before the party, fix a paper plate for each team, marking numbers 1-5 on the plate. On each plate put a small amount of five different foods (strawberry jelly, baby food, etc.). Be sure the food and numbers on each plate match.

To play choose several contestants. Each chooses a partner. Blindfold one member of the team. The other member feeds the blindfolded teammate a taste of the first item. She tries to guess what it is,

Programs for Ladies

and the teammate writes down her guess. Continue until all the foods have been tasted. The team with the most correct answers wins.

Teams can take the taste tests at the same time by going into separate areas of the room and working quietly. Or they can take it one team at a time while the other teams wait outside the room for their turn.

Names for Mom

Give each lady a piece of paper. Allow three minutes for them to write down all the names for mom. Titles such as taxi driver are not acceptable. *Mom, mother, mama* are a few names. Foreign words are accepted.

For a variation, list names of grandmothers.

Ask the lady with the longest list to read it. Give her a small prize.

Get Acquainted

If possible, pair up women who do not know each other. Each lady may ask three questions of her choosing. The partner answers each question with one sentence. The object is to find out as much as possible about the other lady, asking only three questions. Choose several pairs to share their questions and answers with the group.

Purse Scavenger Hunt

Give an award to the woman who has the most of these things in her purse. The clues in parentheses tell where such items might be found. Do not give the clues to the players until the count is taken to determine the winner.

        Bunch of dates (calendar)
        Guy with a rod (chap stick)
        2 carpenter tools in 1 (nail file)
        Picture of president (on dollar bill)
        A book of numbers (address book)
        Receipt from Wal-Mart
        The newest (or oldest) penny
        A money factory (mint)
        A musical assistant (Band-Aid)
        Food for Polly (package of crackers)
        An inkless pin (safety or straight pin)
        A musical chord (key)

MISCELLANEOUS

Word Association

Give each player a copy of this quiz or print it on the program. It can be worked by the ladies as they wait for the program to begin.

Match the phrases with the art.

1. A bunch of dates.

2. A swimming match.

3. Sweet sixteen.

4. Never borrowed, never lent.

5. Seen at a ball game.

6. Out for the night.

7. "Remember" this Bible woman's fate.

8. Branching of a river.

9. One of the causes of the American Revolution.

10. A spring flower.

11. Ready to be licked.

12. A paradise on earth.

13. Birthplace of Burns.

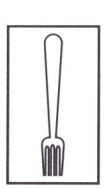

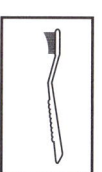

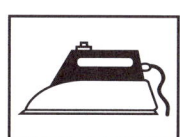

Programs for Ladies

Another Purse Search

Give gag gifts to the winner of each category.

1. One with most pennies. In case of a tie, give the gift to the youngest.
2. One with most keys. In case of tie, give the gift to the one who lives the farthest from the banquet location.
3. One with the fewest credit cards. In case of tie, give the gift to the one with the next birthday.
4. One with the biggest comb. In case of a tie, give the gift to the one with the longest hair.
5. One whose driver's license gives her correct weight. In case of a tie, give the gift to the one who has been driving the longest.
6. One with the oldest coin. In case of a tie, give to the oldest person.
7. One whose social security number contains any two consecutive numbers (1-2, 5-6, etc.). In case of a tie, give to the one whose consecutive numbers add up to the most, example: $1 + 2 = 3$, $5 + 6 = 11$; so the one with the 5-6 sequence would win.

Donut Game

For each team attach a piece of yarn or fishing line to a dowel rod. Tie a powdered sugar donut to the end of the yarn.

Choose four or more teams of two people. Place chairs back to back and ask partners to sit down.

You may wish to make vests from plastic garbage bags. Split these up the middle and cut out holes for the neck and arms. Or bring towels and pin them at the shoulders.

Give one partner the dowel rod and instruct her to hold it over her head and move it so her partner can eat the donut. She cannot look behind her, and the partner eating the donut cannot use her hands.

The team that eats the donut first wins.

Finish the Saying

Players can give the correct ending, or for more fun, they make up a new ending. (The answers are given on page 314.) This game can be copied and worked as a pre-banquet filler, or it can be given orally.

1. A woman's work . . .
2. A happy house . . .
3. Behind every successful man . . .
4. The path of true love . . .
5. My house is . . .
6. When the cat's away . . .
7. A woman's place . . .
8. When the going gets tough . . .
9. A stitch in time . . .
10. Variety is . . .
11. A man's home . . .
12. True love . . .
13. Marriages are . . .
14. A watched pot . . .
15. If the shoe fits. . .
16. Home is . . .
17. Too many cooks . . .
18. A penny saved . . .
19. The road to a friend's house . . .
20. The way to a man's heart . . .

Or you can switch this game by giving the answers (endings) and having the players fill in the beginnings.

Name the Candy

Purchase several candy bars. Cut them open and place a slice of each in a numbered baggie. As the bags are passed around, the players write the name of the candy bar on a numbered paper.

Give the candy to the one who correctly identifies the most bars.

Programs for Ladies

Seasoned with Salt

1. Lot's wife became a _____ of salt.

2. The _____ _____ _____ is in Utah.

3. Where Sodom and Gomorrah used to be is now the _____ _____ _____.

4. _____ put salt in a city's water supply to heal it.

5. A Christian's _____ should be seasoned with salt.

6. Prisoners used to have to work in the _____ _____.

7. A fountain cannot yield both _____ and _____ water.

8. In the Old Testament the _____ offerings were sprinkled with salt.

9. In Mark 9 and Luke 14, it says, "Salt is _____."

10. "Ye are the salt of the _____."

11. When a person exaggerates, we say, "_____ _____."

12. An efficient, capable person is "_____ _____."

13. Some grandmothers have _____-_____-_____ hair.

14. In olden days many women carried _____ _____, in case they started to faint.

15. People used to take _____ _____ for a laxative.

16. At the end of a hard day, it is nice to relax in a _____ of _____ _____.

Sheet Folding Contest

Ask for five or six volunteers. Give the prize to the one who folds a fitted sheet the fastest and the neatest.

Theme Songs

What Bible characters might have these theme songs as the story of their life?

1. "I Feel Like Traveling On" _____
2. "I'll Fly Away" _____
3. "Submission" _____
4. "I Won't Have to Cross Jordan Alone" _____
5. "Behold the Lamb" _____
6. "Fishers of Men" _____
7. "The Wind Is Blowing Again" _____
8. "Ye Must Be Born Again" _____
9. "I Should Have Been Crucified" _____
10. "Rise Again" _____
11. "In the Garden" _____
12. "The Holy City" _____
13. "Standing on Holy Ground" _____
14. "Harvestime" _____
15. "It's Raining" _____
16. "You Can't Do Wrong and Get By" _____
17. "Anointing, Fall on Me" _____
18. "O I Want to See Him" _____
19. "Springs of Living Water" _____
20. "Just a Closer Walk with Thee" _____

If you were to have a theme song that would describe your life and/or relationship with the Lord, what would it be? _____

Programs for Ladies

What's Cookin'?

Fill in the blanks with the name of foods.

1. The elusive _____ fly.

2. Her cheeks are like _____ and _____.

3. He tells the _____ iest jokes.

4. Quit yer _____ in'!

5. Come on, scaredy cat. Don't be a _____.

6. It wasn't the _____ on the tree that caused Adam and Eve their problem; it was the _____ on the ground.

7. "Men are glorified mudballs, but women are _____ _____," said our pastor.

8. _____ your claim.

9. "Where is my _____ makeup?" she asked her mother.

10. The Scripture says that if the fathers eat _____ _____, the children's teeth are set on edge.

11. That car he bought was a _____.

12. I don't care _____ about what she thinks.

13. "We're really in a _____," she said as she looked at the traffic.

14. "_____/_____ all bow our heads and pray."

15. It was fifteen _____ gold.

16. She is always _____ ing for compliments.

17. "_____ and _____ and all things nice."

18. "But we _____ _____," she cried. "I want a big wedding."

19. "Just _____ your teeth and bear it," he said.

20. "There's a spider. Quick, _____ it!"

Unwrap the Gift

Pair of gloves, 2 hats, prize wrapped in several layers of wrapping paper, boxes inside boxes, tissue paper, etc.

The group stands in a circle. The gloves, hat, and wrapped box are placed in the center. Play music and pass the hat around the circle. When the music stops, the person holding the hat hurries into the center, puts on the gloves and hat. She starts to unwrap the package. Start the music and continue passing the hat. When the music stops again, the person holding the hat goes to the center. The person in the center stops immediately and takes off the gloves and hat, gives them to the new person, and she goes back to the circle. The game continues like this until the gift is completely unwrapped.

The lady who unwraps the last package/paper receives the prize.

Potpourri of Ideas

Napkin Folding
Http://interiordec.about.com   Do a search on napkin folding.

Napkin Rings
Cut 1-1/2" diameter PVC pipe into 1" pieces. Sand edges until smooth. Paint. Cover with fabric or glue items to these inexpensive napkin rings.

Cloth Napkins
Purchase at Linen Outlet Stores for fifty cents each.

Purchase men's handkerchiefs and use them for napkins. Dye the handkerchiefs to match the décor.

Purchase old floral handkerchiefs at resale and antique shops. Ladies in your church may have some of these tucked away in a drawer. Fold in half and in half again, gather and tie with ribbon. Let each lady keep hers as a memento of the day.

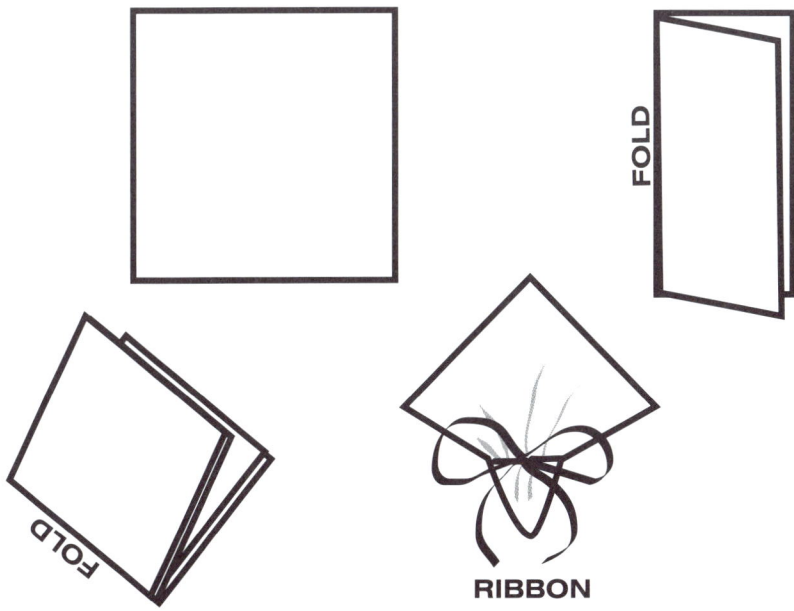

Programs for Ladies

Flatware

Restaurant suppliers sell spoons, forks, and knifes by the dozen at reasonable prices.

Plates

Buy clear glass plates from antique shops, resale stores, and garage sales. They do not have to match.

Garden Ridge Pottery is a good source for clear plates.

Favors

Gold Apples (red Christmas apples spray-painted gold). Attach a 3/4" x 2" card printed with Proverbs 25:11 to the stem with a ribbon. Tie curly ribbon to the stem. Curl the ribbon and shred it.

Tear Bottles. Use small bottles with lids or corks. Spray the lids gold. Fill the bottles with water. A drop of food coloring may be added for color. Tie curly ribbon to the neck of the bottle, curl, and shred the ribbon. Attach a card 3/4" x 2" on which you have written Psalm 56:8 (NASB), *"You have taken account of my wandering. Put my tears in Your bottle. Are they not in Your book?"* Or the TLB translation, *"You have seen me tossing and turning through the night. You have collected all my tears and preserved them in your bottle! You have recorded everyone in your book."* Attach the card to the neck of the bottle with a ribbon.

Tea Party. Trace a teacup pattern onto a wallpaper scrap that has been folded in half. (Ask for old wallpaper sample books.) Glue the edges together. Insert a tea bag in the top of the cup. Or instead of a tea bag, place a Scripture card or a card with theme of the banquet and the date. (See reproducible art on page 315.)

Teacup Candles. Collect teacups. Purchase wicks, wax, and fragrance at a craft store. Follow the instructions on the wax and pour into the teacups. Inexpensive teacups and saucers, boxed by the dozen, are available at floral supply companies around Mother's Day.

Easy Favors can be made by putting candy in small zipper locked bags and stapling the baggies to printed cards.
   Gummy Bears—"You are beary special."
   Hershey Treasures—"You are a treasure."
   Dove's Promises—"God's promises are sure."

Spoonful of Kisses. Place two Hershey Kisses on a plastic spoon. Wrap tulle around the bowl of the spoon and tie a narrow ribbon around the tulle and the handle.

Wagons and Wheelbarrows. Check for pastel colored wagons and wheelbarrows right after Easter. Use these for centerpieces and favors at banquets with floral and gardening themes.

Diapers. Baby Showers. Fold a 6" square of flannel in half to form a triangle. The fold should be on the bottom. Bring the side points to the center of the triangle. Bring the lower point to the center, covering the other points. This will form a diaper. Pin the points together with a small gold safety pin. Dip in melted paraffin wax and set on wax paper until dry. Fill with nuts or mints.
You may use felt to make the diaper. Put nuts or mints into small plastic bags or squares of tulle. Tie the tulle with a ribbon and insert into diaper.

Sweetheart Social. Cookie Cutters. Attach a card printed with "You were cut out for each other."

Make Memories
At every banquet decorate an area for taking pictures. Attendees can bring their cameras, or arrange for an amateur or professional photographer.

Decorating
Tall columns enhance many decors. These may be made from 10" or larger PVC pipe (purchase at plumbing suppliers). The base for the

Programs for Ladies

column is 3" thick wood with a hole cut through it. The pipe slips into the hole. The top base is also 3" thick wood, grooved to sit on top of the pipe.

Drape the columns with fabric or ivy garland.

Concrete pouring tubes also make great columns. These come in various diameters and lengths. Purchase from a concrete company (any length) or home improvement store (up to 4' only). The columns may be painted. For textured columns add texture to paint (home improvement stores) or use stone texture (found near the spray paint).

Centerpieces

Grape clusters. Slide purple Christmas ornaments into a brown chenille stem (pipe cleaner) to form a cluster. Twist the ends of the stem together and attach silk grape or ivy leaves. Place one grape cluster in the center of each table.

Tea Party. Use teapots filled with fresh or silk flowers. Place floating candles in teacups.

When using oblong tables, it is not always necessary to have a centerpiece. Favors can double as table décor. Purchase china cups at garage sales or resale shops. Arrange silk or real flowers in each and use as favors.

Mother's Memorial

Fill My Cup. Give each lady a teacup and ask her to fill it for Mother's Memorial. Ladies bring their filled cups to the banquet or to Sunday school on Mother's Day. The person with the most money in her cup wins a prize. Of course, the lady who writes a check will have the most, so you may have to give a prize for the largest check and to the lady with the most cash. Teapots are nice gifts for this contest.

Mother of the Year. Print a form letter on church stationery, explaining that *(name)* is working to be the Mother of the Year at the First Pentecostal Church. Every dollar given counts as a vote, and the woman with the most votes is the winner. Include an explanation of Mother's Memorial and the church address so the donation can be mailed to the church. Announce the winner at a Mother-Daughter banquet or on Mother's Day. Give the winner a bouquet of flowers and a gift engraved, "Mother of the Year, *the Church's name, and the date."* Present second and third place winners with gifts.

Resources for Skits

The Amelia Bedelia series of children's books by Peggy Parish contains a multitude of ideas that can be easily adapted into skits. The skit "No Place Like Home" on page 65 was adapted from one of these books. One book, *The Surprise Shower,* can be adapted into a skit for a wedding shower. Check these books out at your public library or any bookstore.

Another great resource for skits is *Stories that Sneak up on You* by John Duckworth, published by Fleming H. Revell, 1994. This book contains thirty modern-day parables that can easily be adapted into skits or monologues. The idea for the skit, "Sunny Skies," on page 11 came from "The Man Who Built His House upon a Rock" in this book. If you are into skits, you definitely need this book.

Recipes

Desserts

Dirt Cake

1 large pkg. Oreo or other cream-filled chocolate cookies
1/4 c. (1/2 stick) margarine
1 8 oz. pkg. cream cheese
1 c. powdered sugar
3 1/2 c. milk
2 (4 oz.) instant French vanilla pudding
1 (8 oz.) container Cool-Whip, thawed

Also needed:
 flowerpot, clay or plastic
 plastic or silk flowers
 Gummy Worms
 candy rocks
 trowel for serving

Crush the cookies in a blender and set them aside.
Cream together the remaining ingredients.
Layer in a pot: crushed cookies, pudding mixture, crushed cookies, pudding mixture, until the pot is full.
Top with crushed cookies. Place worms or rocks throughout the cake. Put several worms sticking out the top and insert flower stems into cake before serving.

The recipe may be doubled for large flowerpots. For Christmas, substitute cookies with green filling and pistachio pudding. Stick a silk poinsettia into the cake.
This may also be done in small flowerpots for individual servings. The flowerpots can be painted with names for table decorations.

Programs for Ladies

Pumpkin Roll

3 eggs
1 c. sugar
2/3 c. canned pumpkin
1 t. ginger
1/2 t. nutmeg
2 t. cinnamon
3/4 c. flour
1 t. lemon juice
1 1/4 c. chopped nuts (if desired)

Beat the eggs at high speed for 5 minutes. Add the sugar, pumpkin, and lemon juice. Mix the flour and spices together and add to the pumpkin mixture. Add nuts. Place in a greased and floured cookie sheet. Bake at 375° for 15 minutes. (Check for doneness.)

Let cool for 10 minutes. Turn out on towel or paper towel sprinkled with powdered sugar. Roll the towel and cake together lengthwise. Let it set 30 minutes or longer.

Mix filling ingredients.
    1 1/4 c. powdered sugar
    1 (8 oz.) cream cheese
    4 T. margarine
    1 t. vanilla

Unroll the cake and spread the filling on it. Roll cake again, wrap in foil, and chill. May be frozen. Slice in thin slices to serve.

Pumpkin Rolls are great fundraisers. Whole rolls sell for $10.00 each, or the cake may be rolled crosswise and cut in half. Half rolls sell for $4.00-6.00.

Rainbow Cookies

3 pkgs. slice and bake sugar cookies
food coloring
1 can white icing

Place one package of cookie mix in a bowl. Add a few drops of food coloring. Knead the dough until it turns the desired color. Roll into long roll. Cut lengthwise into three sections.

Repeat with the other two packages of cookie mix, using different colors. Place one section of each color together and press together firmly (or roll together).

Slice and bake according to directions on package.

When cool, spread icing on one cookie and top with another cookie.

Drinks

Party Punch

Punch Base
    3 pkgs. unsweetened strawberry Kool-Aid
    3 pkgs. unsweetened cherry Kool-Aid
    3 pkgs. unsweetened raspberry Kool-Aid
    1 (6 oz.) can orange juice
    6 oz. lemon juice
    1 lg. can of pineapple juice
    7-8 c. sugar

Divide the base into 3 equal parts. Mix 1 part base with enough water to make one gallon of punch.

Fruit Tea

    4 to 5 T. unsweetened instant tea
    4 c. water
    1 1/2 c. sugar
    12 oz. can frozen lemonade
    12 oz. can frozen pineapple orange juice

Stir together tea, water, and sugar in pan. Bring to boil, remove from heat.

In a gallon container mix the lemonade and pineapple orange juice. Add the tea mixture and enough water to make one gallon. Refrigerate. Serve over ice.

Programs for Ladies

Raspberry Tea Punch

5 single-serving tea bags
4 c. boiling water
1/4 c. orange juice
1 T. sugar
1 1/2 c. fresh or frozen loose-pack red raspberries, thawed
1 (6 oz.) can (2/3 c.) frozen lemonade concentrate, thawed
2 c. cold water

Place 4 cups water in a pan, add the tea bags. Bring to a boil, remove from heat. Steep 5 minutes. Remove tea bags. Stir in orange juice and sugar.

Place fresh or thawed raspberries in a blender. Blend until smooth. Strain to remove seeds.

Add the raspberry puree, lemonade concentrate, and 2 cups cold water to tea mixture. Stir gently to mix. Serve over ice. Makes 16 (8 oz.) servings.

Finger and Snack Foods

Hurt Yourself Dip

It's so good you will eat too much and hurt yourself!
4 (8 oz.) pkgs. of cream cheese (softened)
2-3 packages (to taste) Hidden Valley Ranch Dip
1 small can Ortega diced green chilies
1 small can black olives, chopped
1 (4 oz.) jar pimento

Mix and serve with tortilla chips.

Picante Pinwheels

2 (8 oz.) pkgs. softened cream cheese
1/2 c. picante sauce
flour tortillas

Mix the cream cheese and picante sauce. Spread on the tortillas. Roll the tortillas tightly.
Chill 2 hours. Cut into 1/2" slices.

Queso

5 lbs. American cheese
3 1/4 c. water
1 1/2 c. finely chopped onion
1 c. finely chopped celery
1 1/4 c. finely chopped bell pepper
6 finely chopped fresh jalapeno peppers (Cut the pepper in half. Remove the seeds and flesh holding the seeds. Chop the remainder of the pepper).

Place water and cheese in top of a double boiler. Bring to a boil, stirring every 5 minutes.
While the cheese is melting, place chopped vegetables in a saucepan with 1/4 cup of water. Stir constantly until the vegetables come to a light boil.
When the cheese is melted, add the vegetables to cheese.
Serve hot with tortilla chips. May also be used over enchiladas.
This recipe fills a large crock pot. It may be halved.

Ranch Pinwheels

2 (8 oz.) pkgs. softened cream cheese
2 medium green onions, chopped
1 small jar diced pimento
4 1/2 oz. can sliced ripe olives
1 pkg. ranch dressing mix
4 12" flour tortillas
1 (4 oz.) can green chiles

Mix the cream cheese, ranch dressing mix, and onions. Spread on tortillas. Drain olives, pimento, and green chiles. Sprinkle on top of the cream cheese. Roll the tortillas tightly.
Chill for 2 hours or longer. Cut into 1/2" slices.

Programs for Ladies

Soups and Salads

Broccoli and Artichoke Salad

1 head broccoli, broken into small pieces
1 jar marinated artichokes, chopped
1 small jar sliced green olives with pimento
1 bottle Kraft Italian salad dressing

Mix together and let marinate 1 hour before serving.

Broccoli Bacon Salad

6 T. sugar
1 c. mayonnaise
1/3 c. white vinegar
2 heads broccoli, cut into bite-sized pieces
1 lb. bacon, cooked, drained, and crumbled
1 purple onion, finely chopped
1 c. pecans
1/2 c. finely grated cheddar cheese (if desired)

Combine the sugar, mayonnaise, and vinegar. Blend well. In a large bowl, toss together the broccoli, bacon, onion, and pecans and cheese (if used). Pour the dressing over all. Toss. Chill.

Tea Room Soup and Salad

A 3-Salad Plate consists of chicken salad, fruit salad with dip, and pasta salad.
Serve one scoop of each salad on a plate covered with leaf lettuce.
Add a slice of nut bread or pumpkin roll.
Serve with a cup of Broccoli Cheese Soup.
Place homemade bread sticks or croutons on the table.

Chicken Salad a la Teresa

5 boneless skinless chicken breasts
2/3 c. celery, finely chopped
5 t. crushed chicken bouillon (can purchase granulated)
12 oz. cream cheese
1 c. mayonnaise
2 t. dill spice
Chopped nuts or sliced grapes may be added, if desired.

Boil the chicken and chop into small pieces.

Mix all the ingredients together. May add more bouillon or dill to taste.

Use a plastic ice cream scoop to measure servings. With one scoop per serving, this recipe makes about 16-18 servings. It is very rich, so the servings do not have to be large.

Pasta Salad

1 lb. spiral noodles, cooked and drained
1 bell pepper, diced
1 bunch green onions, chopped
1 cucumber, chopped
1 basket of cherry tomatoes, cut into fourths
1 large bottle Viva Italian Salad Dressing
1 bottle McCormick Salad Supreme (this is available on the spice aisle at the grocery store)

Combine all the ingredients. Refrigerate until served.

Fruit Dip

8 oz. cream cheese
8 oz. jar marshmallow crème
apple juice

Mix cream cheese and marshmallow crème together. Add apple juice until the dip is smooth. Consistency should be such that it can be dipped with a spoon, but not runny.

Serve with fresh fruit salad.

Programs for Ladies

Broccoli Cheese Soup

1 lb. processed cheese (such as Velveeta)
1 pt. half-and-half
2 c. water
3/4 t. salt
1/2 t. pepper
1/2 c. cornstarch mixed with 1 c. cold water
1 1/2 lbs. broccoli

Steam the broccoli until tender. Place half-and-half, water, cheese, salt, and pepper in top of a double boiler. Heat until the cheese is melted. Add the broccoli. Mix cornstarch and water together. Stir into the cheese mixture. Heat in top of the double boiler until the soup thickens.

Makes 10 (1 cup) servings. Soup may be thinned with water, as it thickens when refrigerated.

Resources

Web Sites

www.churchdrama.org/links.htm (this site links to many other sites for free skits)
www.skituations.com/samples.html
www.carey.ac.nz/drama
http://members.nbci.com/heartdrama/home.htm
www.justynw.com/main.htm
www.discover-net.com/~dcpeters/kathy.html (great ideas to correspond with themes in this book)
www.lillenas.com/drama
www.macscouter.com/skits/bbskits_contents.html
www.christiancrafters.com
www.fea.net/bobsnook

Decorating

Stumps Prom and Party (decorating ideas and supplies)
(800) 348-5084
http://www.stumpsparty.com
http://www.stumpsprom.com

Andersons Prom and Party (decorating ideas and supplies)
(800) 328-9640
www.andersonsparty.com

Favors and Decorating Supplies

Oriental Trading Company (favors)
(800) 228-2269 or (800) 875-8480
www.oriental.com

Terry's Village (favors)
(800) 200-4400 or (800) 876-5822
www.terrysvillage.com

Programs for Ladies

Dillon Importing Co./M-G Novelty
300 N. MacArthur Blvd.
Oklahoma City, OK 73127
(405) 948-1234 / (800) 654-3696
FAX (405) 942-4705
Slight charge for a catalog

Books and Other Resources for Women's Ministry

Pentecostal Publishing House
8855 Dunn Road
Hazelwood, MO 63042
(314) 837-7304 Ext. 7

Answers to Games and Puzzles

By Their Feet Ye Shall Know Them

Find the Shoes

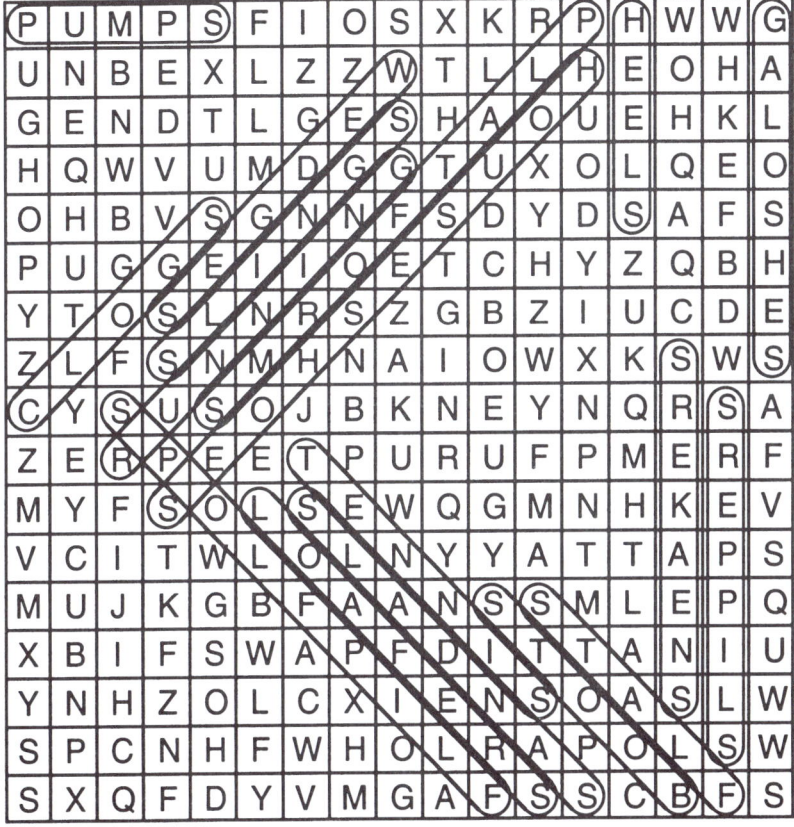

BOOTS
CLOGS
FLATS
FLIPFLOPS
GALOSHES
HEELS
HOUSESHOES
LOAFERS
PLATFORMS
PUMPS
RUNNING
SANDALS
SLINGS
SLIPPERS
SNEAKERS
TENNIS
WEDGES

Programs for Ladies

Bible Trivia
1. The dove that Noah sent from the ark (Genesis 8:9).
2. In the waters of the Jordan (Joshua 3:13).
3. Zacharias (Luke 1:67, 79).
4. Peter (John 13:6).
5. The gate of the Temple which is called Beautiful (Acts 3:2, 7).
6. Abraham (Acts 7:5).
7. Jacob (Genesis 49:33).
8. A wall (Numbers 22:25).
9. Blood (Leviticus 8:23-24).
10. Preparation of the gospel of peace (Ephesians 6:15).
11. Swell (Deuteronomy 8:4).
12. Saul (I Samuel 24:3).
13. Asher (Deuteronomy 33:24).
14. Joshua (Joshua 5:15).

Chosen Vessels

Chosen Vessels from God's Word
1. B—Rahab (Joshua 2:3, 21)
2. B—Sarah (Genesis 17:15-17)
3. D—Priscilla (Acts 18:2, 3)
4. C—Ruth (Ruth 4:13, 17)
5. D—Esther (Esther 2:17)
6. A—Miriam (Exodus 15:20)
7. D—Jael (Judges 4:21)
8. C—Abigail (I Samuel 25:23-25)
9. B—Phebe (Romans 16:1-2)
10. C—Deborah (Judges 4:4, 10)

Christmas Tea

Christmas Wordies. (1) watch over flocks; (2) great joy; (3) "Away in a Manger"; (4) highly favored; (5) Christmas tree; (6) "The Night before Christmas"; (7) Of His kingdom there shall be no end or endless kingdom; (8) fall and rising of Israel; (9) "Silent Night"; (10) "Deck the Halls"; (11) "We Three Kings"; (12) The glory of the Lord shone round about them; (13) "O Little Town of Bethlehem"; (14) "O Holy Night"; (15) "Noel."

Where's My Line? (1) "Silver Bells"; (2) "Here Comes Santa Claus"; (3) "A Holly Jolly Christmas"; (4) "Rudolph the Red-nosed Reindeer"; (5) "Santa Claus Is Comin' to Town"; (6) "Have Yourself a Merry Little Christmas"; (7) "I Saw Mommy Kissing Santa Claus"; (8) "O Come, All Ye Faithful"; (9) "Let It Snow! Let It Snow! Let It Snow!"; (10) "I Heard the Bells on Christmas Day"; (11) "God Rest You, Merry Gentlemen"; (12) "Hark! The Herald Angels Sing"; (13) "Joy to the World"; (14) "I'll Be Home for Christmas"; (15) "Silent Night"; (16) "O Little Town of Bethlehem"; (17) "What Child Is This?"; (18) "O Holy Night"; (19) "We Three Kings of Orient Are"; (20) "Jingle Bells."

Gift Baskets

What's My Line?

1. Dorcas was known for her charitable acts, made garments for others.
2. Martha, Lazarus's sister, was a hostess whose responsibility weighed heavily upon her. She was "cumbered about with much serving."
3. Mary of Bethany, Lazarus's sister, sat at the feet of Jesus and listened.
4. Hannah prayed for a son and dedicated him to the Lord.
5. Ruth left her family to follow her mother-in-law. She worked in the harvest.
6. Abigail, wife of Nabal, was an intercessor. Because of her wise actions, she prevented a bloody battle between the forces of David and her husband. She was called "a woman of good understanding."
7. Miriam, the sister of Moses, was a praise singer.
8. Lydia, a seller of purple, was a convert of Paul's who showed his evangelistic party hospitality.
9. Phebe was a servant to the church at Rome. (See Romans 16:1.)
10. Rizpah diligently kept wild animals and vultures from the bodies of her dead sons.
11. Joanna, wife of Chuza Herod's steward, followed Jesus and the disciples and ministered to them. Along with other women she accompanied Jesus on His last journey from Galilee to Jerusalem and was present when His body was laid in the tomb.
12. Deborah was a prophetess and judge.

Programs for Ladies

Hand 'n Hand

Handy Answers. (1) hand washable; (2) handcrafted or handiwork; (3) handkerchief; (4) hand-me-down; (5) Praying Hands; (6) handlebar; (7) hand tool; (8) handbag; (9) handball; (10) handmaid; (11) handbill; (12) handcuffs; (13) handicap; (14) handpick; (15) handgun; (16) handclasp or handshake; (17) handwriting; (18) handyman; (19) handout; (20) hand organ.

Gloves Crossword Puzzle.

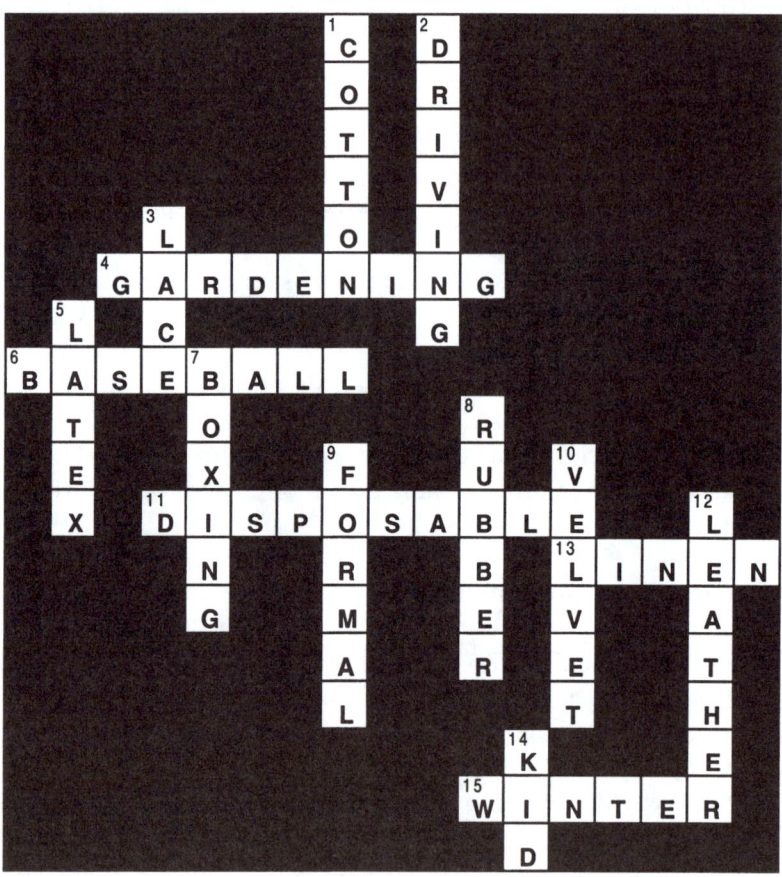

Home Tweet Home

Who Lives Here

Answers may vary from these. (1) king and/or his family; (2) birds; (3) lions, bears, etc.; (4) President and his family; (5) chicken, rooster; (6) bees; (7) ants; (8) fish; (9) cows, various farm animals; (10)

MISCELLANEOUS

horses; (11) pigs; (12) birds, lions, etc.; (13) rabbit, mole, gopher, etc.; (14) spider; (15) sheep; (16) pauper, miner; (17) bears, etc.; (18) criminals; (19) rich person.

Say It with Flowers

Identify the Flowers. (1) aster; (2) bell flower; (3) black-eyed susan; (4) camomile; (5) carnation; (6) daffodil; (7) gladiolas; (8) lily; (9) magnolia; (10) rose.

Phonetically Speaking. (1) bluebell; (2) carnation; (3) crocus; (4) iris; (5) mum; (6) pansy; (7) snapdragon; (8) tulip; (9) sunflower; (10) goldenrod.

Sunbeams and Rainbows

Arrange the Tiles. "I do set my bow in the cloud, and it shall be for a token of a covenant between me and the earth" (Genesis 9:13).

A Color-full Puzzle. (1) red cross; (2) coat of many colors; (3) blue blood; (4) black sheep; (5) orange juice; (6) black book; (7) green with envy; (8) little brown jug; (9) blue Christmas without you; (10) black out; (11) Red China; (12) yellow fever; (13) silver spoon; (14) black lie; (15) blue jay.

Just for Fun Games

Word Association Game

A bunch of dates—calendar
A swimming match—match in the bottle
Sweet sixteen—jar of candies
Never borrowed, never lent—toothbrush
Seen at a ball game—pitcher
Out for the night—candle
The fate of a woman in the Bible—salt
Branch in a river—fork
One of the causes of the American Revolution—tacks (tax)
A spring flower—butter cup
Ready to be licked—stamp
A paradise on earth—dice on plate of dirt
Birthplace of Burns—iron

Programs for Ladies

Finish the Saying
(1) is never done; (2) is full of laughter; (3) is a woman; (4) never runs smooth; (5) your house; (6) the mice will play; (7) is in the home; (8) the tough get going; (9) saves nine; (10) the spice of life; (11) is his castle; (12) conquers all or waits; (13) made in heaven; (14) never boils; (15) wear it; (16) where the heart is; (17) spoil the broth; (18) is a penny earned; (19) is never long; (20) is through his stomach.

Seasoned with Salt
(1) pillar; (2) Great Salt Lake; (3) Salt/Dead Sea; (4) Elisha; (5) speech; (6) salt mines; (7) salty, fresh; (8) meat; (9) good; (10) earth; (11) "take her with a grain of salt"; (12) "worth her salt"; (13) salt-and-pepper; (14) smelling salts; (15) Epsom salts; (16) tub, bath salts.

Theme Songs
(1) Abraham; (2) Elijah; (3) Mary of Nazareth; (4) Joshua; (5) John the Baptist; (6) Andrew/Peter/James/John; (7) Peter; (8) Nicodemus; (9) Barabbas; (10) Lazarus; (11) Adam/Eve; (12) John the Revelator; (13) Moses; (14) Ruth; (15) Noah; (16) Achan; (17) David; (18) Bartimaeus; (19) the Samaritan woman; (20) Enoch. Others names may fit; these are just the most obvious answers.

What's Cookin'?
(1) butter; (2) peaches, cream; (3) corn; (4) beef; (5) chicken; (6) apple, pair; (7) prime rib; (8) steak; (9) pancake; (10) sour grapes; (11) lemon; (12) beans; (13) jam; (14) lettuce; (15) carrot; (16) fish; (17) sugar, spice; (18) cantaloupe; (19) grit; (20) squash.

Patterns

Programs for Ladies

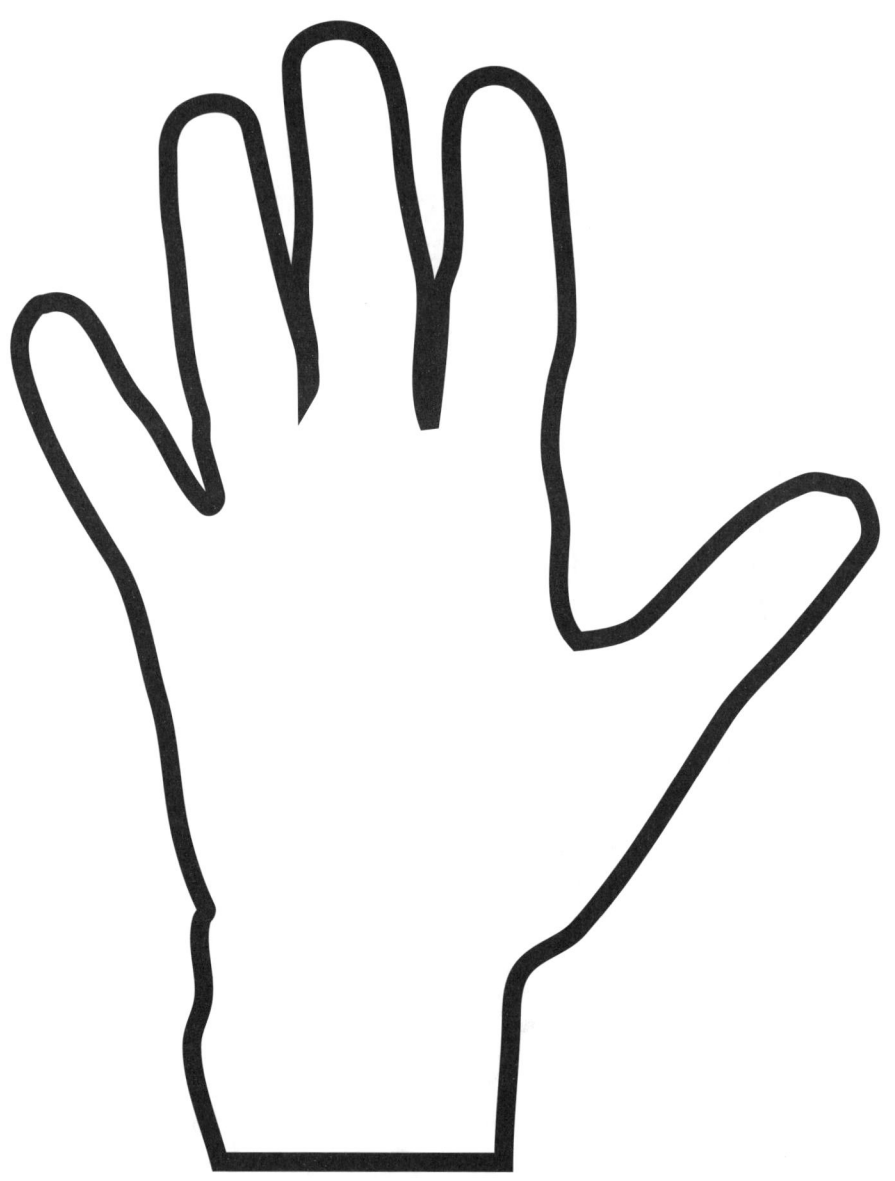

MISCELLANEOUS

Programs for Ladies

Identify the Flowers

On this page there are ten different flowers. How many can you identify?

MISCELLANEOUS

Phonetically Speaking

Put the pictures in each frame together to find the name of a flower.

  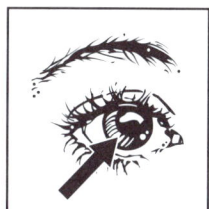

 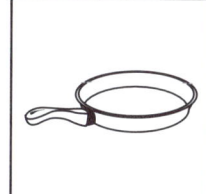 

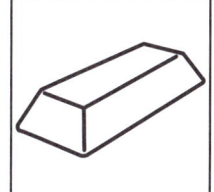 

Index

Audience Participation

All Hands on Board 57
Balloon Release. 26
Charades of Motivational Gifts. 50
Door Prizes 9, 63, 283
Find the Insects 71
Handy Tips 57
Know What I Did? 36
Let's Get Acquainted 283
Make a Vessel 23
Old-Fashioned Sing-Along 72
Prayer Handkerchiefs 57
Teacup or Gift Exchange 32
Timed Drawing for Door Prizes 283
Unwrap the Gift 291
Whose Shoes? 18

Contest

Sheet Folding 289

Dramas

A Wake-Up Call 145
The Bridge Builders. 95
The God of Hagar 187
The Parable of the Teacup 111
Treasures of the Heart 127
Women of the Kingdom 225

Fundraising Ideas

Pumpkin Rolls. 300

Games

A Flowery Answer 82
A Sensitivity Test. 64

Programs for Ladies

Another Purse Search 286
Ants 71
Arrange the Tiles. 88
Basketball Relay 71
Bird Watching 83
Can You Remember? 82
Charades of Motivational Gifts. 50
Construction Crews. 10
Donut Game 286
Drive It In. 10
Feet in the Bible 17
Get Acquainted 284
Herd the Sheep 71
How Many?. 23
Identify It 10
Identify the Tool 10
Let's Race. 17
Memory Ball 71
Name the Candy 287
Names for Mom. 284
Penny Game 50
Purse Scavenger Hunt 284
Taste Test 283
The Mystery Gift. 50
What Is It? 283
Word Association 285

Ideas for Speakers

By Their Shoes Ye Shall Know Them (Outline) 19
Give It to God (Illustrated Sermon) 26
Identifying Your Gift 53
Sunbeams (Outline). 89
The Wise and Foolish Man (Chalk Talk) 11

Monologues

A Daughter's Day 273
Sunny Skies 11
The Bridge Builders. 95

Poems

Reproof 26

MISCELLANEOUS

Program Specials
Beautiful Feet (Puppet Presentation) 18
Consider the Ant. 72
Demonstrations for Making a Home Tweet Home 64

Puzzles
A Color-full Puzzle. 86
Christmas Wordies 30
Find the Shoes (Word Search) 16
Gloves (Crossword Puzzle) 59
Phonetically Speaking 81

Quizzes
Bible Trivia—Feet 17
Chosen Vessels from God's Word. 22
Finish the Saying. 287
Handy Answers 58
Identify the Flowers. 80
Seasoned with Salt. 288
Theme Songs 289
What's Cookin'? 290
What's My Line? 49
Where's My Line? 31
Who Lives Here?. 63

Recipes
Broccoli and Artichoke Salad 304
Broccoli Bacon Salad. 304
Broccoli Cheese Soup 306
Chicken Salad a la Teresa 305
Dirt Cake 299
Fruit Dip. 305
Fruit Tea. 301
Hurt Yourself Dip 302
Party Punch 301
Pasta Salad 305
Picante Pinwheels 302
Pumpkin Roll 300
Queso. 303
Rainbow Cookies. 300
Ranch Pinwheels. 303

Programs for Ladies

    Raspberry Tea Punch 302
    Tea Room Soup and Salad 304

Skits
    An Open Door 50
    Choose Me, Lord 24
    Let Me Call You "Uhhhh, Sweetheart" 38
    No Place Like Home 65
    The Party Line 277

Songs
    "Beautiful Feet" (Puppet Presentation) 18

Stories for Readings
    The Cave and the Light 88

BARBARA WESTBERG has authored several books, including *Programs for Ladies* and *Programs for Ladies, Volume 2*. The dramas in this book were written for and produced at the Oklahoma District Ladies' retreats.

Her radio scripts are often heard on Children's Bible Hour, and many of her devotionals for children have been published in Tyndale House's *One Year of Devotions for Boys, One Year of Devotions for Girls* and *One Year Book of Family Devotions*.

She is currently Children's Editor for Word Aflame Publications. She lives in Cushing, Oklahoma, where her husband pastors the United Pentecostal Church. Her greatest joy is being grandmother to six beautiful grandchildren.

TERESA BOHANNON is the Beginner Editor for Word Aflame Publications.

She has served as a member of the adjunct faculty of Texas Bible College, teaching courses in children's ministries and puppetry.

Born and raised in California, Teresa met Reverend Lynn Bohannon of Houston, Texas, on an International Youth Corps trip to the Philippines in 1975. Married in 1976, they have pastored in Lockhart, Texas, served on the Associates In Missions program to Kenya, East Africa, and for a short time assisted the Reverend Rick Keyes in Santa Maria, California.

They currently reside in La Marque, Texas, where Brother Bohannon pastors Faith Tabernacle. They have two children, Jason and Ashley. The Bohannon family ministers in camps, children's crusades and teacher training seminars across the country. They founded the Children's Ministries Workshop, held each February in La Marque. In her spare time she operates a puppet-making business.

Known for her creativity and organizational skills, Teresa has taught classes at the University of Texas in Austin, after-school and community education programs, co-directed summer day camps, served as crafts director for the Texas District Crusader Camp, and coordinated city Christmas festivals.